Living *with* Arthritis

Living
with
Arthritis

A Practical Guide for All Canadians

RODERICK JAMER

Whitecap Books
Vancouver / Toronto

The information in this book is true and complete to the best of our knowledge. All recommendations are made without guarantee on the part of the author or Whitecap Books Ltd. The author and publisher disclaim any liability in connection with the use of this information. For additional information please contact Whitecap Books Ltd., 351 Lynn Avenue, North Vancouver, B.C., V7J 2C4.

Edited by Elizabeth McLean
Proofread by Lisa Collins
Cover design by Steve Penner
Interior design by Tanya Lloyd
Special thanks to Margaret Ng
Printed in Canada

Canadian Cataloguing in Publication Data
Jamer, Roderick
   Living with Arthritis

   Includes index.
   ISBN 1-55110-407-5

   1. Arthritis—Popular works. I. Title.
RC933.J35 1996   616.7'22   C95-911136-0

This book is not intended to be a substitute for consultation with a physician. Neither the author nor the publisher take medical or legal responsibility for the reader who uses the contents of this book as a prescription.

The publisher acknowledges the assistance of the Canada Council and the Cultural Services Branch of the Government of British Columbia in making this publication possible.

ACKNOWLEDGEMENTS

A book such as this is never the fruit of one person's efforts alone. While I bear full responsibility for its shortcomings, I deserve only partial credit for whatever strengths it may have. Over the years, hundreds of people with arthritis, health-care professionals, researchers, and others have freely shared their experience and expertise with me. Only a handful of them appear between these covers, but this book is a reflection of all their voices. I hope it does them justice.

My thanks to The Arthritis Society, which has provided a platform (in the *Arthritis News,* which provided the basis for much of the material in this book) for my continuing education. Thanks to Dr. Carter Thorne and the health-care team of The Arthritis Program at York County Hospital in Newmarket, Ontario, who not only let me sit in on their sessions, but then took the time to comment on and correct my depiction of their unique program in arthritis care.

Dr. Cy Frank in Calgary read and commented on the surgery chapter; Dr. Mary Bell in Toronto read and commented on the final chapter; and Dr. Carl Laskin, also in Toronto, read and commented on much of the remainder. I'm extremely grateful to them all.

Thanks to those who gave me permission to borrow from their work. They include Terry Trussler in Vancouver, in "Mastering Wellness," in chapter 5; Tim Lougheed in Ottawa, in the last section of chapter 12; Marie Chambers in Newmarket, Ontario, and Dennis Jeanes in Toronto, who allowed me to borrow freely from their superb summary of arthritis medications, which originally appeared in *Arthritis News;* and the following authors and publishers for permission to quote from: *Strong Medicine: How to Save Canada's Health Care System* by Michael M. Rachlis, M.D., and Carol Kushner. Published by Harper-Collins Publishers Ltd. 1994; *Shooting the Hippo,* by Linda McQuaig,

1995. Reprinted by permission of Penguin Books Canada Limited; *Whose Country Is This Anyway?* by Dalton Camp, 1995. Reprinted by permission of Douglas & McIntyre Ltd.; and *Scientific American* magazine.

I owe a special debt to Dennis Jeanes. As editor of *Arthritis News*, Dennis assigned my first arthritis article and supervised me in the decade that followed. Ironically, in early 1995, an arthritis-related back problem forced him to hand over the magazine's reins—by which time he and I had already drawn up an outline of this book and done a rough draft of the introduction. Although he was forced to sit out the rest of it, he lent me the benefit of his counsel and experience—in suggestions, research, advice, and encouragement—without which this project would have been vastly more difficult.

And finally, to Laura and Louise: my heartfelt thanks for your endless patience, love, and support.

CONTENTS

INTRODUCTION

The Sleeping Giant

If you're fifty, were, or plan to be, if you have aging parents or growing children, if you're a Baby Boomer (someone born between 1946 and 1966), you need this book. Buy it. Borrow it, if you wish. But read it.

We were the immortal generation. We were never going to grow up, never get sick, never die. Well, we did, some of us, and Mick and Keith and the boys—the touchstones of our endless youth—are now older on average (by four months at last count) than sitting members in the British House of Commons.

We're late thirties, forty-somethings; in 1996, the first of the Baby Boomers turned fifty. The Camelot of our youth has become George Bush's kinder, gentler America, Newt Gingrich, Ralph "Scissorhands" Klein, and Mike Harris's common-sense revolution—life in a funhouse mirror, except nobody's laughing. Our kids are growing up and our parents are growing old, and we're all living under a cloud—not The Bomb, but the smoke rising from a thousand attacks on our expectations and comfort zones.

Most of us now know more about RRSPs than R.E.M. (that's a rock group, for those of you already out of the loop). Just as we've begun (reluctantly) to think about it, health care in Canada is in crisis, beset by ruinous fiscal policies, rising costs, medical mismanagement, and the increasing weight of an aging population.

There's a crunch coming, and you *will* be affected, one way or another. Here are a couple of things to consider: First and foremost is arthritis. If it isn't already part of your present, it will be part of your future, directly or indirectly, as sure as winter frost in Frobisher Bay. The second point follows from the first: Arthritis is going to cost—big time. It already costs far more than most people imagine, not only in pain and suffering and reduced quality of life, but also in hard, cold cash; like it or not, we're all going to have to pay the piper. This text is your guidebook to managing the impact of arthritis, and handling the coming crisis.

Arthritis is a *major* problem. There's no cure; even its causes remain unknown. Nor is it just a disease of the elderly, though its prevalence does increase dramatically with age. And, since our population is rapidly aging, arthritis is a problem with real growth potential. As Dennis Jeanes, former editor of *Arthritis News*, puts it, arthritis is the sleeping giant of Canadian health care.

Just so you understand how big that potential really is, here's a snap quiz: How many people actually have arthritis—right now? One in a thousand? One in a hundred? Only your Great-Aunt Agnes and a few bridge partners at Golden Villa? The answer is: none of the above.

Arthritis has been mistakenly dismissed as a more or less "benign" condition by health policy planners (and even many doctors, who should know better). But there are a few studies and surveys that help to put the issue in clearer perspective. According to the 1984 U.S. National Health and Nutrition Examination Survey I, for example, slightly more than 16.3 per cent of all Americans age twenty-four to seventy-four have some form of arthritis or related disorder. That's about one in six adults. We're in much the same boat in Canada. The 1990 Ontario Health Survey revealed that 18.5 per cent of the population sixteen and over reported having arthritis; 15.2 per cent specifically identified arthritis as a long-term, chronic health problem.

Lest you be tempted to think that arthritis "happens" only to others, here's a way of figuring out your odds, based on accepted prevalence rates: If you have children under the age of fifteen, the risk of their developing juvenile arthritis is about 1 in 1000. If you're between thirty and fifty, the risk of your developing rheumatoid arthritis—arguably the most devastating form of the disease—is about 1 in 100. If you're over fifty, your chances of developing osteoarthritis (OA), the most common form of arthritis, are 1 in 10; by age sixty-five, the odds close in on 1 in 4. Over seventy-five, it's a toss-up: You—or your parents—have a 50-50 chance of developing OA.

Until recently, at least, Boomers' parents could count themselves lucky. With the "greying of society," theirs was the last generation that could expect to have sufficient numbers of caregivers (something the grim shadow of health-care cuts is likely to change). How's that? Well, right now, Canadians of retirement age represent only about 11 per cent of the total population. Statistics Canada estimates their numbers will almost double by the year 2021—to about 20 per cent, or a fifth of the projected population. That means the number of Canadians with OA-associated disability in 2021 will be almost twice (nearly 200 per cent) what it was in 1986, while the total adult population is only expected to increase by 30 per cent.

As Dr. Elizabeth M. Badley, director of The Arthritis Community Research and Evaluation Unit at Toronto's Wellesley Hospital Research Institute, points out, the increase in the number of people with arthritis disability "will take place against a backdrop of a static number of people sixteen to forty-five, the age group that traditionally supplies the largest share of formal [and informal] caregivers."

Put bluntly, just when Boomers are going to need the services—in unprecedented numbers—of not only GPs (general practitioners), but rheumatologists, orthopedic surgeons, physio- and occupational therapists, nurses, social workers, and so on, they're very likely to find that the well has all but run dry. Good help is going to be hard to find, and some people are going to need a lot of it. At its mildest, arthritis can be an easily managed collection of symptoms: moderate, even negligible restriction of movement in one or more joints, perhaps a few dismissable aches and pains. No big deal. But, at its worst, arthritis can develop with all the devastating impact of a major traffic accident. Caught between those extremes are hundreds of thousands of Canadians whose lives, to greater or less extent, are seriously compromised by the ravages of the disease.

We'll explore the personal impact of arthritis a little later. For now, let's talk money. To get to the bottom line, you have to start with what researchers call "morbidity factors"—nasty little tics like chronic health problems, long-term disability, recent restriction of activity, consultation with a health professional, and taking prescription and non-prescription medication. As Badley noted in the March 1994 issue of *The Journal of Rheumatology*, arthritis and related musculoskeletal disorders are at the top of the list of villains in a recent survey of causes of "morbidity indicators." "No other disease group," Badley wrote, "not even circulatory disorders (including heart disease), had such a consistently high rank."

What is the economic impact of all this? Not surprisingly, given that arthritis has been accorded short shrift from the powers-that-be in terms of such essentials as research funding (it ranks twelfth in federal funding, below dental research), there have been few attempts made to tally up the costs. There's one set of figures available, though, courtesy of Health and Welfare Canada, called "Economic Burden of Illness in Canada, 1986." Published in 1991 as a supplement to Health and Welfare's series *Chronic Diseases in Canada,* the study estimated the cost of musculoskeletal (MSK) conditions—including arthritis and related disorders—at just over 8.2 billion 1986 dollars, which accounted for 10.4 per cent of all health costs in this country. MSK disorders accounted for almost a third of all chronic disability costs.

Keep in mind that that was then, this is now, and 2021—when the first Baby Boomers will already be seventy-five—is going to be a whole new ball game. Let's face it, we grew up in a land of plenty. Many of us never faced a more intractable dilemma than how to weasel floor seats to the next Rolling Stones or U2 concert.

Well, the times (as another aging Boomer once said) they are a'changin'. Since the prevalence of all illness and the requirement for medical care increase exponentially with age (arthritis is only the most common among many chronic disorders that affect the elderly), Boomers are in for a rude awakening: Not only will there be a radical shortage of young and healthy caregivers, but Medicare—the much-vaunted birthright of every Canadian since 1966, the sine qua non of national identity—is, in all probability, going to be lying supine in intensive care (a subject we'll return to in chapter 14).

Our health-care system has always been among the best in the world, but it's bursting at the seams, and something's got to give. As *Maclean's* reported in 1994, "Aside from world wars, health care may be the most spectacular venture this country has ever taken."

We can't afford to fight a war on that scale anymore, yet over the last generation or so, health-care costs have risen faster than a cheap condo. Let's look at the big picture: In 1995, health care cost Canada some $72 billion, about 10 per cent of gross domestic product (GDP). That's close to $2500 for every man, woman and child in Canada—$10,000 for a family of four—a far cry from the $200 per capita envisioned in 1966 by the late Justice Emmett Hall, the father of Medicare. Not even Nostradamus could have imagined, though, that the cost of everything (except pocket calculators) was going to go through the roof. In 1975–76, the total bill for Canadian health care was a mere $9.5 billion; four years later, it was $15.1 billion. A decade later, health care had become a sucking chest wound, bleeding $41.6 billion out of the total federal budget, a figure that seemed astronomical until we picked up the '93 tab.

Everything's more expensive, and there's so much more that modern care facilities have to have: A standard electric hospital bed costs about $5000 these days—a relative pittance, since hospitals are using fewer and fewer of them, as they move to a greater reliance on outpatient services, particularly in the treatment of arthritis. But, at the same time, sophisticated diagnostic tools, such as magnetic resonance imaging (MRI) scanners, are often seen as essential parts of the doctor's brand-new bag. (They're especially useful in revealing the effects of arthritis on soft tissue, which doesn't show up on ordinary x-rays.) Adding one of these to a clinic costs $250,000—about as much as fifty hospital beds—to say nothing of CAT scanners, electron microscopes, extraordinary new medications. . .

It's a dismal equation: an increasingly aging population plus increasing prevalence of age-associated chronic disease plus soaring costs and dwindling health-care resources equals. . . well, it equals that crunch time we referred to earlier.

Governments, federal and provincial, have already begun shutting off the IV of cash Baby Boomers grew up believing was their birthright. Increasingly, bankers and bondholders and currency speculators here and abroad are dictating the scope of Canada's social policies, as fiscal policies are implemented to service combined federal-provincial deficits, which devour an enormous chunk of Canada's GDP. Those policies are misinformed and unfair (we'll come back to that in chapter 14), and none of us can afford to ignore them, because they threaten to blow Medicare right out of the water.

In the meantime, Medicare is undergoing major surgery, and the prognosis for its ideals of equal access, portability of benefits, and uniform high-quality service have dimmed considerably. They're no longer sacred cows, and by the time Boomers sit down for their cut of the health-care steak, there may be nothing but hamburger left on the table. There are things each of us can do about the situation, but, whatever happens, a good many of us are going to have to become (and it's to our benefit to become) arthritis self-managers, because—it can't be stressed too often—arthritis *is* going to play a role in our future.

This book is an attempt to cover everything you need to know to minimize its impact on your life: There are detailed descriptions of many types of arthritis; how these various conditions are treated by health professionals; effective strategies for maintaining control over your life, despite the inevitable ups and downs of the disease; what services and other resources are available; where research is headed; and what the "health-care crisis" *really* means.

1

A Substance That Flows
An Overview of Arthritis

Of Change, the which all mortall things doth sway...
—*Spenser,* The Faerie Queene

Life, as an old pop song put it, is a carnival, a kaleidoscope of experience and events, a dizzying sequence of changes, of growth, maturation, and decline. Change is the salt sea in which we swim. In the course of life's voyage, we learn to adapt to each shifting current, every eddy and flow, riding the crest of a wave or bailing out of its trough.

For millions of Canadians, arthritis is one of those changes. If they're lucky, it's little more than an annoyance, an occasional discomfort or limitation; by far the majority of people with arthritis lead otherwise normal lives with only minor problems attributable to their disease; some people even claim that having the disease has made their lives *better*, because they've learned to re-examine their values and priorities and discover what's truly meaningful in their lives, forge new friendships and re-evaluate old ones, or simply become stronger.

Some people thrive on a little adversity—but make no mistake, that's what it is, and when it's more than a little, it can be daunting indeed. Of the 4 million-plus Canadians with arthritis, more than 600,000 have some degree of disability that hobbles their ability to perform everyday tasks. According to Arthritis Society figures, three-quarters of them need occasional help with everything from household chores to washing, dressing, and preparation of meals; three out of ten have trouble getting in and out of a bathtub or turning on the taps; and more than half of all adults disabled by arthritis have been knocked out of the labour force by their condition.

At its most severe, arthritis can impose change with the force of a tsunami, a tidal wave so high and strong it threatens to swamp people completely. Yet most learn to adapt. They learn to use whatever resources are available—friends and family, organizations such as The Arthritis Society, community health workers, medical professionals, etc. They learn to swim against the current and find a patch of high ground, sometimes, admittedly, after an exhausting struggle.

But there are others—the unlucky few—who are totally overwhelmed by arthritis, relegated to a shortened life of severe, often constant pain, deformity and ever-increasing disability. Technically arthritis isn't a fatal disease, but it *can* be deadly, albeit rarely. Systemic forms, such as lupus (see page 25) and RA (see page 17), can cause serious complications, including inflammation in major organs, such as the heart, liver, and kidneys. If such conditions aren't correctly diagnosed and treated, they can be fatal.

For a small percentage of people, the "cure" proves deadlier than the disease: Every year, some 1900 Canadians die from ulcers caused by NSAIDs (non-steroidal anti-inflammatory drugs), an extremely important and normally extremely valuable component in the treatment of inflammatory arthritis. What makes such deaths doubly regrettable is that most of them could have been prevented with more careful monitoring.

That said, it has to be stressed again that most people with arthritis do live full, active lives, despite the impositions of their disease. To minimize the damage arthritis causes, arm yourself with understanding. The most effective route to managing the disease is expressed in a simple maxim: Know thy enemy.

What Is Arthritis?

Arthritis is an umbrella term for more than a hundred different conditions. Strictly speaking, arthritis is inflammation (from the Greek *itis*) in a joint (*arthron*), but it's come to refer to almost any painful condition that attacks the musculoskeletal system—the bones, joints and the soft tissues that connect them. They include such obvious entries as rheumatoid arthritis (RA) and osteoarthritis (OA), plus lupus, gout, scleroderma, ankylosing spondylitis, fibromyalgia syndrome—even soft-tissue problems such as bursitis and tendonitis.

These discrete conditions are known as rheumatic diseases, a term that dates back to the first century A.D., when various and sundry ailments were described as *rheuma,* Greek for "a substance that flows." They were believed to be caused by *phlegm,* one of the "humours," mysterious fluids that supposedly originated in the brain, causing illness wherever they happened to flow in the body. The term "rheumatologist," meaning a doctor who specializes in arthritic conditions, was only coined in the 1940s. Its use didn't much predate the decline of the term "rheumatism"—at least among most medical professionals—a vague, catch-all term used to describe almost any pain or swelling in joints and surrounding soft tissues.

What actually causes arthritis is still unknown, though researchers appear to be closing in on the triggering factors in a number of conditions. Certainly within the last generation, they've made tremendous advances—in medications, surgery, and the roles of rest, exercise and nutrition, pain control, and occupational therapy—in treating just about every form of arthritis. There's also greatly increased understanding in the role *you* can play in the self-management of your disease, as a key member of your health-care team.

Most forms of arthritis affect the joints and the surrounding tissues, either through inflammation, as in RA; cartilage erosion, as in OA; or both (RA again). For you to cope effectively with your condition, you have to know what's happening and why, so let's start with a skeletal review.

Joints (also called articulations) come in three basic categories. All joints (you have more than a hundred) are connections between 2 or more of your 206 bones, as in the hip or knee. Most are designed to allow a certain amount of motion, though some, called synarthrodial joints, are fused, allowing only enough motion for normal growth. The cranial bones of the adult skull—as solid as a breadbox—are the best example. Amphiarthrodial joints, as in the vertebrae, are tightly bound together by flexible but tough tissue that permits only slightly greater motion.

The third category, the diarthrodial joints, are your big movers and shakers. They're the most numerous and allow the greatest range of motion. Because these joints all have a synovial membrane (described below) that contains synovial fluid, these joints are more commonly referred to as synovial joints. There are several kinds, each a tiny lesson in engineering excellence: ball-and-socket (hips and shoulders), saddle joints (which connect thumb to hand), hinge joints (fingers and knees), and pivot joints (wrists).

Normal Joint

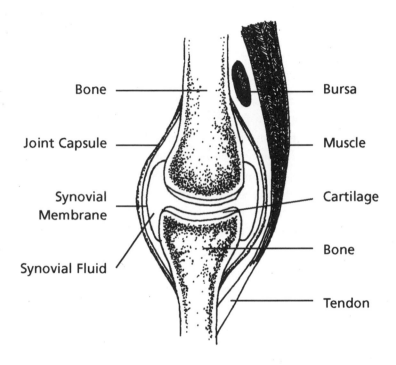

Bone — Bursa

Joint Capsule — Muscle

Synovial Membrane — Cartilage

— Bone

Synovial Fluid — Tendon

Holding the ends of (usually) two bones together are tough, elastic tissues called ligaments, which give the joint much of its stability. Further stability (and movement) is provided by the sheaths of muscles surrounding a joint and the tendons that anchor the muscles to bone. Muscles and tendons take up much of the load placed on a joint through normal activity, including the shock of weight-bearing. Bursa are small, liquid-secreting sacs that ease the passage of tendons over the hard surfaces of bone and other muscles.

Joint interiors are where most of the action takes place in arthritis. The bone ends, to begin with, are capped with articular cartilage, a resilient, fluid-filled material that acts as a kind of hydraulic shock absorber, squeezing its inner fluids to the greatest stress points during load-bearing. If the cartilage is damaged (as in OA), the bones of a joint can start to grind against each other, causing pain, increasing loss of mobility, and sometimes deformity.

Between the bones in a synovial joint is the joint cavity, which gives the bones room to move. It's enclosed by a synovial membrane, the synovium, which secretes a viscous substance that lubricates the joint and digests bacteria and debris (synovia means "like egg white"). The synovium itself is extremely thin, well lubricated and flexible. For clarity, it's usually depicted in illustrations as a fairly generous, fluid-filled space; in fact, in most normal human joints, the synovium collapses in on itself and the articular cartilage it encloses, keeping joint space to a minimum. If you cut into a synovial joint, you're likely to find a tacky coating on the cartilage and synovial lining—they're more tar pits than pools. The joint is surrounded in turn by a strong, flexible capsule that helps protect the joint against dislocation. The joints of the body are indeed elegant constructions: flexible, long-lasting and tough, but vulnerable.

— —

We'll be talking more about inflammation in the pages that follow, since it's involved in most types of arthritis, even OA, which, generally speaking, isn't considered an inflammatory form of arthritis. Inflammation is one of the body's natural healing responses to infection or injury, a strategic marshalling of immune system components in the blood (such as infection-fighting white blood cells) to the trauma site. This "immune cascade" causes redness, heat, swelling, pain, and decreased function in the affected area—proof that your body is doing its job, inducing you to immobilize and rest the injured area while it takes care of business.

In inflammatory arthritis, though, the defence force is overzealous. It goes out of control, attacking the body's own tissues as though *they* were the enemy. What causes this autoimmune response, as it's called, isn't known, but the results are clear: The synovial lining becomes thickened and the joint becomes clogged with white blood cells, which begin excreting enzymes and growth hormones that erode the cartilage on the bone ends, as well as surrounding soft tissues and even the bone itself. Unchecked, the process causes increasing levels of pain, deformation, and disability.

In OA, the principal issue is cartilage degradation; there's usually little inflammation, though it's sometimes present because of bits of eroded cartilage irritating the synovial lining. OA used to be considered strictly a "wear-and-tear" condition brought on by trauma (as in sports injuries) or years of wear on weight-bearing joints: hips, knees, ankles, feet, and spine. It's now known that other factors are also at work, including joint misalignment and, in some cases, heredity. OA also strikes the fingers, particularly the end joints and the base of the thumb, but it can develop in the ribs or the jaw or the elbows—just about any joint. Again, the result is pain, sometimes deformity, and decreased function.

Another term you might hear is synovitis, which simply refers to inflammation of the joint lining, one of the hallmarks of inflammatory arthritis. Diseases of attachment (known as enthesopathy, as in ankylosing spondylitis, one of the few forms of arthritis that predominantly affects men) attack the sites where ligaments and tendons are anchored to bones, initially causing inflammation, but often leading to tissues becoming thickened and scarred and sometimes hard and bony. Gout and pseudogout are another story. They're due to excess deposits of crystallized salt in a joint, causing synovial inflammation and, of course, pain. Arthritis can also be caused by infections that invade a joint (see page 53), either directly, as in a wound or from an operation, or indirectly, via the bloodstream from another site in the body.

Diagnosing Arthritis

Again, what causes most types of arthritis isn't clear, though it's believed there are multiple factors at work, including genetic predisposition (in a few though not all types of arthritis), injury, and viral or bacterial infection. Despite innumerable claims, no study has ever shown a definite link between arthritis and food (see page 186), though it's possible that in certain individuals an allergic reaction to something they ate could trigger an arthritic episode. Other than weight loss, which can reduce potential risks of developing OA in susceptible people, there's nothing you can do to prevent arthritis, as you can reduce your risk of heart disease, say, by quitting smoking. And, although certain forms of the disease, such as OA, increase in prevalence with age, there's nothing in the aging process that provides a clear link to arthritis.

The first signs of arthritis may include any or all of the following (it doesn't always start with joint pain):

- redness, or warmth in a joint that you can actually feel with your hand;
- swelling in one or more joints;
- stiffness, especially in the early morning;
- recurring pain or pain not attributable to a traumatic injury that persists in one or more joints for two weeks or more;
- decreased ability to move a joint normally, especially if moving the joint causes pain;
- an unexplained rash;
- sudden weight loss, fever, or persistent fatigue and weakness combined with pain in muscles or one or more joints.

Note: These are only warning signs; they don't mean you *do* have arthritis. A skin rash could be caused by allergies or any number of dermatological problems, and an aching jaw might mean you need a root canal, not a rheumatologist. The last thing you should consider is any kind of self-prescribed regimen of treatment, based on friends' advice— or for that matter, the information in this book: Only a doctor can make the diagnosis, and it isn't always easy, even for specialists. Many forms of arthritis are notoriously difficult to diagnose, especially in the early stages. It's not uncommon for people with conditions such as fibromyalgia or lupus to suffer low-grade symptoms for months (even years in some cases) without getting a correct diagnosis and treatment, even though they've been examined by doctors. Think about it: You're feverish, you have achy, painful joints, you're immobilized with fatigue, and you're having the devil of a time sleeping—it could be anything from the onset of "the flu" or hemorrhagic fever to RA or one of the more obscure forms of arthritis.

With some forms of arthritis, particularly OA, your GP may be able to make a quick diagnosis and prescribe suitable treatment, but in many cases it's anything but obvious. If your GP suspects arthritis but can't positively identify it, he or she will refer you to a rheumatologist. Making a diagnosis often requires a good deal of specialized detective work. The process begins with a detailed medical history—a summary of current and past medical problems, as well as a review of your family's medical problems, since some kinds of arthritis have a genetic component.

The doctor will need as accurate and detailed an account as you can provide of your symptoms, so be prepared to answer a lot of questions: Where does it hurt? Which joints have been giving you problems? For how long? Did you sustain an injury to the affected joint? Have you noticed any pattern to the symptoms—for example, do you experience the most intense pain and stiffness in the morning? Do certain activities increase your discomfort? Is there any fever? Have you lost a noticeable amount of weight recently? Are you overly tired, having trouble sleeping, depressed? The answers to such questions can provide valuable clues.

You'll also be given a thorough physical examination, with careful attention to all of your joints. Putting your joints through range-of-motion tests is a way of assessing whether or not you have "normal" function. Hands are key indicators: Pain and swelling in the small finger joints could be a tipoff of OA, whereas the same symptoms in the middle joints and the large knuckles could indicate RA. The doctor will also look for deformities caused by the disease, such as painless lumps, or nodules, that are typical of RA, or a tophus—another kind of lump—caused by crystal deposits in gout.

X-rays are useful in distinguishing between OA and RA where diagnosis has proved difficult. In OA, for example, the narrowing of the joint space is uneven, bone may have thickened, and outgrowths, called spurs, or osteophytes, may have formed on the bone and small cysts under the cartilage. In RA, the joint space narrowing is more even, there's more soft-tissue swelling and no bony accumulation.

Less frequently, a physician will ask that a small tissue sample be surgically removed from a joint for examination (a biopsy), fluid aspirated from the joint space (drawn out with a needle under local anesthetic), or suggest that the joint be examined and assessed arthroscopically (see page 223).

Lab tests—mainly blood tests, though a urinalysis can reveal arthritis-related problems in kidney function—are the most common diagnostic procedure. Blood carries a heavy burden of chores in its ceaseless flow, transporting oxygen to every part of the body, hauling food, waste products and hormonal messengers, and marshalling the armies of the immune system in the body's defence against invaders. Left to settle in a beaker and treated with salt, it will divide into three distinct layers: a thick layer of clear, colourless liquid known as plasma at the top, a narrow band of white blood cells (leukocytes) in the middle, and a large layer of red blood cells (erythrocytes) at the bottom. Inflammation can disrupt that measured order, causing the white count to soar (leukocytosis), sending the red count plunging (anemia), or elevating the platelet count.

While a complete blood count (or CBC) can reveal these changes, it can't confirm arthritis by itself. Anemia can just as easily be caused by blood loss or vitamin deficiency, and a high white count may simply reflect the presence of an infection.

For that matter, people with lupus can have extremely low white cell and platelet counts (platelets play a key role in blood clotting), despite intense inflammation. Inflammation can also be detected with a test known as a sed rate (for erythrocyte sedimentation), which measures the rate at which blood settles in a tube: The more inflammation that's present, the faster red cells settle. Again, though, it's not a conclusive test, since inflammation can be caused by other conditions in addition to arthritis.

Similarly, the presence of an antibody known as rheumatoid factor (RF) in the blood is a strong indicator of RA, but not a sure bet—only about 80 per cent of people with RA have RF in their blood. People with OA generally don't have RF in their blood, and often have a normal sed rate, but if there's inflammation present, their sed rate could be elevated. Antinuclear antibody (ANA) is a strong clue in testing for lupus (some 95 per cent of people with lupus have ANA in their blood), but since half of all RA patients also test positive in ANA tests, it's not proof positive for either condition.

There are other blood tests that can be done, though none, taken alone, is sufficient to confirm a diagnosis. Considered as part of the overall picture, though—along with the medical history and physical exam—a diagnosis is usually possible. If it isn't, your doctor will ask you to monitor your condition closely and come back for an examination and further tests. (For more on lab tests, see page 154.)

Getting a diagnosis, of course, is just the beginning. Most forms of arthritis are chronic, though they may go through periods of remission (a temporary or, in some lucky people, full abatement of symptoms) and exacerbations, or flares, when the symptoms take a turn for the worse. Arthritis can be a real roller-coaster ride. Before we look at how you can keep your seat through the ups and downs, though, let's take a closer look at some of the many forms arthritis can take.

2

All Features Great and Small
Common Forms of Arthritis

My bones are pierced in me in the night season,
and my sinews take no rest.
                    —*King James Bible,* Book of Job

Arthritis is a many-headed beast, a shape-shifter with a hundred and some disguises. Many of its incarnations are extremely rare, some are among the commonest conditions in the population. Many predominantly affect women, a few predominantly affect men, and a surprising number—given that arthritis has for so long been considered "an old person's disease"—affect children, as well. Some types involve inflammation; some don't. Some people are severely debilitated; some are barely affected at all. Arthritis can attack bones and the connective tissues of joints and, in systemic forms, wreak havoc in the heart, lungs, kidneys, liver, or in fact any system in the body, including the skin.

Over the last hundred years, most forms of the disease have been identified and defined, and effective treatment regimens developed. Some forms that might have been fatal in a majority of cases only a generation or so ago have largely succumbed to the fruits of research and advances in surgery and medications. In the next two chapters, we'll take a detailed look at some of the most prevalent forms of arthritis, with brief summaries of some of its less prevalent manifestations.

Rheumatoid Arthritis (RA)

"I never knew I had arthritis," says Ray Lockwood, forty-three, "never had any indication, until twelve years ago. I was heavily involved in curling, and I started to hurt in my hands and feet. I felt like I'd been beaten with a stick. Within a month, I was too sick to curl."

The pain, he says, "was excruciating. It really hit me hard." He was hospitalized in mid-December of that year, and the problem in his fingers was diagnosed as Raynaud's phenomenon (see page 46), a narrowing of the blood vessels in the extremities, a condition that more often strikes people with scleroderma and lupus. "By that time, my fingers were black. I can't even describe what the pain of that is like. It's like putting your finger in a vise and never letting go. There's no position you can put your hands, not up, not down, not anything. It was there constantly."

Lockwood was home for Christmas but shortly after was sick again—so sick, he says, "I didn't even know my own name." A friend and his wife, Debbie, literally carried him to his car and drove him to Sunnybrook Hospital in Toronto, where he was immediately admitted.

Lockwood stayed for three or four weeks while his condition— rheumatoid arthritis (RA)—was diagnosed and stabilized. "Never in my wildest imagination did I think I had arthritis," he says. "I thought I had some severe flu bug or a virus. My wife and my friends thought I was dying. I couldn't sleep for more than five minutes at a time. You can't eat, you can't do anything. I was sick for a year."

Over the next couple of years, Lockwood was treated with large doses of Tylenol 3 and intramuscular gold, with an occasional cortisone shot in his shoulders. Although he's since had no problems with his shoulders ("I find my arms get tired quicker than I'd think"), that first severe attack left damage in his left hip and right wrist.

The first sign was pain, then slowly increasing disability. Finally, about six years ago, his rheumatologist told him the only thing to be done was to have his hip replaced. Because of his age, though, he suggested Lockwood try to postpone it as long as he could.

By 1993, Lockwood's quality of life had deteriorated to the point that he couldn't do anything without suffering tremendously: "If I cut the grass, I couldn't walk for two days. Play a round of golf—well, I couldn't get past nine holes with a cart. The worst pain I felt was trying to sleep; I'd be up ten times a night. I couldn't do anything with my kids, with my daughter, with my son. Life just wasn't any fun any longer. So, I made the decision to do it."

Lockwood hasn't had any trouble keeping things in perspective. His son, Matthew, has a progressive genetic disorder, which is more on his mind, he says, "than anything that would ever happen to me.

It's called Hunter's disease, a mucopolysaccaride storage disease, very rare. He just turned thirteen, and I didn't think he'd live this long. So, you talk about the hip. That's nothing. My whole focus has been on trying to cope with his disease, and his problem. He was active at one point, walking and talking. Now he can't do anything for himself. The arthritis," he says with a wry laugh, "that was secondary."

For the last three years, Matthew's been in a wheelchair and has needed almost full care. Lockwood's wife, an R.N., has a bad back, "probably from nursing," and was having trouble manoeuvring Matthew into the bath and handwalking him to the table to eat. Lockwood found he wasn't much help: "I had to get myself looked after to be able to look after him."

Lockwood's surgeon told him that, after the surgery, he'd be able to do everything he'd been able to do before, up to a point. He'd have to modify his curling style a little, but he could play, and although impact sports were out, he could get back to cross-country skiing, golf, and swimming.

What the doctor didn't say was that it might not be a walk in the park; Lockwood discovered that for himself: "I had a harder time than most people with my operation. The pain in the hip was excruciating. The operation triggered another arthritic attack, which I hadn't had in years, and I had a lot of swelling in my leg, right down to the ankle. I couldn't even put a shoe or a sock on for the first two weeks."

Once the swelling went down, though, the arthritic pain—that continual ache in the hip—was gone. Nearly two years later, Lockwood still hadn't regained his full strength, probably because he didn't follow his physiotherapy regimen as diligently as he should have. "I wasn't disciplined enough to put myself through the hour-a-day routine," he admits. "There were a number of exercises, as often as you could do them, that are beneficial. You could even do them sitting down watching TV."

But then, Lockwood's got other things to keep him active, such as his daughter, Alyssa, and of course Matthew, the son he's now able to take care of. And, if there's any time left over, he might squeeze in a bit of curling, or a round of golf...

It isn't easy to put RA in perspective. For some people, it's a manageable imposition; for others, it's devastating. In fact, the recognition of just how serious RA can be is a relatively recent one. Only in the last decade, after a series of long-term studies, have physicians and researchers belatedly concluded that they've underestimated the long-term severity and overall impact of the disease. Because of that long-held misapprehension by medical professionals, RA has never been accorded the attention it warrants.

Although RA has nowhere near the prevalence of osteoarthritis (it affects about one in a hundred people, as against OA's one in ten), it has an enormous impact in terms of long-term disability and its effect on the health-care system, simply because a greater proportion of the people with RA are more cruelly afflicted. People with severe RA are often more seriously debilitated, requiring aids, assistive devices, wheelchairs, and so on. They may require help to perform the simplest tasks of everyday life and, among those who are disabled, a great percentage are unable to hold a job and are dependent on medical insurance, disability payments, and social welfare. RA sufferers represent countless hours in lost wages and lost productivity, they require more medication for a longer time, and they see physicians more often.

From x-rays, it's now known that more than half of all RA patients have some degree of cartilage and/or joint damage within the first two years of the onset of the disease, with progressive erosion occurring in nearly all patients during the first five years. RA may be relatively mild over the short term, but in the long run "most patients" will suffer joint erosion and damage in affected joints, noted Dr. Theodore Pincus at a 1993 symposium on RA.

"Most patients experience functional declines, work disability, and comorbidities [illnesses secondary to their RA] over a decade or longer," said Pincus, a rheumatologist from the division of rheumatology at Vanderbilt University in Nashville, Tennessee. "Increased mortality rates with shortening of lifespan by up to ten to fifteen years has been seen in some studies."

Not surprisingly, mortality rates increase with the severity of the disease: In patients with the most severe form of the disease, they're comparable to the mortality rates of people with three-vessel coronary artery disease and stage IV Hodgkin's disease. In other words, they have only a 50-50 chance of surviving the next five years.

Now, having redressed the standard misapprehension of RA's seriousness, let's take a step back: Yes, RA can shorten life (if not directly, then through secondary conditions; some studies suggest that, overall, men and women with RA have a life expectancy reduced by seven and three years respectively). However, the majority of people *don't* have a severe form of the disease, and, with early, appropriate care, mild to moderate RA can usually be managed quite effectively, with little disability or joint deformity.

RA is an autoimmune disease, that is, a disease in which the body's own defences mistakenly turn on itself. What causes it is unknown, though it's now believed that a bacterium or other infectious agent may trigger the inappropriate immune response in susceptible people. Most researchers believe more than one element is involved, including one or more triggering factors, heredity (though just because someone in your family has the disease doesn't mean you'll get it, too), and environmental factors.

Because RA affects more women than men, and because it often begins at menopause, it's likely that hormones play some role in its onset or development. The hormone theory has gained additional credence from long-term studies that showed a reduced incidence of the disease in women using contraceptive pills. Women with RA who become pregnant also often notice a reduction of symptoms (RA doesn't appear to affect fertility or harm a developing fetus), but they may experience a flare of symptoms after the birth of the baby. (Like all pregnant women, women with RA have to be careful about taking medications while they're pregnant: Medication can pass through the placenta and harm the baby. If you're planning on becoming pregnant, consult with your doctor beforehand if possible.)

Symptoms

As noted above, RA affects approximately one in a hundred people (some 300,000 Canadians), women two to three times more often than men. It can begin at any age, from early childhood to old age, but typically begins between twenty-five and fifty. The older you are when it begins, the less likely you are to have a severe form of the disease.

Its cardinal symptom is synovitis, an inflammation of the lining of a joint capsule caused by an invasion of the synovial membrane by immune cells. This causes the typical redness, swelling (sometimes heat), stiffness, and pain in a joint with inflammatory arthritis. As this autoimmune activity progresses, the synovial fluid becomes engorged with immune cells (synovial proliferation), leading to a thickening of the synovial lining itself ("pannus"). RA usually attacks the large knuckles and middle joints of the fingers, the hands, wrists, elbows, shoulders, knees, ankles, and feet, but it can affect any of the joints in the body, usually symmetrically (if one hip is affected, usually the other is too). People who suffer deformities in their joints are the most likely candidates for disability later on.

Tendons and ligaments may also be affected, especially in the smaller joints. Fingers may become misshapen, causing swan neck and boutonnière deformities in the small joints, or, in the large knuckles, causing the fingers to turn, away from the thumb (ulnar drift). Hands sometimes become painfully weak and functionally limited, and it may be difficult to grasp any kind of utensil with ease; a range of modifications may have to be made to your environment.

Some people develop RA in the joints of the neck, leading to erosion of the cervical vertebrae, which causes periodic headaches, a most unsettling cracking sound and, if severe, progressive disability. People with RA also often suffer painful involvement in their feet; in fact, RA can impose severe disability limitations on any joint it invades, reducing range of motion, and causing great pain and stiffness. As the disease progresses, you may have to learn whole new ways of accomplishing the simplest tasks, using assistive devices, for example, to wash and dress or to prepare meals.

RA is a systemic disease, capable of affecting nearly any of the body's major organs and systems. There may be inflammation of the membrane surrounding the heart (pericarditis) or the lungs (pleurisy), and some people develop dry mouth and eyes due to inflammation of the salivary and lacrimal glands, a condition known as Sjögren's syndrome (see page 59). More rarely, people with RA develop vasculitis, an inflammation of the blood vessels that can affect the skin, nerves, and other organs and tissues.

Many people experience fatigue and flulike symptoms or low-grade fever, as well as rashes, or develop lumps called rheumatoid nodules under the skin, particularly over bony areas, such as the elbows (they can also appear elsewhere, including the internal organs).

Morning stiffness, or stiffness after having been sitting for a while (known as "the gel phenomenon") are typical; some people suffer loss of appetite, weight loss, anemia, and/or depression—a not uncommon side effect of almost any chronic illness. Some symptoms are a useful gauge of your condition. For example, your condition may be improving if your morning stiffness only lasts fifteen or twenty minutes (as against two or three hours).

RA can start slowly, with a gradual onset of fatigue and weakness before any joint pain, or come on like a freight train, with multiple joints suddenly swollen, tender and painful, causing excruciating pain with the slightest movement. As with all forms of arthritis, it's highly individual: The course of the disease may be relatively mild or severe, with a steady progression of symptoms, or following an up-and-down pattern, with frequent flares and remissions. In some 10 per cent of cases, the disease goes into permanent remission after less than a year.

Diagnosis and Treatment

Where RA is suspected or diagnosed by a GP, it should be immediately referred to a rheumatologist, who's knowledgeable about the many permutations the disease may present over time. Diagnosis proceeds from a detailed family history and an account of your symptoms, a full physical examination, which includes range-of-motion tests and the number and distribution of inflamed joints, and a battery of lab tests and x-rays. While useful, x-rays are insufficient in themselves. They can reveal joint-space narrowing, but they can't show any of the underlying processes of the disease itself.

Blood tests also reveal telltale signs of disease activity but, again, they're not conclusive—nor are they infallible. Perfectly healthy people sometimes test positive for disease indicators, and not everybody who's ill registers positive either. For example, some 80 per cent of people with RA are seropositive, that is, they have a protein called rheumatoid factor (RF) in their blood, but 20 per cent of RA patients are seronegative: Even though they have the disease, they *don't* have RF in their blood. (RF is an autoantibody—a protein that provokes an autoimmune response against its own body—that usually appears in higher quantities in people with RA.) In those who *do* have RF in elevated levels, it's usually indicative of a more severe case of the disease.

There's no cure for RA, and although 10 per cent of all people with the disease may go into complete remission, the remaining 90 per cent will have to learn to deal with a life-long problem. As with any chronic illness, your job will be to learn to manage the disease, rather than be managed *by* it. It may not be an easy task. You may have to make tremendous adjustments and modifications to your lifestyle and environment and maintain an ongoing struggle for emotional balance. For your sake and the sake of your family, avail yourself of whatever help and support is available, including doctors, nurses, pharmacists, occupational and physiotherapists, social workers, and so on. If you're not sure what kind of help and advice you can enlist, ask your doctor or any other health professional you're dealing with, or phone your local chapter of The Arthritis Society (see page 295 for a list of resources).

In the meantime, there's a good deal that can be done to treat your RA, thanks to substantial advances in the understanding of the disease and the development of far more effective medications.

The manifold goal of treatment is to reduce inflammation, relieve pain, maintain function, and prevent deformities, with a view to preserving quality of life and slowing disease progression. Certainly those who take the time and trouble to educate themselves in the nature and management of their disease experience the best possible outcomes. Become an arthritis self-manager: Learn everything you can about RA, what your medications are for and when you should take them; develop strategies for dealing with pain, and learn to schedule rest and physical therapy into your activities. Eat well, get plenty of gentle exercise, practise joint protection, and try to reduce stress and activities that leave you overly tired.

As you undertake to manage your arthritis, reduce pain, and maintain joint function, remember that you're not alone. Ask your doctor for his or her advice, and don't hesitate to ask for a referral to a physio- or occupational therapist. They can help you devise a rest-and-exercise program, learn about joint protection, prepare working and resting splints and assistive devices and, if necessary, redesign your home or work environment to reduce stress and strain on arthritic joints.

Ask your doctor or your pharmacist about your medications; don't just follow orders blindly—it's important that you understand them so that you can judge the relative severity of side effects and make the right decisions to deal with any that crop up. Almost without exception, everyone with RA will have to take some form of medication—perhaps many different medications over the years—for pain, to reduce inflammation, and to try to arrest the progress of the disease. Virtually all RA medications involve potential side effects, but many people with RA experience tremendous benefits from them. Some people even experience temporary or permanent remissions—thanks to medications—providing they're started early enough and used wisely, in careful consultation with their physicians.

Although your RA may not seem particularly severe to you, your doctor will in all likelihood suggest an aggressive approach to your treatment, by prescribing powerful "second-line" medications right from the outset. There is an increased risk of side effects from such drugs, but the approach is based on a relatively new and more complete understanding of the disease process. It's now understood that the route to achieving the best possible outcome is to fight the disease early, before it's had a chance to effect permanent damage and lasting disability. (For a fuller explanation of this concept, see Dismantling the Treatment Pyramid, on page 126.)

Surgery is sometimes an option in RA, to repair soft-tissue damage and to realign or replace badly eroded joints, but usually only after more conservative strategies have been exhausted.

Finally, if you need advice with medical plans and insurance, or you're losing your emotional footing, talk to a social worker or a psychologist; they can help you sort out problems you don't feel able to deal with alone and—together with other members of your health-care team—they can help you develop coping strategies that work.

Systemic Lupus Erythematosus (Lupus, or SLE)

Lupus is Latin for wolf. The name comes from a red rash that spreads in a characteristic butterfly pattern over the bridge of the nose and cheeks of some people with lupus, lending its bearers, it's said, a wolflike appearance. That's certainly one explanation for the origin of the name. It was a Parisian dermatologist, Pierre Cazenave, in 1851, who coined the term "lupus erythematosus," the latter half from the Greek word *erythema,* meaning redness. Cazenave may have meant to echo the term for skin lesions, known as lupus pernio (*pernio* is Latin for congestion and swelling of the skin due to cold), that he'd seen in patients with sarcoidosis (see page 56). A more whimsical notion is that he associated the shape of the rash with a type of mask worn by society ladies at costume balls, popularly called *un loup.*

Nearly half a century later, Sir William Osler, the great Canadian-born physician, realized that many of his patients with the rash had more than a skin condition. The rash was merely a telltale sign of a far more "systemic" ailment—a descriptive modifier he appended to more appropriately describe the overall disease.

Lupus can and often does cause nausea, weight loss, and muscle weakness, as well as chronic inflammation in many different parts of the body, including the skin, muscles, and joints (the connective tissues), lymph nodes, and spleen. Lupus also poses a risk of kidney damage, in which inflammation impairs the organs' ability to filter waste products from the blood. The result may be uremia, a poison buildup in the system, which can cause nausea, vomiting, and extreme fatigue, or proteinuria—an excess of protein in the urine, which may in turn lead to edema, swelling in various parts of the body due to fluid accumulation.

Serositis is another potentially severe problem, often taking the form of pleuritis or pericarditis (inflammation of the lining of the lungs or heart, causing chest pain, difficulty breathing, and sometimes fever). In fact, any of the vital organs can be affected. Even the blood vessels of the brain (in rare cases) can become inflamed, leading to paralysis and convulsions.

Many people with lupus also suffer from Raynaud's phenomenon (see page 46). As well, among women with lupus who become pregnant, there's a high incidence of miscarriage, especially in the first three months.

Lupus is often called "the great pretender," because many of its symptoms mimic those of other diseases, making diagnosis vexingly difficult, especially during its early stages. A definitive diagnosis can take a year or more. Lupus strikes about one in two thousand people—fourteen to fifteen thousand Canadians—women eight to ten times more often than men. It usually appears in women between the ages of twenty and forty, although it can occur at any age in either gender and is equally common to both after age fifty. In severe cases, it causes death. In fact, as recently as the 1940s, only one patient in six survived three years after diagnosis.

Thanks to intensive clinical and basic science research, that last grim statistic has been radically upgraded, to something like one fatality in ten cases a decade after diagnosis. By far, the majority of people with lupus live full, basically normal lives, as the disease and its symptoms can usually be treated.

People with lupus often suffer from a double affliction. There's the disease itself, but added to that is an emotionally corroding experience: the misunderstanding and skepticism, sometimes outright disbelief, that many people with lupus are subjected to by colleagues, family members, and friends—even some physicians. It's partly a visibility problem: How can you be sick, someone will ask, when you look perfectly healthy?

Such queries usually reflect the disease's own fickle mercies: Sometimes you're up, sometimes down, victim to an inconstant spectrum of ills. Lupus isn't a "true" form of arthritis; more accurately, it's a connective-tissue disease, though it's classified as a rheumatic disease because its symptoms usually include joint pain and swelling. About half of all people with lupus do develop recognizable arthritis, though very few of them suffer the deformities associated with severe forms of that disease.

There are still major questions concerning the cause, or causes, of lupus, and a real cure is still only a dream. (It's known that some people develop drug-induced lupus from taking medications for other conditions.) It is certain, however, that lupus is an autoimmune disease, a disorder in which the body's own defences turn on itself.

Furthermore, there appears to be an inherited predisposition for the disease, although the specific gene or genes involved have yet to be identified. Current theory suggests that heredity alone can't explain why some people develop the disease and others don't. Some external trigger, perhaps a bacterium or virus, may be responsible for starting the disease process in genetically predisposed people. It could also be the result of one or more environmental factors, such as childbirth, hormonal changes, a traumatic injury, an infection—even sunlight.

Diagnosis and Treatment

That unknown trigger is just part of the reason physicians are at such pains to diagnose the condition. Then there's the fact that no two patients suffer, or present with symptoms, in quite the same way. Symptoms can include anything from hair and weight loss and rashes to ulcerated mouth sores and throat and facial swelling (which may indicate kidney failure). Some people develop mainly joint problems. And any patient can get any combination of the full menu.

Diagnosis begins with a patient's history. A family history of lupus or another autoimmune disorder, such as rheumatoid arthritis, is a strong clue. The doctor then performs a physical examination to confirm suspicions raised by the history. Joint inflammation, for example, would suggest arthritis, but if there's a rash that flares from exposure to the sun (see Photosensitivity, below), or other rashes on the body consistent with lupus, the diagnosis is clearer. There are a number of other techniques a physician can perform to confirm the diagnosis, including tests for inflammation around the lungs and heart. There are also lab tests to identify lupus-associated immunological dysfunctions, including tests for FANA (fluorescent antinuclear antibody), anti-DNA, and anti-Sm (a substance found in cell nucleii that was named after a patient—named Smith—in whom the first "anti-Smith" antibody was found).

The arthritis component is one of the most confusing factors in diagnosing lupus, since many of its symptoms are shared with various rheumatic disorders. As in RA, arthritis in lupus involves synovitis, inflammation of the synovial membrane enclosing a joint capsule, though the intensity of inflammation is less pronounced, and affected joints rarely become disfigured. The range of joints affected is the same, or very nearly so: Any joint in the body is subject to attack, though the most frequent sites in lupus are the wrists, the large knuckles at the base of the fingers, and the middle finger joints.

In the lower body, knees fall victim more often than hips, though hips have their own (admittedly rare) problem—a blood-supply complication called aseptic necrosis (death of tissue without infection). Another major difference between RA and lupus is that, in RA, the inflammatory process leaves bone ends pitted. X-rays of affected joints in lupus almost never show that kind of damage, though the patient may still experience pain, and the joint will be tender to the touch or when it's moved through a range of motion.

Again, only a few lupus patients suffer any joint deformity. When they do, it's most often in the hands and fingers, and they don't lose as much dexterity as someone with a comparable degree of RA. Even the process of deformity is different. In RA, disfigurement results from the erosion of bone; in lupus, it's caused by joint slippage, known as subluxation—a partial or incomplete dislocation.

Today, most cases of lupus are eminently treatable; some people, in fact, require very little treatment at all, depending on their symptoms. Mild forms of the disease can usually be treated with non-steroidal anti-inflammatory drugs (NSAIDs) to reduce pain and inflammation. More serious forms of the disease, especially those involving a major organ, call for stronger medications, such as corticosteroids, though the most commonly prescribed medication for moderate to severe lupus is the antimalarial Plaquenil. Plaquenil has fewer associated side effects than the corticosteroids, though there's a real risk of serious vision impairment, so frequent checkups with your ophthalmologist (at least every six months) are essential. Immunosuppressant drugs, such as azathioprine (Imuran), are reserved for only the most serious cases of lupus, because of their potentially severe side effects. (See chapter 6 for further information on these medications.)

Rest, diet, and exercise programs all have a role to play in the management of the disease. You may find you tire easily and require scheduled rest periods: Don't overdo it—fatigue is sometimes enough to excite a flare-up of symptoms. For the same reason, you should investigate relaxation techniques to keep your stress levels to a minimum. Exercise is important to maintain overall body fitness and joint flexibility (and thus reduce fatigue and promote all-round health), but it should only be done in consultation with a physiotherapist or your doctor.

A healthy diet is important to your general health (as it is in any arthritic condition) but, because of the potential complications of lupus, ask your doctor or a nutritionist for specific dietary recommendations—for example, with regard to how much salt or protein you should allow yourself, and what foods will best control the progression of renal (kidney) disease.

Photosensitivity

About one in seven people with lupus suffers from photosensitivity, or reaction to the light of the sun, specifically ultraviolet (UV) light. A certain amount gets through even on cloudy days, and hats and visors are no guarantee of protection. Even fluorescent lights produce UV radiation. While they only emit minute amounts of UVB, the active band of UV light, their effect is cumulative and, over time, they can have the same effect as the sun.

Not every lupus patient has this photosensitivity, says rheumatologist Dr. Carl Laskin, director, Obstetric Medicine Program, University of Toronto, and staff rheumatologist at The Toronto Hospital, "but the thing that's important about it is, if someone *is* photosensitive, it's not just the rash you worry about. You get photoinduction of the immune system, so that the whole disease gets turned on." People with photosensitive lupus report flare-ups of symptoms after brief periods of exposure, ranging from fatigue and headache to rash, nausea, and joint pain. Some people have even complained of reactions to a half hour's shopping under the fluorescent lights of a large store.

(Ironically studies have also shown exactly the opposite effect— that exposure to some bands of UV light can actually *reduce* symptoms in people with photosensitive lupus. Dr. Hugh McGrath, associate professor of medicine at Louisiana State University Medical Centre in New Orleans, reported that exposing patients to low-dose ultraviolet-A1 radiation in a controlled setting for ten to fifteen minutes a week eliminated headaches, fatigue, and bad rashes. Not only did patients say they felt much better after brief treatments, those who missed treatments quickly reported feeling worse.)

In general, people with photosensitive lupus are advised to stay indoors during the hottest part of the day, that is, from noon to 3 p.m. If, like mad dogs and Englishmen, you simply must go out in the midday sun, slather on a good sun block, with a minimum SPF (sun protection factor) of 15. Cover arms and legs and sport a broad-brimmed hat, but keep in mind that the sun's rays reflect up off sand and a variety of hard surfaces, such as metal (in a boat, for example). For a mild rash or skin eruption, a topical cortisone cream may be all that's required, but a real overdose of sun can cause a reaction requiring emergency hospitalization.

Lupus and Pregnancy

Women with lupus face some special problems when it comes to pregnancy. Some women have trouble becoming pregnant; those who do become pregnant sometimes suffer recurrent miscarriages, and, while some women enjoy a relief from symptoms during pregnancy, many experience a flare-up of symptoms after the baby is born. On top of that, lupus medications can be harmful to the developing fetus. Yet none of these concerns means you *can't* have a child; it simply means you have to be careful. Sit down with your rheumatologist or doctor. There are a number of things you can do to minimize the risks for you and your unborn child.

The first thing to understand is that women with lupus may have a problem with fertility. If you're determined to become pregnant, you can take fertility drugs, but they can cause the disease to flare. Fertility drugs have different effects on different rheumatic diseases. In RA, for example, they may actually settle the disease down, but in lupus they impose a real risk of the disease flaring, so you have to be assessed to determine what kind of risk you have in undergoing fertility therapy. Some lupus patients don't have this sensitivity, says Laskin. "Several years ago it was *verboten* to give a lupus patient birth-control pills, because you ran into a high frequency of flaring of the disease. Now, although no one prescribes birth-control pills to a lupus patient with any sense of security—nobody's that glib—I make sure the patient's under good control. If I'm going to give fertility drugs, we have a session about it, and I follow blood work at least monthly. The blood work will tend to flare before you do clinically, and you have to determine whether or not there's a sensitivity to it."

If you're going ahead with a pregnancy, be aware of the facts: Some 25 to 30 per cent of women with lupus miscarry, because of the disease, and up to 50 per cent lose the baby, either by prematurity, interuterine fetal death, or miscarriage.

Prednisone is generally well tolerated by both mother and fetus, though many anti-inflammatories should be avoided, particularly later in pregnancy, because they can damage the fetus's heart (the problem can generally be treated postnatally with medication). Azathioprine (Imuran) isn't recommended by every doctor, but Laskin believes it to be safe for some women, with careful monitoring. On the other hand, although some authorities say methotrexate is safe, Laskin doesn't recommend it, because it can cause spontaneous miscarriage in isolated cases. And immunosuppressive and cytotoxic drugs are definitely out—they can cause miscarriages and fetal abnormalities. (See chapter 6 for further information on these medications.)

One last thing: If you *don't* want to become pregnant, should you consider an IUD (intrauterine device)? There are physicians who don't recommend them, for fear that they'll cause infections. "Some women do have trouble with IUDs," Laskin admits, "but we use them." Again, be cautious, and discuss any procedure or device you're thinking of trying with your doctor before you go ahead.

Osteoarthritis (OA)

Live long enough and almost all of us will develop osteoarthritis. OA occurs in one in ten Canadians, slightly more often in women than in men. It can develop at any stage in a person's life, but its prevalence increases dramatically with age: One out of five Canadians sixty-five or older is disabled by OA, and, by the time we're seventy-five, four out of five of us will show some degree of osteoarthritic changes on an x-ray.

It's a huge problem. OA is by far the single most serious drain on health-care resources of all the musculoskeletal disorders. According to the most recent edition of *Primer on the Rheumatic Diseases* (1993), OA has a financial impact thirty times greater even than rheumatoid arthritis, despite the fact that RA is generally more severe in its effects—simply because the prevalence of OA is ten times greater than that of RA. And that doesn't even begin to measure the impact of the disease on individuals, which can be enormous, although most people learn to manage their disease and live relatively normal lives.

OA can develop in any joint, in one or many, but it most commonly affects the hips (men slightly more than women), knees, spine, the small joints of the fingers (women especially), and the joints at the base of the thumb and the big toe. Other major joints, such as the wrists, elbows, shoulders, ankles, and jaw, are only rarely affected.

OA's essential characteristic is the breakdown of cartilage in joints, leading to pain, stiffness, decreased function, and in many cases, some degree of deformity. With the progression of OA in a joint, the cartilage becomes soft and pitted and loses its elasticity and strength;

as it's slowly eroded, the bone ends are exposed, rubbing painfully together with every motion. Gradually the bone ends thicken and develop bony growths called spurs, or osteophytes, where ligaments attach to bone. Bits of eroded cartilage and bone may float freely in the joint space, irritating the synovial lining and causing inflammation.

Strictly speaking, OA is not an inflammatory condition, as is RA — it's a degenerative joint disease. Thus some people prefer to call OA "osteoarthrosis," replacing *itis*, which refers to inflammation, with *osis*, which simply means condition. OA should also be distinguished from osteoporosis, a disease that causes loss of bone mass, leaving patients at high risk of breakage, particularly in the wrist, spine, and hips of older women.

Symptoms of OA generally begin slowly as aching and soreness in the joints, particularly after they've been overused. Pain, in fact, usually tends to increase throughout the day, as the joint is used. Morning stiffness is typical (gelling), but it can usually be alleviated with stretching or by moving about, at least at the outset. Some people experience little more than stiffness and discomfort, while a smaller number of people suffer intense, chronic pain. Some people also experience what's known as "referred pain," pain in a part of the body relatively distant from the affected joint. Due to pressure exerted on nearby nerves and muscles, for example, someone with an osteoarthritic hip might feel referred pain down the leg, in the buttocks, or even in the knee.

In any osteoarthritic joint, the ligaments that originally supported the joint gradually loosen, because the cartilage has lost some of its volume, causing the joint to become unstable and more painful. As the pain becomes more protracted, especially in weight-bearing joints, such as the hips and knees, activities such as climbing stairs become more difficult, the beginning of a cyclic decline: As activity levels diminish, muscles become weaker and less supportive of the joint, making exercise and activity still more difficult and painful.

As time passes, you may notice that the appearance of your joints begins to change. In women especially, one of the most obvious changes is the growth of spurs on one or more of the finger joints, giving the hands a gnarled appearance. Spurs in the end joints of the fingers are called Heberden's nodes (a condition that tends to run in families), after the physician who first documented them; spurs on the middle finger joints are Bouchard's nodes. Either can cause redness, swelling, tenderness and pain, though some people experience only a mild tingling or numbness, and some people suffer no real discomfort at all.

Knees are one of the commonest sites for OA. You may feel a slight temperature increase in the affected joint, and, if it's been going on for a while, there could be changes in its alignment. Arthritic knees may become enlarged and tender, and you may experience a grating or crackling sensation (crepitus) when you move the affected knee. If the disease progresses beyond minor discomfort, you'll probably find getting up from a chair or climbing stairs increasingly painful and difficult. Osteoarthritic hips and knees, in fact, are the most common reason for total joint replacement surgery.

In the feet, the large joint at the base of the toe is the most common site of OA, causing swelling, tenderness, and sometimes severe pain. A buildup of bony material at the side of the joint (a bunion) will sometimes develop, especially in people with a family history of bunions. Footwear with a large, boxed toe will provide some relief from overly tight shoes, but if the toe is giving you a great deal of pain and discomfort, surgery may be required to reduce the growth of bone.

OA can also cause a breakdown of joint tissues in the spine, causing stiffness and pain in the back and neck. In some people, this also leads to extra pressure being exerted on the spinal nerves, which can cause chronic pain at the base of your head, your neck, legs, lower back, or down your arms, and stiffness in your neck or lower back. Some people also experience a weakness or numbness in their arms or legs and at times have difficulty using their arms or walking.

What actually causes OA is still unknown, but a number of contributing factors have been identified. OA is now divided into two classes, primary and secondary. Primary is the kind that, theoretically at least, we'll all get—age-associated OA: After years of normal activity, cartilage simply breaks down and begins to erode (which isn't to say that everyone *is* going to develop OA).

Secondary OA can usually be linked to some instigating event— an accident, a sports injury, perhaps a sprain or fracture that never really seemed to heal. Any kind of trauma (or congenital misalignment) that leaves a joint even slightly out of whack can result in OA, sometimes decades later. Years of overuse can have the same result. Athletes especially are prone to developing secondary OA from years of running, jumping, throwing, or hitting a ball, but anyone in a profession that exposes a joint to long-term, repeated stress or impact (a carpenter, say—even a dentist) can be affected. (See also Repetitive Stress Injuries, page 65.)

OA can arise secondary to RA, and it now seems fairly clear that heredity plays a role in some people's OA. Scientists are also investigating the role of metabolism in the development of OA: Some people may be at greater risk because of an underlying hormonal imbalance.

A long-time suspicion on the part of many clinicians—that weight is a factor—was confirmed by a long-term study in the States. The findings were released several years ago in the *Annals of Internal Medicine*, based on a survey carried out on a substantial portion of the adult population of Framingham, Massachusetts, since 1948. It was found that overweight women, middle-aged or older, who lost weight over a ten-year period—and kept it off—cut their chances of developing OA of the knee by half. Subsequent studies and a wealth of clinical observation have concluded that obesity also places hips at risk. Thus, diet and exercise have a key role to play in the management of the disease.

Diagnosis and Treatment

Diagnosis of OA begins with the usual detailed medical and family history, a history of pain and a joint examination, with lab tests to rule out other kinds of arthritis. X-rays are generally taken to help the doctor make a definitive diagnosis. "When we look at the x-rays," says Dr. Mary Bell, a rheumatologist at the Sunnybrook Health Science Centre in Toronto, "what we're looking for is confirmation of what *you* feel and *we* see, and that comes through the x-rays. We look for that joint space narrowing and a little bit of extra bone being added on in certain places where it shouldn't be. This helps confirm a diagnosis and helps us make a plan for management with you."

Treatment in OA is keyed to managing symptoms of the disease, with a view to reducing pain, increasing flexibility, and maximizing joint function. "Management is working with you to try to maintain the basic human goal of preserving independence and our ability to enjoy our lives," says Bell. It begins with education, through support and information groups, outreach and out-patient programs, literature, videotapes—anything that helps you to learn what your disease is all about, what the treatment options are, and what you can expect from them.

"We try to target pain as something to relieve with time," Bell says, "and to improve joint and physical function through a combination of exercise, attainment of fitness, and improvement of activity levels in everyday life." Pain is an unfortunately unavoidable component of OA; for some people, it's a major hurdle on the road to managing their arthritis. While there aren't any medications available that work on the disease process itself (as there are for inflammatory forms of arthritis), there are effective analgesics and a wealth of non-medicinal techniques in pain reduction (see chapter 5).

Exercise is a key part of OA management. The body not only requires rest, it requires work. Even a moderate amount of activity promotes the biochemical processes that maintain the strength and vitality of a joint's tissues, and a regular exercise program helps promote better overall health and strengthens the muscles that stabilize and support an injured joint. If you're overweight, it can also be a first step toward losing some of those excess pounds.

Diet is also important, and some people will have to consider lifestyle changes to reduce stress on tender joints. If possible, consult a physiotherapist (PT) or occupational therapist (OT) for advice. PTs and OTs can instruct you in joint protection, custom-tailor exercise regimens, help you find ways to modify your activities, and suggest ways to redesign elements of your home or workplace to adapt to your changing capacities. An OT can also fit you for working and resting splints or orthotics and recommend other assistive devices, braces, walking aids, and scooters that can make life with disabling arthritis much easier.

Inevitably, some people will require surgery on one or more affected joints. Don't think of it as a last-ditch effort; as we'll discover, surgery is just one component in your overall disease management. For many people, in fact, surgery proves to be an extremely successful intervention when conservative strategies have proven ineffective.

Oil for Creaking Joints

Move any arthritic joint and it's going to hurt. For some people with OA of the knee, at least, there may be a solution—literally: a viscous liquid called hylan that temporarily replaces the natural fluid in a joint that's been reduced because of OA. When that fluid is lost, the natural inclination is to use the joint less, thus reducing the natural processes that maintain the elastic properties of the joint. It's a kind of self-perpetuating process that leads to the destruction of the joint.

Hylan, says Dr. Bell, "is a concentrated material designed to have the same shock-absorbing and lubricating properties as a normal material in the joint called hyaluronic acid [HA] or hyaluronan. [Synthetic hylan] is clear, thick, and for therapeutic purposes it comes in a prepared syringe. Under sterile conditions, and under local anesthetic, it can be injected into an osteoarthritic knee and improve the internal environment, the lubrication of the cartilage, and the circulation of fluid in the joint. This results in marked improvement in pain and mobility."

The process is known as viscosupplementation, the brainchild of American researcher Dr. Endre Balazs and his biotechnology firm, Biomatrix Inc. They devised a purified and concentrated form of HA (it was used initially to help race horses recover from injuries) generically termed hylan and marketed under the name Synvisc. The body recognizes the substance as chemically identical to its own HA and accepts it without mounting an immune response. In clinical trials in Europe, Japan and, most recently, Canada, some 70 per cent of participants have enjoyed improvement in function and alleviation of pain in their knees.

Despite being several times stronger and more elastic than natural HA, hylan is gradually absorbed from the joint space, making its way through the lymph system and the blood to the liver, where it's broken down and eliminated from the body. It can be injected into a knee joint without adverse effects, with treatment promising to deliver six months or more of pain relief. Its clinical success in treating OA of the knee follows from the fact that it works mechanically, rather than chemically, on a problem that's essentially mechanical. Posing no threat to the body's immune system, an injection of hylan temporarily protects the knee's pain receptors with virtually no side effects, permitting normal joint movement, which in turn permits the joint to restore its natural mechanism for maintaining healthy cartilage.

Health and Welfare Canada's Health Protection Branch has classed hylan as a device, rather than a drug, and it isn't covered under many medical insurance plans. A single regimen of three injections, spaced a week apart, costs about $300, but at least now you have a choice: Synvisc has a competitor (called Replasyn, from Bioniche Inc.). So far, neither has been approved for use in other joints, but there are early indications that it may have beneficial application to hips, as well.

Fibromyalgia Syndrome (FMS)

"I've had two days in seven years that I woke up and felt normal and went to bed feeling normal," says Lee Shimano, thinking back. "The first time I didn't know what was going on. The second time I was afraid. It was almost like I wanted to jump up and say, 'I'm cured!' Two days. And they were so depressing, because the next day I didn't feel that way anymore. It was kind of like a glimpse of the past."

Shimano has fibromyalgia syndrome, a much-misunderstood neuromuscular disorder that affects millions of North Americans (probably between three and five per cent of the population, though some estimates put the figure much higher), the majority of whom suffer for years without a proper diagnosis or, worse, are subjected to misdiagnosis and outright disbelief. Despite steadily mounting clinical evidence, despite two decades of studies, despite the acceptance of diagnostic criteria by international medical authorities, including the World Health Organization, recognition and understanding by physicians has been tragically slow.

Diagnosis and Treatment

Because FMS shares many symptoms with other illnesses, it's often mistaken for something else. The result, Shimano says, is "two schools of thought": Some doctors accept that the symptoms are real, but start looking for something else because "fibromyalgia's not really a disease in their minds." Others think "it's just a crock, or it's nothing, like saying you've got a stiff neck or something."

People with FMS *might* have a stiff neck, as well as a host of other ills, the most common being widespread—often constant—musculoskeletal pain, stiffness, nonrestorative sleep, chronic fatigue, and cognitive disorders, such as problems with memory and concentration. What differentiates FMS from a host of apparently similar disorders, though (including chronic fatigue syndrome, myofascial pain, and recurrent pain syndrome, not to mention various forms of arthritis and lupus) is a set of well-documented, precisely located "tender points." They don't normally cause real discomfort, but they're exquisitely sensitive to exact pressure, a painful fact, but an invaluable diagnostic criterion.

As yet, there's no cure for FMS, and its cause is unknown. It may be brought on suddenly after an accident or minor illness such as the flu, or symptoms may begin with no discernible "trigger" whatsoever. In Shimano's case, it began after the birth of her second daughter, then gradually grew more serious; at times she's been immobilized for up to six months from complications from her condition, and she's been hospitalized several times.

At times, though, she's enjoyed a kind of semi-remission from symptoms—not "a good remission," but enough to allow her to work part-time as a psychiatric assistant at the Clark Institute in Toronto. A former psychiatric nurse, Shimano would often find the job uneventful, even dull, but at the same time it could be extremely stressful, physically and emotionally. The day after tough shifts, she'd wake exhausted and would sometimes experience numbness in her right hand so intensely she couldn't write.

A competitive swimmer for most of her life, Shimano believes exercise helps keep her from "getting into big flare-ups." Exercise, in fact, is the subject of much debate. Some doctors (and patients) are convinced that a regular regimen of low-key exercise does help to reduce symptoms, but not everyone agrees. Some people with severe forms of the syndrome not only don't seem to benefit, but any kind of even moderately stressful exercise may provoke a flare of their symptoms. Even for those people, though, it's important to maintain a minimum level of activity, if only to keep muscles from becoming weak and joints from stiffening, which can intensify pain.

Pacing is another important facet of FMS management. Because fatigue is constant, you have to learn to rest before and after activities, rescheduling others when your pain is in a flare. Learn what your capabilities are, and learn to prioritize: If something doesn't have to be done, don't do it if you know you're going to suffer for it afterward, or postpone it until you feel stronger. Determine when your energy levels are highest—morning, afternoon, or evening—and try to schedule activities (or exercise) for those times, and try to keep stress to a minimum.

Despite your best efforts, though, sometimes things "just happen," without any discernible cause, Shimano says: "I'll suddenly break out in hives, then my joints flare up, and it just goes on and on—sometimes when I'm most at peace and restful and not stressed out at all."

Occasionally the hives and rashes are so bothersome she can't sleep. Chronically cheerful, she jokes about "huge, red, puffy rings" around her eyes and "big lumpy blotches" on her face. And some days her shoulder's "really hot," to the point that she has trouble dressing. Such episodes are baffling. "If I'm busy at work or goofing off on a weekend," she says with an ironic laugh, "I deserve to have some pain and stuff, and I take it quite nicely, but if it just kind of attacks me, it's very frustrating, because they can't really put a finger on it."

FMS is an insidious condition. Remission or no remission, Shimano has almost constant pain, sometimes less, sometimes more, in addition to frequent fatigue and recurrent episodes of a host of other symptoms. "I'm not good at being a sick person," she says. "I feel like I'm a healthy person. Everyone thinks I'm a healthy person. They think I just have *things* every so often: 'Oh, she's hurt her back. She's hurt her shoulder swimming'—that kind of thing."

There are medications that help with sleep disturbances, others that help with pain, but none is recommended explicitly for FMS—another indication of its lack of recognition as a distinct entity. For mild to moderate pain, non-medicinal strategies are your best bet (see chapter 5). Because FMS involves chronic pain, it's unwise to build a dependency on medication, because you'll gradually build up a tolerance to whatever you're using and thus need progressively stronger doses, with all the potential side effects that can entail. For periodic episodes of more extreme pain, regular Extra-Strength Tylenol may be sufficient, though some people who experience severe chronic pain will inevitably require prescription-strength medication.

Medications that mute the characteristic FMS sleep disturbance are, however, more widely used and more widely recommended. Sleep modifiers help to improve the quality of your sleep, and thus improve your pain tolerance. They don't help you go to sleep—as do sleeping pills, which are usually narcotic, and thus potentially addictive—they merely help you to sleep *deeper*, which can improve the quality of your sleep and relieve some of the achiness you may feel. The most commonly prescribed are amitriptyline (such as Elavil) and cyclobenzaprine (such as Flexeril). Keep in mind that neither is described as a sleep modifier: Many people stop taking amitriptyline when they discover it's actually an antidepressant drug ("*I'm* not depressed!"), but, in sleep-modifying doses (10-25 mg, compared to 300 mg for depression), it has little or no anti-depressant effect. Cyclobenzaprine is a muscle relaxant, which helps relieve some of the tension in muscles that may be contributing to non-restorative sleep.

Shimano isn't keen on taking anything if she can avoid it. A self-confessed "type A" personality—a go-getter—Shimano only rarely takes any medication: They're simply too sedating for her taste. She does use topical creams, particularly for the rashes, and "herbal things," and she'll occasionally take a Tylenol tablet, but unless absolutely necessary, that's about it: "I really have a strong preference not to get into that whole round. If I have to, I do, but I always feel sicker in the end. It doesn't do my body well."

She's learned to cope as best she can, in other words, with exercise and rest, in judicious measure. "I think it does work. I think it's the difference between me and the next guy. I don't know for sure, but I know how good I feel when I feel good. I know how bad I feel when I feel bad, too, and I wouldn't want to feel bad all the time—and I don't. I mean, some days aren't so bad. *Many* days aren't so bad."

3

A Litany of Laments
Less Common Forms of Arthritis and Associated Conditions

"Complaints is many and various,
And my feet are cold," says Aquarius.
—*Robert Graves, "Star Talk"*

Systemic Sclerosis (Scleroderma)

Scleroderma (*sclero* means hard, *derma* means skin) is an umbrella term for a variety of connective-tissue disorders characterized by an excessive production of the protein collagen, which acts as a kind of mortar in connective tissues, including skin, bone, ligaments, and cartilage.

Collagen plays an important role in maintaining connective tissues by replacing dead and decaying cells, but in scleroderma, fibroblasts (the cells that generate collagen) multiply at a furious rate, and once soft, supple skin—particularly on the face and fingers—thickens and becomes as tight and shiny as shrink-wrap. In the systemic form of the disease, excess collagen builds up in joints, blood vessels, muscles, and some internal organs, altering both appearance and function.

An autoimmune disease, scleroderma can cause anything from mild skin disturbances to severe, even life-threatening, complications. Changes to blood vessels, due to an abnormal growth of cells lining the vessel walls, may lead to vascular problems, such as Raynaud's phenomenon.

Scleroderma is relatively rare, though its prevalence is disputed. By some calculations, about 5000 Canadians are affected (children only rarely), most often between the ages of thirty and fifty, but some studies put the number as high as 20,000 or more. Women are affected two to four times more often than men, except during child-bearing years, when the ratio soars to fifteen times more often.

The exact cause of scleroderma is unknown. Heredity seems to play a role, and scientists have linked scleroderma-type symptoms to industrial toxins, such as the vinyl chloride monomer used in manufacturing PVC plastic, as well as the hydrocarbons and silica found in coal dust. Moreover, patients treated with certain anti-cancer drugs have either developed scleroderma or displayed characteristic symptoms.

Scleroderma was first described by a physician in Naples, Italy, almost 250 years ago. There are two basic types: The localized form is self-limiting (that is, it clears up independently of treatment), its active stage lasting two to five years. Early symptoms include persistent skin swelling and redness and thick, waxy patches of skin called morphea on the body and occasionally on the face and limbs. Localized scleroderma doesn't usually involve the internal organs or progress into the systemic form of the disease.

Systemic, or generalized, scleroderma is a very different—and often far more serious—disease. There are actually two kinds of systemic scleroderma. The milder form, which affects about half of all people with scleroderma, is called the CREST syndrome, an acronym that neatly sums up its characteristic symptoms: C is for calcinosis, referring to painful calcium deposits in skin and/or muscle; R stands for Raynaud's phenomenon (see page 46)—blood vessel constrictures in the fingers caused by exposure to cold or emotional stress; E is for esophageal difficulty—trouble swallowing, often accompanied by heartburn and constipation; S refers to sclerodactyly, in which the skin of the fingers, hands, and sometimes toes thickens; and, finally, T is for telangiectasis, a dilation, or widening, of the capillaries (small blood vessels) visible just beneath the skin that leaves mottled red spots on the hands, face, and tongue.

With few exceptions, people with the CREST syndrome do fairly well, with only limited changes to the skin of the hands and face and only rarely any complications in the internal organs. The more severe, generalized form of systemic scleroderma is not so sparing: Fibrous tissue may develop in the gastrointestinal tract, lungs, heart muscle, and kidneys, leading to potentially fatal complications.

The first signs of the disease are usually pain and swelling in the

joints, especially the hands, and Raynaud's phenomenon, which virtually everyone with scleroderma develops in the early stages of the disease. In the so-called edemic phase (*edema* means swelling), the fingers
and hands, and occasionally the feet, become swollen and shiny, resem-
bling sausage. Biopsies taken at this point reveal a glut of inflammatory
cells in the subdermal (interior) layers of the skin. As the skin becomes
taut and hardened, the creases in the skin and the blood vessels usually
visible beneath it disappear. Hands affected in this way will almost
inevitably be stiffer and less capable of fine motor movements.

As the disease progresses, the skin in affected areas—in mild cases,
usually only the hands and fingers; in more severe cases, the arms, face,
and upper body, as well—may darken and become rough and dry, as
sweat glands cease functioning. In very severe cases, tissue buildup in
the heart can cause arrhythmia (irregular heart beat) or heart failure, and
lung capacity may become reduced, causing shortness of breath after
even mild exertion.

Diagnosis and Treatment

As with many other forms of arthritis and arthritis-related conditions,
there's no single test or pattern of symptoms that will in itself confirm
a diagnosis of scleroderma. It may take time and several consultations
with rheumatologists or dermatologists (skin specialists). The first step
is a thorough medical history, followed by a physical examination, with
a view to identifying changes in skin, or joint problems. Your doctor
may wish to do a skin biopsy (extract a small tissue sample under local
anesthetic) to look for microscopic changes to connective tissue. Muscle
biopsies may be done to confirm any myopathy (muscle weakness
without inflammation) or myositis (muscle weakness *with* inflammation). Digestive-system involvement can be confirmed by measuring
the muscle pressure of the esophagus, and blood tests can reveal any
immune-system imbalances. There are also tests to determine whether
there's any involvement in the lungs or kidneys.

In most mild to moderate cases, scleroderma can be controlled
with medication, and there are a number of treatment strategies that
provide symptomatic relief. Some people experience a remission in
which the fibrosis in skin and internal organs slows, but about 30 per
cent of those with the systemic form of the disease suffer rapid

deterioration and have a shortened life expectancy.

Treatment usually includes exercise, skin care, and careful attention to meal planning if the digestive system is involved, with treatment modalities changing as the disease changes. Medications have a definite role to play, but they can do little to halt the skin disease or tissue buildup in the internal organs. Some physicians have tried using vitamin E preparations, potassium para-aminobenzoate (Potaba), and the anti-gout drug colchicine to treat skin manifestations, but, so far, none has proved very effective.

Where there's evidence of arthritis, NSAIDs (non-steroidal anti-inflammatory drugs) may be prescribed to control joint inflammation. Anti-hypertensive drugs, such as propranolol (Inderal) and minoxidil (Loniten), may be prescribed for renal (affecting the kidney) hypertension. The most common medication for modifying the disease progression, though, is nifedipine (Adalat), which is also effective for Raynaud's phenomenon. Medications are only part of the treatment, however. Massage, stretching, and regular exercise help keep skin flexible, reduce flexion contractures (joints immobilized in bent or deformed positions due to fibrosis), and maintain circulation. People with joint involvement should also learn joint-protection measures.

- To reduce blood-vessel constrictions, try to keep your skin warm—without becoming overheated and sweaty. Perspiration cools the body, so it's best to wear thin cotton garments next to the skin or wool underwear and thermal socks lined with cotton, which absorbs perspiration and minimizes the cooling effect. Loose, non-restricting boots and shoes are also a good idea. For a little extra warmth for hands and feet, try reheatable skiers' gel packs.
- Take care not to let your skin become too dry. Stay away from strong soaps, detergents and other compounds that irritate the skin, and experiment with soaps, lotions, bath oils, and moisturizers until you find the best formulas for your skin—despite manufacturers' claims, not every compound is effective, nor does every product work the same way for everyone.
- Quit smoking: Smoking causes blood vessels to constrict, decreasing blood flow to the fingertips, which may trigger

attacks of Raynaud's phenomenon. Smoking can also damage the lungs and heart, which are already at risk from scleroderma.

- Since emotional stress contributes to reduced blood flow, it's also important to reduce stress levels. Try to avoid situations that get you all wound up emotionally; be sure you get enough sleep, and consider learning relaxation techniques, which not only help to reduce stress but reduce pain, as well (see chapter 5).
- Another stress-reduction technique that some people find helpful is biofeedback (chapter 5), which can actually teach you how to increase blood flow and reduce blood-vessel constriction.
- If your digestive system is affected by the disease, learn to eat slowly and chew thoroughly, and drink a tall glass of water with meals to soften and wash down food. You can also ease the digestive load by eating smaller meals, or give digestion a boost by staying active for three to four hours after a large meal.

Despite advances in understanding in the last twenty years, scleroderma remains a frustratingly difficult disease to treat—and to live with. Fortunately, in most people, the disease remains limited to a few areas and progresses very slowly. In those whose disease is worsening more rapidly, there are measures that have proven helpful—even though the process itself cannot be halted.

Raynaud's Phenomenon

Raynaud's phenomenon is a narrowing of the blood vessels in the fingers, which causes numbness, tingling, and sometimes a burning sensation. The fingers may change colour (first white, then blue) when exposed to cold (even the cold in a refrigerator or tap water) or in response to stress. Although Raynaud's can occur by itself, it's often associated with other forms of arthritis, including scleroderma, RA, and psoriatic arthritis. (It's also occasionally seen in people who operate machinery, such as jackhammers and other pneumatic drills, that transfer their vibrations to the hands and arms.) In most cases, it's little more than a nuisance, however painful, but in extreme cases severe blood vessel constriction can cause gangrene.

Because smoking causes blood vessels to constrict, decreasing blood flow to the fingertips, it's obviously not recommended: It may trigger Raynaud's attacks. Emotional stress and tension can also reduce blood flow and thus trigger an attack in susceptible people. Try to get enough sleep to minimize tension, avoid stressful situations whenever possible, and practise relaxation techniques. Some people are able to learn to actually increase blood flow and limit blood vessel constriction through biofeedback; if necessary, there are vasodilating medications that "open up" constricted vessels, and anti-hypertensive drugs used to treat high blood pressure.

To protect their hands, some people wear latex gloves under ordinary mittens or gloves in cold weather, and reheatable skiers' gel packs can be stuffed into extra large mitts and boots. If diving into the fridge for a snack is enough to trigger Raynaud's, hang an extra pair of gloves near the fridge door that you can slip on before hunger strikes.

Polymyalgia Rheumatica (PMR)

Not long ago, most physicians probably knew polymyalgia rheumatica—if they knew of it at all—as the "surprise arthritis," because its symptoms were said to strike so suddenly. Their colleague, the rheumatologist, probably characterized it as difficult to conclusively identify—so difficult, in fact, that a patient's swift and satisfactory response to drug therapy was often taken as confirmation of the diagnosis.

It would be gratifying to say that time and science have put matters right, that PMR is known and completely understood, but the most that can be said is that PMR is *better* understood. It *is* now known that patients have good reason to be optimistic.

PMR rarely affects anyone under fifty, strikes twice as many women as men, demonstrates a mild family connection (though it doesn't seem to be strongly hereditary), and—like some other rheumatic conditions—almost all reported individuals are Caucasian.

PMR is rarely life-threatening, says Dr. Bevra Hahn, professor of medicine and chief of rheumatology at UCLA in Los Angeles. Nor is there much likelihood of the sort of joint deformation common to other forms of arthritis. "That's quite unusual," says Hahn. And the really good news is that in some 50 to 60 per cent of patients, the disease goes into total remission after one to two years.

— —

"Polymyalgia rheumatica" is a good summary of the ailment, *poly* meaning many, *myo* meaning muscle, *algia* meaning pain, and *rheumatica* referring to an inflammation of connective tissue, such as muscles and ligaments. Patients complain of usually symmetrical pain and stiffness in the neck, shoulders, pelvic girdle, thighs, and buttocks. Location is one of the reasons PMR can be difficult to identify, says Dr. Gene Hunder, chair of the division of rheumatology at the Mayo Clinic in Rochester, Minnesota, and professor of medicine at the Mayo Medical School: There's often a mild synovitis (joint inflammation) associated with the disease—"mild in the sense that there's not a lot of swelling"—but since it's often the hips or shoulders that are involved, "there's no way the hip joints, for instance, can be palpated [felt or examined by hand, because the joints are so deep beneath the tissues]."

Hunder estimates that about one in two hundred people over fifty are at risk, but there's a marked difference in the symptoms patients experience. "Someone with the more severe disease could have a low-grade fever," says Hunder, "marked fatigue, and anorexia weight loss." Hunder describes one of his patients, who was confined to a wheelchair because of involvement in her hips and thighs, who was so stiff that she was having a hard time washing her face and combing her hair. "On the other hand," he says, "PMR can be very mild. The patient limbers up in an hour in the morning and has few symptoms the rest of the day. They feel a little fatigue or stiffness after sitting for an hour, but they don't have a systemic sickness. PMR covers a broad spectrum."

Is it a "surprise arthritis"? "It's highly variable," says Hahn. "Some patients can tell you the time and date it started to hurt, others no. But the same is true with rheumatoid arthritis. You can wake up with rheumatism in every joint, or it can creep up over a period of months. It's the same for most rheumatic diseases."

Diagnosis and Treatment

Hunder claims that making an accurate diagnosis isn't really all that difficult: "By taking a careful history of the patient's symptoms, you can elicit the typical features of the syndrome. If a patient can sit in a comfortable position, for example, the symptoms would be less, and they might not even be present at times." The morning stiffness is also very characteristic: "We look for that. During the first easy movements—turning over in bed, pushing the covers down—that would accentuate the discomfort. Then, after one or two hours, the symptoms would tend to subside, only to return after another period of inactivity."

There's also a blood test that measures the sed rate (see page 15): Most people with PMR have a characteristically high rate. All of that—plus age over fifty, pain location, "and the absence of swelling in peripheral parts of the body," says Hunder, "which might suggest RA"—contribute to a diagnosis of PMR.

Then there's patient response to drug treatment—usually the corticosteroid prednisone. "PMR responds abruptly and very well to it," says Hunder, "so some people see it as a diagnostic test. But there are a number of types of rheumatic disease that respond to prednisone, so I think it should be seen as just one point in the diagnosis. I don't usually use it as a diagnostic tool, because I hope to make an accurate diagnosis before starting the patient on prednisone."

If a patient's condition can be managed with NSAIDs or ASA, it should be. Prednisone is a powerful drug—"a two-edged sword," says Hunder. Possible side effects of long-term use include fluid retension, hypertension, easy bruising, diabetes, psychological effects—anxiety, hyperactivity, stimulation, or depression—even osteoporosis. "The idea," says Hunder, "is to use the least dose for the shortest period of time that satisfactorily suppresses the disease."

Giant Cell Arteritis (GCA)

There's a far more serious condition associated with PMR. In a typical study Hunder conducted, 15 to 20 per cent of patients with PMR had a condition called giant cell or temporal arteritis; about 50 per cent of patients with GCA also have PMR. It affects the external carotid artery in and around the head and scalp, occasionally the branches of the arch of the aorta, and sometimes the bigger abdominal arteries. The walls of the arteries thicken and narrow, allowing clots to form or ruptures of the arterial wall, occasionally causing a stroke or heart attack.

The most characteristic effect, though, is clotting in the vessels supplying the retina of the eye, causing sudden and permanent blindness. At one time, says Hunder, "up to 50 per cent of patients with GCA became blind. Nowadays, it's more like 10 per cent. That's still scary, and it means that physicians should be aware and start treatment early, because prednisone will prevent blindness in most patients."

Patients with PMR, though, should be their own first line of defence against GCA. Headache is the most important sign, says Hahn: "Headaches, visual symptoms, pain in the jaw while chewing, or very tender scalp—these are clues to inflamed blood vessels in the cranium. [Prednisone] doesn't cause any of those symptoms, so it's almost certainly the disease. Fortunately, most of the time you have time to get to the doctor and change your medicine."

Despite the potential hazards, patients with PMR should feel optimistic, says Hunder. "PMR is diagnosable. We don't understand it completely, but it's treatable, and, if carefully followed, the side effects to prednisone can be minimized in most patients. The eventual outlook is good. They should recover."

Spondyloarthropathies

This mouthful of a word describes a group of related diseases, including ankylosing spondylitis (AS), psoriatic arthritis, and Reiter's syndrome, as well as arthritis with inflammatory bowel disease. Their primary similarity is implicit in the name: *spondylo* refers to the spine, *arthro* to joints, and *pathy* to disease; each involves inflammation of the joints of the spine. All are also seronegative, meaning patients' blood tests come up negative for rheumatoid factor (RF; see page 15), a feature that helps doctors distinguish them from rheumatoid arthritis (RA), though it's not a certain diagnostic criterion. Spondyloarthropathies also have a tendency to run in families; all may involve inflammation of the sacroiliac joint (where the spine attaches to the pelvis) and the tissues that join ligaments and tendons to bone (enthesopathy). Symptoms are so similar, in fact, that AS is sometimes difficult to distinguish from Reiter's syndrome (see page 53).

Ankylosing Spondylitis

Ankylosing spondylitis (AS), also known as Marie-Strümpell disease, is a chronic, inflammatory form of arthritis—one of the few arthritic conditions that strikes men more often than women. It affects one in a thousand Canadians, chiefly in late adolescence or early adulthood (in their twenties and thirties), rarely after age forty. Younger children are sometimes affected by a milder form of the disease, known as juvenile ankylosing spondylitis.

The name properly describes advanced cases of the disease ("ankylosing" refers to stiffness, "spondylitis" to inflammation of the spine), but is less appropriate to milder forms of the disease, which are far more prevalent. AS usually begins with dull pain in the lower back, buttocks, thighs, and knees, sometimes the hips, shoulders and—especially in women, who generally have mild AS—in the small joints of the fingers.

When there's widespread peripheral joint involvement, it may be difficult to distinguish AS from RA; lab tests (nine out of ten people with AS have the HLA-B27 genetic marker—HLA stands for "human leukocyte antigen; see page 257) and x-rays of the spine and sacroiliac can help make a differential diagnosis. A family history of the disease is a strong clue, and your physician will also make a further determination from a physical exam and disease history.

Pain is often intermittent, sometimes disappearing for weeks at a time; many people have trouble sleeping, since their discomfort is worst at night. There may be sciatic-like pain radiating from the lower back and down the legs, and there may be additional pain and stiffness from muscle contractures around affected joints.

Like other forms of inflammatory arthritis, AS is a systemic disease; some patients experience mild fever and fatigue, weight loss, skin problems, and inflammatory eye problems. In a small percentage of people with AS, the disease progresses to the point that bony ridges form between the spinal vertebrae, fusing the joints and causing increasing stiffness; the inflammation may also affect the tendons and ligaments joining the spine and the pelvis (the sacroiliac joint), and severely affected people may be forced into a permanent stoop.

Most of the more serious consequences of the disease can be prevented with appropriate early treatment, most often NSAIDs, which are usually sufficient to control the disease. Where there's peripheral joint involvement, sulfasalazine is sometimes prescribed, and corticosteroid injections may be used in stubborn enthesopathy or synovitis (though oral corticosteroids have no therapeutic value in chronic care of AS).

Exercises to strengthen muscles and maintain flexibility are an important component of disease management; even deep breathing exercises may be of help, where there's a problem with the tendons and ligaments joining the ribcage. A consultation with a physiotherapist is an excellent idea; he or she can instruct you in the importance of good posture, joint protection, and stretching routines. Only a few of those with AS will suffer any long-term disablement from their disease; most will be able to live relatively normal lives, with only mild to moderate symptoms of the disease.

Psoriatic Arthritis (PA)

Psoriasis is a miserable skin condition caused by abnormal cell growth. Why it happens isn't clear, but immune, genetic, and environmental factors, such as bacterial infections, seem to play a role. The results are flaking skin, itchy red lesions, and sometimes yellow-white scales as the disease progresses on various parts of the body, especially the scalp, the back of the elbows, knees, umbilicus (belly button), and genitals. It can also appear as flaking skin between the toes, leading some people to dismiss it (or attempt to treat it) as athlete's foot. It affects from two to four per cent of the white population (far fewer blacks are affected), and it has one nasty wrinkle: Some people with psoriasis—five to ten per cent—also develop arthritis.

In fact, in psoriatic arthritis, arthritic symptoms usually develop first, with the skin condition trailing by months, even years in some cases. PA is gender-neutral, affecting men and women equally. It's rare to see it in children under thirteen; the usual age of onset is between thirty and fifty. Nearly all PA sufferers (about 95 per cent) have peripheral joint involvement; the remainder have exclusive spinal involvement, though 20 to 40 per cent of patients have both. In some people, inflammation may develop in the periosteum (a blood-laced membrane that surrounds and nourishes bones), in tendons, and the points where tendons attach to bone (enthesopathy). Others are only affected in the end joints of fingers and toes; finger- and toenails may develop pitting or ridges; and inflammation and swelling of the flexor tendons can cause fingers to take on a characteristic "sausage digit" appearance.

Clinically PA may resemble both Reiter's syndrome and RA; a diagnosis of PA is only confirmed with evidence of skin or nail changes typical of the condition. The systemic component of PA, though, is generally limited to eye inflammation (such as iritis, episcleritis, or conjunctivitis).

Treatment consists of the same regimens used for other inflammatory conditions—ASA and NSAIDs for mild to moderate cases, for example. For more intractable cases, DMARDs (disease-modifying anti-rheumatic drugs) may be prescribed, including gold, chloroquine, and methotrexate; antimalarials, such as sulfasalazine, are effective for some people, and soft-tissue involvement may be treated with corticosteroid injections. Suppressing the skin disease (with topical skin creams and corticosteroids) is sometimes helpful in controlling the arthritic aspect of PA; where the psoriasis proves especially recalcitrant, a dermatologist may be called on for further treatment.

Education is a big part of treatment to ensure that patients understand and practise joint protection, do regular joint exercises to maintain maximum range of motion, and use splints where necessary. A minority of people with PA suffer long-term problems and joint destruction, but most cases of psoriatic arthritis are mild, and most patients—probably 80 per cent—do quite well.

Reiter's Syndrome (RS)

From the log of his second voyage to the New World, in 1493, we know that Christopher Columbus had Reiter's syndrome, but it wasn't until 1916, when a Prussian army doctor named Hans Reiter described the symptoms of the disease in a young World War I cavalry officer that RS was clearly identified. And it wasn't until 1985, when Pope John Paul II visited Midland, Ontario, that a clear link was made between certain types of bacterial or viral infections and onset of the disease. On that day, some 1600 Ontario Provincial Police (OPP) officers nibbled on box lunches prepared for them; nearly 500 of them came down with diarrhea and associated gastrointestinal problems due to salmonella poisoning.

Unlucky for them—but a nice break for researchers, who had a contained study group. When nineteen policemen developed symptoms of arthritis within three weeks of the Pope's visit, Dr. Robert Inman, a rheumatologist and immunologist at Toronto Western Hospital, and his colleagues were able to prove a definite link between RS and the HLA-B27 genetic marker.

RS is a form of reactive arthritis, which is caused by an infectious agent—a bacterium, virus, or fungus—that passes via the bloodstream into a joint (or enters directly through surgery or injection).

Other types of reactive arthritis include gonococcal arthritis (sexually transmitted), Lyme disease (via the bite of a tick that feeds on infected deer), viral arthritis (from hepatitis, rubella, etc.), and rheumatic fever (following a streptococcal infection). RS is the most common form, affecting an estimated 3.5 people per 100,000, usually men (perhaps twenty times more often than women, and rarely in children).

Arthritic symptoms typically appear within one to three weeks of an inciting urethritis (inflammation of the urethra) or diarrhea; there may be low-grade fever (or high fever and weight loss in some people), followed by joint stiffness, muscle pain, and low-back discomfort, particularly in the sacroiliac joint. As in PA, the low-back pain may radiate into the buttocks and thighs, and it's actually worsened by bed rest and inactivity. Knees, ankles, feet, and wrists are most commonly affected, usually in an asymmetric pattern; they may be slightly swollen and stiff, tender to the touch, and difficult to move through a full range of motion without pain.

A distinctive feature of RS is inflammation where ligaments and tendons attach to bone (enthesopathy), as opposed to a synovitis (inflammation in a joint), which helps to distinguish it from RA. Fingers and toes may take on the appearance of "sausage digits," which can lead to confusion with psoriatic arthritis; the hind part of the foot may become swollen and tender, and the Achilles tendon, and plantar fascia (a tough band of tissue on the sole of the foot) may also become inflamed (plantar fasciitis).

Some 40 per cent of all RS patients also suffer conjunctivitis ("pink-eye") early in the disease, though it's usually mild and self-limiting. A more serious concern is uveitis (see page 63), which is often acute and generally begins in only one eye. If you're experiencing pain or inflammation of the eye, you should be seen as soon as possible by an ophthalmologist. Most problems can be easily dealt with using appropriate medication, but if it's not treated, eye damage can result.

NSAIDs are the medication of choice for most of the inflammatory symptoms of RS, with corticosteroid injections sometimes prescribed for enthesopathy problems, such as plantar fasciitis. More intractable cases may be treated with methotrexate or azathioprine. Bed rest is sometimes helpful where there's little lower-back pain, and range-of-motion and isometric strengthening exercises are highly recommended.

Some people only suffer a single, self-limiting experience of arthritis with RS, but as many as half of those with the condition undergo an up-and-down course over an extended period, and approximately one in five people suffer a chronic, even disabling form of the disease.

The best advice for avoiding RS is simply to watch what you eat: If that sandwich you're eyeing has been sitting out in the sun, pass on it. You can always eat later.

Crystalline Arthritis (Gout and Pseudogout)

To most people, gout is Henry VIII, foot propped on a stool, his big toe purple and swollen. What few people recognize in this picture is that Henry has severe inflammation in the joint of that royal toe—a form of arthritis. Strictly speaking, it's not inflammatory arthritis, though: Gout is crystal-associated arthritis, in which needle-sharp crystals of monosodium urate settle in a joint, often, but not exclusively, in the big toe. Why it's so consistently selective isn't known; what is known is that the crystal deposits are the result of excessive concentrations of uric acid (hyperuricemia), a waste product from the breakdown of purines, which are found in meats, especially organs, such as heart and liver.

The other thing that's not generally known about gout is that it's one of rheumatology's biggest success stories. We know what causes it, and we know how to treat it.

Gout primarily strikes middle-aged men (women are seldom affected, and those who are are usually post-menopausal) with a taste for certain rich foods and copious amounts of alcohol. Not everyone with hyperuricemia develops gout, however; there may be a metabolic imbalance in susceptible individuals, or their kidneys are failing to excrete enough uric acid (certain medications, such as diuretics, can also contribute to gout by blocking the elimination of uric acid in urine).

Flare-ups of gout often subside by themselves, but for the pain of an acute attack, colchicine is the medication of choice, though it should be started within two days of onset for maximum effectiveness. Unfortunately it can cause nausea, vomiting, and diarrhea—perhaps a small price to pay for what some people describe as the most intense pain they've ever experienced. NSAIDs (not ASA; it's too slow) may also be useful, and, in especially resistant cases, corticosteroids may be employed. Sometimes aspirating the joint (drawing out fluid through a syringe) is sufficient to reduce the pain and inflammation.

Diet is an important part of treatment. Low-fat foods are recommended, and purine-rich foods, such as fatty and organ meats and many seafoods, should be eliminated or greatly reduced. Try to keep your weight under control, and drink plenty of fluids (though you should limit your intake of coffee and other drinks containing caffeine)—and restrict your alcohol consumption.

Pseudogout (*pseudo* means false) is also caused by depositions, but in this case calcium pyrophosphate dihydrate (CPD) crystals are the culprits. It attacks the knees, wrists, ankles, and shoulders, rarely the big toe; a differential diagnosis is made by identifying the crystals in joint fluid. Both gout and pseudogout cause joint inflammation, heat, redness, swelling, and pain, but they have different causes and treatment.

An acute attack of gout generally lasts from seven to ten days; in very severe cases, it can last for three weeks, especially if there are massive deposits of urate crystals; pseudogout attacks may last from two weeks to a month. Pseudogout also develops later in life, usually around age sixty-five, and affects both genders equally. Because of the age of onset, there may be some osteoarthritic change in an affected joint, which may make determining how much pain is attributable to the pseudogout and how much to the OA difficult.

What causes pseudogout isn't known; it may result from a metabolic imbalance, surgery, or an underlying medical condition. Unlike gout, there's no medication to dissolve CPD crystals, though NSAIDs or aspirating a joint are often effective. Diet (other than normal, healthy eating) isn't a factor in its treatment. Nonetheless, most cases of pseudogout are effectively controlled with appropriate medication.

Sarcoidosis

For six years I have been suffering an incurable affliction, aggravated by imprudent physicians. Year after year deceived by the hope of an improvement, [I am] finally forced to contemplate the prospect of a lasting illness, whose cure may take years or even be impossible...

Ludwig von Beethoven, *Heiligenstadt Testament*

It's tempting to speculate what the "Shakespeare of Symphony" might have left us had he lived longer or in better health—perhaps an even richer legacy of pure orchestral genius. But the fierce German composer, born among the burghers of Bonn in 1770, died at fifty-seven, after thirty years of sickness had stolen his hearing, devoured his body, and left him in unrelenting pain and emotional anguish.

Beethoven's medical history after 1802, when he penned the "Heiligenstadt Testament"—a letter to his brothers, never sent—was a litany of fevers, infections and abscesses, bronchitis, rheumatism, anxiety, and bouts of prostration from severe abdominal pain and colic. By 1817, a full decade before his death, Beethoven was all but stone deaf. Four years later, he had jaundice and the year after that was diagnosed with "thoracic gout." Severe pain in his eyes for most of the next couple of years caused him to shun the light and bandage his eyes at night. His last years were as hellish as his final music was divine.

Yet, had Beethoven lived today, much of his suffering might have been alleviated. He would almost certainly have lived longer. That, at least, is the opinion of Dr. Tom Palferman, a rheumatologist at the Yeovil District Hospital in Somerset, England, an amateur cellist, and a Beethoven enthusiast. In 1990, Palferman startled the separate worlds of music and medicine with a paper in the *Journal of the Royal Society of Medicine,* in which he drew new conclusions about Beethoven's ills and cause of death. Until then, the most widely held view was that Beethoven, the son of a heavy drinker, was himself a tippler and his death due to cirrhosis of the liver.

Not very likely, Palferman asserted. During ten years of careful reading, he became "increasingly curious about the influence and the particular effect Beethoven's medical history might have had on him." Fortunately there was almost no end of material. Beethoven's letters run to three volumes, Palferman noted, "and he had quite a number of medical student and doctor friends. He wrote to them from quite an early age, and this was helpful. For one thing, it gives us some idea of his early approaching deafness.

Everything he read convinced Palferman that Beethoven was "closer to an ascetic than an alcoholic," but he found the autopsy results—"the description of the liver was quite unlike what one would expect from a cirrhotic liver from alcohol"—conclusive. In his postmortem diagnosis Palferman suggested that Beethoven suffered from an obscure disorder called sarcoidosis. It appeared to explain all of his ills—even the deafness.

Sarcoidosis is a puzzling systemic disease that can affect the lungs, skin, eyes, and almost any other organ or tissue in the body in either its acute or chronic forms. Although its cause is unknown, researchers have speculated that it may be caused by a viral or bacterial infection, an immunologic disorder, or even an allergic reaction. It can occur at any age but is most common between ages twenty and forty, with slightly more women affected. Almost unknown in China and Southeast Asia, it afflicts as many as 20 people per 10,000 in Ireland but only one in 10,000 North Americans. About one in every six patients develops arthritis.

Had Beethoven lived today, much of his condition might have been treated. A regimen of corticosteroids "would have been highly effective," Palferman says. "I've no doubt we could have had a more accurate diagnosis and treated him very successfully, and he would have had a much more comfortable existence."

He may even have lived to a ripe old age, Palferman says, "but whether that would have been a service to mankind I'm not sure." Having made a study of the "possible relationships between suffering and creativity," Palferman is convinced there's a case to be made for suffering as an inspiration. Beethoven's most famous symphony, the Ninth, with its rousing final chorus on Schiller's "Ode to Joy," had its first performance only three years before the maestro's death. And, Palferman wrote in his *Journal* paper, "as Beethoven's decline accelerated during the last year or so, his music became more innovative and profound. Arguably his greatest masterpieces are the five late string quartets, including the Grosse Fugue which Stravinsky, more than a century later, acknowledged as being 'eternally contemporary.'"

Possibly Beethoven's disappointments and struggles against the curse of ill health "resulted in the darker side of his nature," Palferman opined. "Yet maybe those same adversities provoked and released emotions which were translated into the apocalyptic, sublime music left to us. Callous though it might appear, perhaps Beethoven's increasing wretchedness and misery were ultimately to the benefit of mankind."

Diagnosis and Treatment

Diagnosis can be tricky, because so many different parts of the body can be affected in different ways. A tissue sample taken from the lymph glands or the lungs is usually conclusive, but it can be misleading, says Dr. Arthur Bookman, a rheumatologist at The Toronto Hospital, because it can look like certain other maladies, including tuberculosis and certain fungus infections.

The most common symptom of sarcoidosis is the formation of small inflammatory nodules known as granulomas in different parts of the body, most often in the lungs. Some patients may develop a dry cough, shortness of breath, and chest pain, though only a few will have trouble breathing. Other common symptoms include a painful rash on the shins called erythema nodosum (EN), inflammation of the eye, and enlarged spleen or liver. Between 10 and 35 per cent of patients also suffer granulomas on the face, hands, feet, buttocks, and/or shoulders that, fortunately, usually clear up without scarring (though a form called lupus pernio, which appears on the face, especially the nose, cheeks, and chin, can damage skin tissue and leave scars).

Although sarcoidosis is generally a chronic condition, lasting for several years or a lifetime, its onset may be acute, then disappear without treatment after several months. About one in six people (most frequently women) also experiences joint inflammation in ankles, knees, elbows, wrists, or fingers—that is, arthritis. It's especially common with the acute form of sarcoidosis, often accompanying EN, but it can occur years after the disease began.

Fortunately the acute arthritis "often responds quite nicely to colchicine, the same drug we use for gout," says Bookman. A doctor may also recommend an NSAID to reduce joint inflammation or prescribe an exercise program as joint protection, and relatively mild medications to relieve muscle aches and treat skin sore from EN or granulomas. For more serious cases, a corticosteroid, such as prednisone, may be prescribed to reduce joint pain and inflammation and granulomas that may have formed in, say, the lungs.

Sjögren's Syndrome

"I had dozed off in the chair, which was a bad mistake, because I woke up with two flannel blankets in my mouth....I felt terrible." That's

Raymond Chandler's hard-boiled private eye Philip Marlowe talking. Gumshoes are always waking up with thick tongues and sore heads in Chandler stories. It seems to come with the territory. A couple of pages later, though, the flannel in their mouths has always disappeared, faster than a fifth of bootleg whiskey.

But how tough would Philip Marlowe be if it *didn't*? What's it like to wake up *every* day (not to mention in the middle of the night) with flannel in your mouth? That only begins to describe the effect of Sjögren's syndrome—next to rheumatoid arthritis (RA), the second most common autoimmune rheumatic disorder. Sjögren's (pronounced "show-grens") is a chronic, inflammatory condition characterized in a single word: dryness. Its most common manifestation is the result of diminished lacrimal (tear duct) and salivary gland secretions. People with Sjögren's often complain that their eyes feel as though there's sand or grit under the eyelids. They tear less and may experience burning, itching, redness, eye fatigue, and sensitivity to light.

The other common problem is dry mouth. Patients may have trouble chewing and swallowing dry foods such as crackers, food particles may adhere to the mucosal surfaces of their mouth, and, no matter how much fluid is ingested, Sjögren's can be unquenchable—and we're not talking about thirst: Even a *lot* of water doesn't provide anything like normal relief from dry mouth.

There are a number of other causes of extreme oral and ocular dryness, including sarcoidosis, hormonal disorders, and anxiety and depression syndromes. What's commonly referred to as dry eye is caused by a withering of the lacrimal (tear) glands, usually with aging, while in ordinary dry mouth (xerostomia), a dysfunction of the salivary glands may be symptomatic of an underlying disease or a side effect from medication (not to be confused with the flannel mouth you woke up with after your sister's wedding reception). None of these conditions is caused by an immune system disregulation, none is systemic, and none is so potentially serious.

Named for Swedish ophthalmologist Dr. Hendrik Sjögren, who documented the condition in 1933, Sjögren's (also known as sicca syndrome) affects not only the lacrimal and salivary glands, but all the mucous membranes and glands in the body, including oil and sweat glands and the vagina. It can be either primary (occurring by itself) or secondary to another autoimmune disorder, such as RA, lupus, systemic sclerosis, vasculitis, or chronic hepatitis, among others. Typically it occurs in middle-aged women, but it can begin at any age and in either gender.

In some people, Sjögren's is confined to the exocrine glands, as they're called, but about half of all patients develop a systemic (extraglandular) form of the disease that slowly—about eight to ten years after onset—begins to affect the lungs, kidneys, blood vessels, and muscles; complications may also include kidney or bone disease. Perhaps the most serious complication of both primary and secondary Sjögren's is a Hodgkins-like disease involving the lymph glands, though the types of lymphoma Sjögren's patients develop are usually responsive to treatment, and some are even curable.

Usually the first sign of Sjögren's is that dry or gritty sensation in your eyes, which may be crusty and hard to open in the morning because of a buildup of discharge during the night. As the condition progresses, infections and corneal ulcers are not uncommon, which contribute to redness and discomfort in the eyes.

Oral problems are another clue, beginning with chronic dryness in your mouth—people often notice that they can barely tolerate food without something to wash it down—and you may notice a sharp deterioration in the condition of your teeth, despite regular maintenance: Saliva performs a major role in flushing the bacteria and sugar particles from food out of the crevices between teeth; when the flow of saliva is diminished, those food particles attack and decay the teeth. Nor is there enough saliva to combat common types of mouth fungus, such as *candida albicans,* which can lead to infections.

Diagnosis and Treatment

Like many another rheumatic condition, Sjögren's may be relatively easy for a specialist to diagnose, but the average GP may have a harder time pinning it down. The gradual onset of symptoms can also complicate matters. An ophthalmologist can easily diagnose Sjögren's by means of a Schirmer test, in which a small strip of filter paper is hung from the lower eyelid—the quantity of tears wetting the paper (less than 5 mm in five minutes) confirms the diagnosis. There's also a technique called Rose Bengal staining that reveals corneal pitting (called punctate corneal ulcerations) and damage to the conjunctiva (the mucous membranes lining the eyelids) in a slit-lamp examination.

Saliva can be measured, usually by an ear-nose-and-throat specialist or a dentist, by simply having you lift your tongue and waiting to see if pools of saliva form. If such tests prove inconclusive, the diagnosis can also be confirmed with a biopsy from the minor salivary glands underneath the upper or lower lip. Lab tests may be especially revealing, since people with Sjögren's often have large concentrations of antibodies, such as rheumatoid factor, in their blood.

There's no cure for Sjögren's, but it can be treated and the impact of symptoms greatly reduced with careful maintenance and hygiene. Fluid intake is a high priority: Try to drink a dozen large glasses of water a day, and consider a saliva substitute for times (during travel, say) when stopping for a refill isn't convenient. Eye drops help, but get a recommendation from your ophthalmologist or doctor; some drops are irritants—that's why they make your eyes tear. There are no medications specific to Sjögren's, though you may be prescribed anti-inflammatories or other drugs for any accompanying illness.

Neither primary nor secondary Sjögren's (which tends to be more severe) is life-threatening on its own, but both are associated with an increased incidence of lymphoma, pneumonia, bronchitis, and lung abcesses, as well as corneal ulcerations, which can be serious. For that reason, it's important to book regular visits with an ophthalmologist to check your eyes and your rheumatologist or other specialist to monitor your blood on a regular basis. Complications are always less serious if they're caught early.

Because of the potential for oral problems, including rapid tooth decay and infections, immaculate daily oral hygiene is a must. Brush your teeth after eating *anything*, and learn to floss. Enlist your dentist or oral hygienist in the fight; get them to show you the proper way to maintain a high level of dental care, and plan regular visits—at least four times a year—for cleaning. If you need dentures, you might also need a dental adhesive to keep your new choppers secure, since you don't have the saliva that would normally help form the occlusive seal.

Candies and gum promote saliva flow, but make them sugarless, and watch what you eat: You may find that foods you previously ate with impunity are now irritating and/or drying. Salted nuts, chocolate, and undissolved salt are good examples. So are potencies like vinegar, strong cheese, and high-acid foods, such as tomatoes, unripe and whole citrus fruit and juices, shellfish, and alcoholic beverages, especially wine. If you've developed lesions from mouth fungi, put the spices back in the rack and pack the carbonated beverages back in the fridge.

Finally, if you're still smoking, butt out. Tobacco smoke can be extremely harmful to dry eyes, nasal tissue, and mouth.

As a rule, Sjögren's syndrome is what doctors call "a nuisance condition": It can cause a good deal of pain and discomfort, but only a minority of people suffer serious complications. There are severe cases that are the exception, but most people adapt and lead productive lives.

Uveitis and Other Eye-Related Problems

"With very few exceptions," says Dr. James T. Rosenbaum, a rheumatologist who treats patients with inflammatory diseases of the eye at the Oregon Health Sciences University in Portland, Oregon, "any of the rheumatic diseases can be associated with an inflammation in or around the eye. While the eye is anatomically tiny, it's actually a very diverse structure, with different portions that have very distinct functions and distinct characteristics. Inflammation can affect any part of the eye, and frequently the portion that's affected is characteristic in its association with a rheumatic disease."

Uveitis, says Rosenbaum, "is very analagous to arthritis, except that it's a descriptive term for inflammation inside the eye instead of in a joint. For example, 20 to 40 per cent of patients with either Reiter's syndrome or ankylosing spondylitis sometime in the course of their disease will develop an anterior uveitis."

There are about a dozen specific conditions that affect joints and the uveal tract simultaneously, including juvenile rheumatoid arthritis (JRA), Wegner's granulomatosus, Sjögren's and Behçet's syndromes, relapsing polychondritis, psoriatic arthritis, sarcoidosis, Kawasaki disease and, in rare cases, vasculitis and lupus. There's a specific overlap, Rosenbaum says, "so that, for example, RA typically does not involve the uveal tract, even though it typically involves the eye. It involves distinct structures in or around the eye." One of these is the sclera, the outer layer of the eye; in severe cases of scleritis the entire thickness of the sclera can be affected—leading to a secondary uveitis. Scleritis is also seen in about 20 per cent of all people with RA-associated vasculitis.

The uveal tract is sufficiently different from front to back that the symptoms of uveitis can vary greatly between iritis (inflammation in the iris), say, and choroiditis (inflammation in the choroid, part of the posterior section of the uveal tract). The symptoms also vary depending on whether the disease has a gradual or sudden onset. In ankylosing spondylitis, for instance, a typical presentation would begin with a red, painful eye, specifically in an area called the nimbus, which is where the cornea ends and the white of the eye, the sclera, begins. In pauciarticular JRA, on the other hand, the eye typically is neither red nor painful; some children may have it without even knowing it.

There are various degrees of severity. Rosenbaum notes that approximately one out of four children who get chicken pox develop a form of uveitis so mild that it doesn't even require treatment, while the JRA form of uveitis is often "a more significant part of the disease than the arthritis, because it may lead to blindness." Furthermore, he says, "the arthritis in a majority of cases, though not always, will go away, whereas the uveitis tends to last a couple of decades."

Despite its many incarnations and associations with different forms of arthritis, uveitis isn't the most common ophthalmological complication of arthritis; that dubious honour goes to dry eye, which can have serious repercussions: Overly dry eyes are susceptible to infection. Many people with RA develop dry eyes, Rosenbaum says, causing abnormal tear function. Why is unclear, but it's not just a side effect of their medication: "The same autoimmune process that we hypothesize attacks the joints also attacks the tear glands. By definition, that's what Sjögren's syndrome is—an autoimmune disease. It can also be a complication of conditions like scleroderma or polymyositis."

There are arthritis medications, though, associated with ocular problems. After prolonged usage, antimalarial drugs such as chloroquine and hydroxychloroquine can cause retinopathy, which can result in permanent blindness if not caught early. Corticosteroids are also associated with ocular toxicities that can lead to cataracts and glaucoma. Patients receiving any of these drugs should have their eyes checked regularly by an ophthalmologist.

People receiving gold therapy are also at risk; they may develop corneal chrysiasis, deposits of elemental gold in the cornea, after prolonged usage, though most side effects, if detected early, can be alleviated simply by discontinuing the treatment.

A well-recognized and serious complication of temporal arteritis, which is often associated with polymyalgia rheumatica (see page 47), particularly in untreated patients, is ocular involvement, sometimes leading to sudden blindness. And lupus patients often report photosensitivity, a reaction to bright sunlight. While it may bring on a flare of symptoms, it's not usually considered ophthalmologically serious.

There is *some* good news amidst all of this ocular woe: There's no eye disease associated with osteoarthritis, the most common form of the disease. Still, says Rosenbaum, "people with osteo tend to be older and should have routine eye screening for cataracts and glaucoma and a disease called macular degeneration [in which a small section of the retina used to distinguish fine detail—the macula—begins to break down]. But the arthritis per se does not have an association."

The bottom line? Don't take chances. If you have eye pain or experience vision problems, call a rheumatologist or ophthalmologist.

Repetitive Stress Injuries (RSI)

Ask people what RSI stands for, and they might guess it's some sort of scholastic institute. Ask the alumnae, and they'll tell you it's the school of hard knocks.

Repetitive stress injuries are a group of painful disorders affecting muscles, tendons, and nerves caused by any repetitive activity or any activity done repeatedly from an awkward posture or position. It goes by a dozen names, among them, repetition strain or motion injuries, overuse syndrome, and regional musculo-skeletal disorders.

Strictly speaking, RSI isn't a form of arthritis. Many people seek medical help for what they believe to be symptoms of arthritis, though, when what they're experiencing are soft-tissue injuries. "It's a condition that causes stress and strain on the joints, muscles and tendons, so it can be a secondary condition in people with arthritis," says Ilene Cohen, an occupational therapist with The Arthritis Society's Consultation and Therapy Service in Toronto. "As a primary condition, though, it's most prevalent in people who don't have arthritis."

In its most celebrated incarnations, RSI exercises its influence in sports, where multimillion-dollar fastballers succumb to rotator cuff injuries. On the courts, pro and amateur alike fall victim to tennis elbow (a condition that can also strike anyone overzealous at raking, window cleaning, floor scrubbing, or pruning with manual clippers). Musicians and dancers, with their endless hours of repetitive practice, have long been prey to various forms of RSI.

Where RSI casts the longest shadow, though, is in the workplace. That's not exactly news, of course—our ancestors suffered weaver's bottom, dustman's shoulder, brewer's back, telegraphist's wrist, and housemaid's knee—but a near-epidemic toll of workplace injuries attributable to RSI a few years ago certainly seemed to signal the start of something unprecedented in scope and international impact.

In its wake, the Canadian Centre for Occupational Health and Safety recognized workplace RSI as one of the "leading causes of significant human suffering, loss of productivity, and economic burdens on society." A 1992 *Time* magazine story estimated that repetitive stress injuries were striking 185,000 U.S. office and factory workers a year, accounting for "more than half of America's occupational illnesses, compared with about 20 per cent a decade ago."

The costs are substantial. It's been estimated that RSI costs North Americans more than $7 billion a year in lost productivity and medical expenses. As the British Arthritis and Rheumatism Council noted some years ago, a constant stream of new technological innovations has lightened workloads, but oftentimes those same technical innovations have led to greater use—overuse, that is—of rapid and repetitive hand, wrist, and upper arm movements.

With them has come an ever-increasing incidence of injuries, to say nothing of lawsuits: Hundreds of injured American workers—telephone reservationists, cashiers, word processors, and journalists—have launched suits against computer manufacturers, blaming the machines for their disabilities. The defendants have included IBM, Apple Computers, AT&T, and Kodak. If every plaintiff chalked up a victory in court, a host of manufacturers could find themselves on the hook, *Time* said, for a payout that "could rival the $4 billion paid on asbestos-related claims."

Computer-related injuries reveal the essence of RSI. Keyboards allow typists to type faster than they could on conventional machines—and without needing to stop to shift the carriage, change the paper, or get up for a file; everything is at the typist's fingertips. And unlike conventional typewriters, which generally have a bit of spring in the keys, computer keyboards have hard bases. Each keystroke is a tiny shock to the minute filaments of soft tissue in the muscles, tendons, and joints of the fingers, hands, and wrists. Used hour after hour, day after day, such unforgiving keyboards eventually exact a toll.

Manufacturers have responded to the problem with ergonomic adaptations, but in a way they're victims of their own success: The ease of computer keyboards encourages lazy hand and arm position. Many people type with their wrists in flexion—bent slightly—which increases the pressure on the soft tissues passing through the joints of the elbows, wrists, and fingers. When these tissues that make up the muscles, tendons, and ligaments become swollen because of the repetitive and awkward motions of typing, the nerves surrounded by them become squeezed or compressed, as in carpal tunnel syndrome (CTS). In CTS, the median nerve, which passes through a space between the carpal bones in the wrist, is pinched by swelling in the surrounding tissues, causing numbness and tingling in the hand.

CTS, though the most common, isn't the only "tunnel syndrome" or "nerve entrapment" disorder. There are also cubital and radial tunnel syndromes, plus pronator and anterior interosseous syndromes (all of which affect nerves in the elbows and forearms), not to mention intersection syndrome and de Quervain's disease, which are forms of tendonitis (swelling of the tendon) and tenosynovitis (inflammation of tendon sheaths) in the wrists.

It's not just computers that cause problems: Anyone performing a repetitive task can fall victim. Most people's first symptom is pain, sometimes accompanied by joint stiffness and muscle tightness, as well as redness and/or swelling in the affected area; some people may also experience tingling or numbness. It's a gradual degeneration, at first obvious only during the activity that causes it or as aching and fatigue afterward. Slowly, though, people with work-related RSI begin to take their pain home. Before long, they may be in such distress they have trouble sleeping, can't pick up their children, or can't do the dishes.

Treatment

The first step in therapy is stretching and range-of-motion exercises to ease stiffened joints and tissues. A variety of passive and active exercises may be employed, either with a therapist's help or with the patient using various apparata to perform non-stressful motions.

Rest, of course, is an important component of therapy—getting away from that repetitive use of the limb so everything has a chance to settle down. Applications of ice and ultrasound are used to reduce pain, numbness, and inflammation. Exercises help muscle fibres stretch out and get the circulation going again to minimize scar tissue formation, followed by a graduated exercise program—usually isometrics—for strengthening. Isometrics involve a full contraction of the tendon and muscle unit, without actually moving the joint, to avoid friction.

In theory, such a program will bring an injured arm and shoulder back to the point that an injured worker will be able to return to his or her job, but all too often the worker has to go back to the same job after an overuse injury and the cycle starts all over again. The only effective way to break out of it is to change the job, which isn't always an option. How many times an injury has occurred and whether the patient fully (or near-fully) recovered are also factors. If patients reach 80 per cent of capacity, they're usually sent back to work.

It's only recently that the problem of RSI has been given the attention that it deserves, Cohen says—"that work situations and environments are causing so many of these musculoskeletal problems we're seeing. It's a major issue for Workers' Compensation, and it will become even more major with time." But it's not just the workplace, Cohen notes: "This also affects people with arthritis, because they can get RSI on top of their arthritis. Because of their joint limitations, they can be working at a mechanical disadvantage, and that's why it's so important to look at their positioning. Someone who's ironing for hours—which they shouldn't be doing—but in a bad position, they're going to end up with problems."

Cohen tries to prevent that from happening "whether at home, in the workplace, or at school. People with arthritis especially should be aware of how they're working, be aware of the proper position, and then try to do that—whether they've got RSI or not. *Everybody* should. That's preventative."

4

A Child's Garden of Curses
Juvenile Forms of Arthritis

Do ye hear the children weeping, O my brothers
Ere the sorrow comes with years?
...The child's sob in the silence curses deeper
Than the strong man in his wrath.
                    —Elizabeth Barrett Browning,
                    The Cry of the Children

Kids get arthritis, too. It doesn't seem fair, but they do, about one in a thousand of them. That's a higher prevalence rate than a mittful of other childhood disorders, including diabetes and cystic fibrosis.

Forms of Arthritis in Children
Juvenile Arthritis
The most common form of arthritis in children goes by the name juvenile rheumatoid arthritis (JRA), though the term isn't entirely appropriate. To begin with, children develop a form of arthritis that's usually quite different from adult rheumatoid arthritis: They not only experience symptoms differently but generally have a more favourable prognosis—partly because of the nature of the disease, partly because kids have marvellous recuperative powers. A better name for the condition is simply juvenile arthritis (JA).

Like the adult form, JA is often chronic, but not always, and, like the adult form, there's no cure, though with proper treatment and therapy most children enter adulthood without any major physical disability. The course of the disease, however, is highly individual. Some children are up and down, suffering flares, or exacerbations (when symptoms worsen), and enjoying remissions (when symptoms subside) for years.

Happily in most children flares decrease in severity and frequency over time. Some actually "outgrow" the disease before they've put away the last of their toys: The longer your child has active disease, the greater the risk of permanent damage, but about three out of four children will eventually go into extended periods with no symptoms or even complete remission of the disease, with little or no disability.

JA is defined as continuous inflammation of one or more joints lasting six weeks or longer for which no other cause can be found. It may follow a routine infection or injury, but neither causes the disease. While the actual cause isn't known, it's believed the inflammation is caused by some sort of immune-system disorder, as in other auto-immune conditions. It can begin at any age, but it's first seen most often in toddlers and teens, girls more often than boys. Although heredity has long been dismissed as a factor, because of certain genetic markers that have been found in some children with arthritis, researchers suspect that some children may have a genetic predisposition to the disease.

Because children don't always complain of pain (or, when they do, have their complaints dismissed as "growing pains"), JA is often hard to diagnose. Morning stiffness or pain in moving the joint are good clues, but inflammation in a joint isn't always obvious. As in adult forms of arthritis, you may have to seek a referral to a specialist, a pediatrician, or a pediatric rheumatologist. He or she will do a physical examination, put your child's joints through range-of-motion tests, and have blood tests and x-rays taken; even then, it may take time to confirm the diagnosis. Sometimes the onset of the disease is so slow and the symptoms so mild that only a combination of tests, clinical examination, and monitoring symptoms over a period of weeks or months will allow a firm diagnosis to be made. Generally a diagnosis will only be confirmed after at least six consecutive weeks of inflammation in a joint or joints; some doctors won't make a designation as to which subtype of the disease your child has until after six months of active disease.

Some forms of JA (the systemic and polyarticular forms especially) can cause growth problems in up to a third of children with the disease. Because of inflammation in affected joints, there may be overgrowth or undergrowth in some bones. A leg with an affected knee may grow faster than the "normal" leg, or inflammation of the jaw may cause the child to develop a slightly smaller jaw. Most growth problems subside, though, when the disease process goes into remission.

Pauciarticular Juvenile Arthritis

In this, the most common form of the disease, less than five joints are affected (*pauci* means few; *articular* means articulation, or joint), usually the knees, ankles, wrists, or elbows in an asymmetrical fashion (that is, one knee, one ankle, etc.). It generally starts when children, predominantly girls, are four or younger; it rarely affects overall health or growth and seldom causes any lasting damage to joints. Many children, in fact, go into permanent remission within a few years of onset.

The one complication you must be aware of is uveitis, an inflammation of the iris, ciliary body and/or choroid of the eye (see page 85). It's a potentially serious condition that affects approximately one in five children with pauciarticular arthritis (some estimates put the figure as high as half of all children with this form of the disease). Bear in mind that children may not notice any apparent signs or symptoms, or complain of any they do experience, but if the condition is left untreated, it can cause visual loss or even blindness. It's therefore recommended that children with pauciarticular JA have regular eye exams—three to four times a year for the first few years after diagnosis—by an ophthalmologist, who can usually treat the condition if it appears.

Polyarticular Juvenile Arthritis

Involving five or more joints (*poly* means many), usually symmetrically, polyarticular JA is more common in girls and can begin at any age, often in several joints at the same time. It may last for just a few months or continue for several years and generally follows a course similar to pauciarticular arthritis. The prognosis is usually good for these children, though a minority, who test positive for the presence of rheumatoid factor in their blood (see page 15), are at greater risk of developing a progressive, chronic form of the disease similar to adult RA, which can cause permanent damage to joints.

Systemic-Onset Juvenile Arthritis (SOJA)

Also known as Still's disease (after the British physician who first reported the condition in 1897), SOJA is different again. It occurs in 10 to 20 per cent of children with JA, equally affecting girls and boys. Its name arises from the fact that it begins with a spiking (rapidly rising and falling) fever, which occurs once or twice a day, often accompanied by a rash on the thighs and chest. Children may have swollen lymph glands and enlargement of the liver and spleen and, in some cases, myocarditis or pericarditis (inflammation of the heart muscle or surrounding tissue). During fever episodes, children may appear listless and experience chills and achiness; if the fever lasts for several weeks, they often lose weight and become weak and anemic (from diminished hemoglobin levels in the blood).

There may be little or no joint involvement at the outset, but that usually changes within the first six months, as a few or several joints become affected. As with other forms of JA, SOJA may follow a pattern of ups and downs, flares and remissions, but even severe cases often go into remission within a few years (though flares may recur long after the disease has apparently subsided). In up to 75 per cent of all cases, the condition goes into permanent remission without inflicting any damage to joints or internal organs.

Spondyloarthropathy

As its name suggests, spondyloarthropathy (*spondyl* refers to vertebra, *arthro* to joint, and *pathy* to disease) affects the spine, particularly the lower back, and often the hips; it occasionally causes heel pain, as well. The only type of JA to affect boys more often than girls, it most often begins at age ten or older, and may persist into adulthood. It's just one of a group of spondyloarthropathies (see page 50) that includes ankylosing spondylitis, Reiter's syndrome, and psoriatic arthritis. In any of these so-called seronegative conditions, blood tests are negative for rheumatoid factor, a result that's often helpful in making a diagnosis.

Juvenile spondyloarthropathy is one of the few forms of arthritis in which there appears to be a genetic link. It may also occur with inflammation of the skin or bowel, either in the child or other family members. Many children with spondyloarthropathy carry a protein called HLA-B27 (see page 257) on their cells, which may help in making a diagnosis.

Juvenile Rheumatoid Arthritis

The one type of JA that can properly be called juvenile rheumatoid arthritis is actually an adult-type RA that begins in childhood. Girls are affected far more often than boys. As with about 80 per cent of RA adults, they'll typically test positive for rheumatoid factor. True JRA is more likely to cause severe joint damage and permanent disability than any other form of the disease, which means that stronger medications are employed to bring the disease under control as early as possible.

Psoriatic Arthritis

Like adults, children can develop psoriatic arthritis, a combination of psoriasis, and arthritis in one or more joints. The arthritis, in fact, usually precedes signs of the psoriasis—which may include nail pitting, ridging, or onycholysis (loosening or detachment of the nail from the nailbed), as well as a rash behind the ears, at the scalp line, or at the umbilicus (the belly button)—sometimes by up to fifteen years. Psoriasis affects from 10 to 15 per cent of children with all forms of JA, girls outnumbering boys two to one, half of them with pauciarticular arthritis. In approximately 40 per cent of cases, there's a family history of psoriasis, which may help in making a diagnosis.

Diagnosis and Treatment

To achieve the best outcome in any form of JA, diagnosis has to be made and treatment begun as early as possible. As Dr. Bernhard H. Singsen notes in the tenth edition of the *Primer on the Rheumatic Diseases,* parents and physicians have to be especially cognizant of children's pain perception: "Many children with...arthritis complain little of joint pain, particularly if they are younger than ten years old, have long-standing disease, or are experiencing adolescent denial. Rather, they limit or modify any motion that would result in pain; thus, pediatric complaints of severe joint discomfort or pain at rest are distinctly unusual."

This can lend a false sense of security about the child's condition; it also makes diagnosis and follow-up treatment extremely difficult. Parents should be especially vigilant of changes a child makes in the way he or she is playing or moving, and be prepared to provide the child's physician with accurate descriptions of any pain, discomfort, or dysfunction they're aware the child is experiencing. In turn, the doctor has to be extremely careful in his or her examination and assessment of the child's joints and overall health.

Treatment of JA aims at relieving pain and stiffness, maintaining joint flexibility and muscle strength, and preventing lasting deformity. Depending on your child's age and the severity of the disease, treatment will likely include medications, rest, exercise and physiotherapy, perhaps splinting, and occupational therapy. Because the impact of developing a chronic illness is often devastating for children (and parents), counselling and psychological therapy may also be appropriate.

Medications are a mainstay of arthritis therapy, even for children. In fact, most of the medications used in adult arthritis are also prescribed for children, albeit in reduced dosages, according to their weight. For periodic pain relief, analgesics (such as ASA and acetaminophen) may be employed, but for longer-lasting relief of pain, the inflammation in a joint has to be reduced, which calls for NSAIDs (nonsteroidal anti-inflammatory drugs). There's a wide variety of these, and your child's physician may want to experiment with different brands to find the one that's best for your child—meaning the most effective with the fewest side effects. You and the physician will have to monitor your child carefully each time his or her medication is changed, but generally an NSAID will be found that's both safe and effective. Try to be patient: NSAIDs take up to eight to twelve weeks to be effective.

ASA (Aspirin, Entrophen, etc.) used to be commonly prescribed in anti-inflammatory doses, and it remains a safe and effective medication for many children with JA, but NSAIDs are usually easier to use (one or two pills a day as against three to ten). More important, there's a slight risk of Reye's syndrome associated with children and ASA after an acute viral infection, such as chicken pox or influenza. Reye's syndrome can cause a sudden onset of brain dysfunction and permanent liver damage; in some cases, it can be fatal. Obviously it's not something to take chances with, but it is extremely rare (discontinuing ASA after exposure to or infection with a virus greatly reduces the risk of developing Reye's); ask your doctor for more details about the condition.

For some children, corticosteroid injections (cortisone) are used to relieve the pain and swelling of an acutely inflamed joint that isn't responding to other treatments. Don't worry: These are *not* the same as anabolic steroids, the muscle-building treatment some athletes have found themselves in hot water for using. Steroid injections are given sparingly, but one injection will often reduce symptoms—with little risk of side effects—for months at a time.

Prednisone—the tablet form of cortisone that's commonly used in the treatment of adult arthritis—is less frequently prescribed, except in short courses, when its potential side effects (including slowing of growth, thinning of bones, and cataracts in the eyes) can be minimized. It's generally reserved for severe systemic-onset JA and other serious forms of the disease.

For moderate to severe cases of JA, your child's physician may suggest a course of DMARDs (disease-modifying anti-rheumatic drugs), such as methotrexate, sulfasalazine, or gold. Known as slow-acting drugs, DMARDs can take up to six months to become effective and are generally continued for six months to a year after the disease is under control or in remission to prevent a recurrence.

Surgery has some applications in JA, generally only after years of severe arthritis. Ligaments and tendons may be surgically lengthened to compensate for arthritis-induced overgrowth in one leg, for example; the misalignment of a joint may be corrected; even poor chin growth can often be dealt with surgically (though arthritis in the jaw may complicate dental work). A synovectomy (removal of an inflamed synovial lining) may be performed to reduce chronic pain and inflammation and slow the progress of the disease in a joint, but total joint replacements are usually inappropriate until a child has stopped growing.

Other non-medicinal interventions are an important part of treatment in JA, especially with respect to minimizing permanent damage to joints and muscles and preserving function. Active and passive physiotherapy may be employed to help stretch muscles and tendons and relieve discomfort, as well as splints for both resting and activity. Splints help keep children from doing what comes naturally: holding an arthritic joint in a bent position to relieve the discomfort in muscles and tendons caused by inflammation. A joint maintained too long in a bent position causes what's known as a joint contracture, in which the muscles and tendons gradually shorten and lose pace with the child's growth. The result is often permanent deformity.

Splints can be for working, which permit a certain amount of movement, or sleeping (for the wrists, say), which keep the child from holding her limbs curled up for comfort. Joints gradually stiffen during the night; without splints to hold them in the correct position, the child will wake up barely able to move in the morning, making activity and therapy that much more of an uphill climb. (A warm bath or shower in the morning can help ease morning stiffness.)

Similarly, exercises (which should always be done in consultation with a physiotherapist) are essential to strengthen the muscles that stabilize joints and build endurance. They should be done at least once a day, working all the joints through a full range of motion. As the child's condition improves, mild exercises can be upgraded to more strenuous ones, but be careful: Overdoing exercises can be just as bad as not doing them at all. Swimming is excellent, because it takes all the load off weight-bearing joints; for preschoolers, bring out the tricycle and let them have a little fun while they're working and strengthening their hips, knees, and ankles.

Exercises are a good way to involve the whole family, something that may help the child feel a little less isolated. If you can, do some of the exercises with your child, or have siblings take part. A brother or sister could even be enlisted to put the arthritic child's limbs through a range of passive-motion exercises.

The flip side of exercise and physiotherapy is rest, and children with JA need lots of it, especially during periods when their arthritis is active. Even during a flare, though, they shouldn't be allowed to stay in bed all day, since that will allow muscles and joints to stiffen up and reduce the child's overall mobility. Insofar as possible, encourage your child to stay active. That not only promotes overall health but encourages a healthier state of mind.

Children have a lot to deal with when they have arthritis, and anything you and your family can do to make a JA child feel "normal" will be good for him. Don't try to do everything for him; that will only create a sense of dependency, and he won't learn to do things for himself. Try not to spare the child from normal discipline, either; that may encourage the child to exploit his disability to his own advantage—a sure route to behavioural problems in later life, when other people aren't nearly so sympathetic.

If there are other children in your family, keep them involved, and try to save as much time for them as you can. Inevitably a child with a chronic illness is going to receive a lot of parental attention, and other children may feel left out. More than one child who's been encouraged to get involved in a sibling's care has developed an acute sense of empathy for the chronically ill and others with limited abilities.

Kids Get Fibromyalgia, Too

All things considered, Kyla Shimano was pretty lucky. Some mothers might have dismissed their six-year-old's complaints as growing pains; heaven knows, Kyla's mom wanted to. Lee Shimano recognized that Kyla's symptoms—she was achy, her joints hurt, and she had trouble sleeping—were disturbingly familiar. She just couldn't bring herself to believe what was happening. "It was one of those denial things," she says. Eventually, though, the evidence became too obvious to ignore: Kyla's complaints sounded just like Lee's own chronic condition. Kyla had fibromyalgia, too (also see page 38).

Fibromyalgia syndrome (FMS) is a chronic, arthritis-related syndrome that subjects anywhere from three to five per cent of the adult population to a host of vicissitudes, the most common being widespread musculoskeletal pain and stiffness, non-restorative sleep, chronic fatigue, and cognitive disorders, such as problems with memory and concentration.

As yet, there's no cure for FMS, and its cause is unknown. What was also apparently unknown and certainly undocumented until only a decade or so ago is that FMS afflicts children, too, most often in the teenage years, but sometimes in children under ten. The symptoms of juvenile FMS seem to mimic adult FMS, though there isn't sufficient data to confirm this. It may be as widespread as the adult condition; again, it's not known.

Until recently, says Dr. Ron Laxer, a pediatric rheumatologist at The Hospital for Sick Children in Toronto, physicians simply weren't aware of FMS as a diagnosis for a wide range of similar complaints in children. Now, he says, "fibromyalgia is the second most common diagnosis we make [after JRA] in new patients referred to our clinic."

Ignorance about FMS has long been a thorny issue with adults with FMS, many of whom endure years of disbelief and medical scepticism before receiving the satisfaction of a diagnosis. It's even worse for a child. Children often have difficulty articulating their discomfort, and their descriptions of generalized aches and difficulty sleeping are easily ascribed to "growing pains" or dismissed as malingering or attention-seeking. "And when you examine them," Laxer points out, "you don't find any abnormalities." More than one child has suffered months or even years of misunderstanding and disbelief before his or her complaints were confirmed by a diagnosis of FMS.

Lee and Kyla Shimano's experience is typical. Lee had been diagnosed with FMS a few years before Kyla began presenting symptoms, which started gradually. There were always "little things," Lee recalls. "She constantly had tonsillitis. Her tonsils were enormous, and she always had a cold or something and felt really crummy."

Kyla's doctor at the time suggested she have the offending tonsils removed, and all the aches and pains would disappear. But about two weeks after the operation, Lee says, "it started again. Her feet hurt, her calves hurt, her knees, her back—constantly. She couldn't get up the stairs sometimes."

Kyla was five. She enjoyed school but was already beginning to miss a lot; she was involved in gymnastics but wasn't encouraged to go because it was hurting her. "It was really a long haul," Lee says. At that point, they tried another doctor. Suspecting Kyla's troubles were FMS-based, Lee told the doctor she had it, too. "And he said," Shimano recalls, still shocked, "'Well, that's like having a hangnail.' I thought, 'I *wish* I had a hangnail. I wish I had *ten* of them.'"

Shimano was stunned into silence: "I thought, 'Well, OK, great. He must be right. This must be something I've created, it's all in my head, and if I get my act together, I'll be fine...'"

But she wasn't. She plodded along for months, trying to convince herself it really was all in her mind, but she wasn't getting any better. Then she had a major flareup that put her out of action. At that point, she realized she'd been kidding herself *and* Kyla: This wasn't all in her mind; she *was* sick, and so was Kyla. "I *know* there's something wrong with this child," she said. "She's not a con artist. She wouldn't miss a day of school if she could help it. She loves it, and she loves her friends—she's very social, so I knew. I know her better than anyone."

Shimano made a call to the Ontario Fibromyalgia Association, which directed her to Laxer. "He knows," she says. "I asked why Kyla's eyes and my eyes are red all the time. They don't know, he said, but it goes with the fibromyalgia. Well, *thank* you. I was so pleased to know that." It was a relief simply to be told it was a related problem, that she didn't have something else to worry about.

— —

Laxer and his colleagues try to be both as optimistic and as realistic as possible with patients and their parents. They explain that FMS isn't a crippling disease, nor will it lead to long-term complications. At the same time, as far as anyone can tell from what little is known, it's not going to disappear either. And that means it's crucial that kids with FMS develop coping mechanisms that span every sphere of their lives, from home and school to extracurricular activities.

"The first problem is that they have pain," Laxer says. That's the worst part, says Kyla, "when my joints hurt, my knees and my ankles, and then I get colds from it. I feel sick and stuff." The second problem, which in some ways is worse, is that "maybe they're not believed," Laxer says. "I think their parents believe them, but there may be a problem with school, with teachers, and gym teachers in particular. They don't see anything obvious, so it's 'Go out and do your pushups or your twenty laps like everybody else.'" That can turn into a major problem if it isn't dealt with, Laxer says. "These kids do miss a lot of school— much more than our worst JAs."

That means parents have to play an active role. It will probably fall to them to make sure teachers and school staff understand that the child with FMS is going to be too tired at times to take part in some activities; she may miss school because of medical appointments and physiotherapy, and she may have difficulty concentrating. Despite that, she needs to be encouraged to take an active part in her studies.

A child with FMS is going to need plenty of reassurance; he needs to feel believed that his pain is real. He'll also need regular injections of hope and encouragement. At the same time, he can't be allowed to start feeling sorry for himself, nor can he withdraw from regular social and physical activities, including—and perhaps most important—whatever physical rehabilitation program he's involved in. Perhaps not surprisingly, parents can become overprotective of their children, says Beverley Tobe, co-ordinator of the Juvenile Arthritis Program at the Arthritis Society's Ontario Division. That only helps children become less functional: "If they aren't motivated to get up and get going, some kids stop going to school and become quite dysfunctional. We try to get them to move toward going to school and improving the way they feel, coping, managing the pain. They need the social context."

Tobe and her colleagues operate a consultation and therapy service that's designed to help kids take charge of their condition. They learn about it, and they learn how to improve their fitness levels and sleeping patterns, so that over time they start feeling better. "We try to get them to be more physically active, to set small goals for themselves," Tobe says. "They do have some control over what's happening to them, but they need to address the issues—their posture, the state of their musculoskeletal system and the fact that they need to accept a committed exercise program as part of their weekly routine—and not to go off on tangents, like diet fads."

Overall fitness levels are a big part of the picture. "If they're spending all their time in bed," Tobe says, "we have to get them up and moving—slowly. Any exercise program we do with these kids is in small increments, because it may make them more sore initially and demotivate them. They may want to stop the exercise completely."

In Tobe's experience, though, kids who stay with it, increasing the level of their activity and enhancing their endurance, "tend to feel better, so they keep it going themselves." How much better exercise can make them feel is open to debate. "They still have aches and pains," Tobe says, "but if they stay on their exercise program, they *seem* to get better. How long they stay better I don't know."

Ignorance is the leitmotif of the syndrome. No one seems to have enough answers; no one can say what will happen—or won't—over a long period of time. Uncertainty is part of the condition, and people who have FMS can't let that get them down. What's also important is that parents of a child with FMS don't let it get *them* down: They can't afford to compromise their role with doubts and evasions. That isn't always easy, but it can be rewarding.

If you think your child may have FMS, consult your doctor, but keep in mind that it isn't always easy to diagnose. You may want a referral to a pediatric rheumatologist. For further information about fibromyalgia, contact your local division of The Arthritis Society.

Septic Arthritis: A Medical Emergency

"It all began in the night time," Rita Sydij says. She glances at husband Orest, takes a deep breath and begins an account of their son's bout with septic arthritis (SA). It's been two years, but the details remain painfully clear. Sitting in the basement office of their Toronto store, the Sydijs take turns with the narrative, while Rory, now six, putters about, as healthy, apparently, as if the SA had never happened.

The story begins on a Friday. Rita had gone to pick up Rory at the daycare after work, and when she arrived the children were in the midst of gym time. Rory and the other kids, Rita says, "were jumping all over the place." There wasn't a hint of a problem. Later, though, at dinnertime, Rory complained that his buttocks were sore. "Right here," he says, interrupting his game to indicate the offending spot.

"We just thought he wasn't sitting properly or something," Rita says, "but after dinner, he was playing in his room, and he came out and said his leg and his feet were sore."

"Throughout the evening," says Orest, picking up the story, "he was favouring that one leg and walking on the pads of his toes."

"Like this," says Rory, tippy-toeing.

"He'd complained before that his ankles were sore," Orest says. "Sometimes there's a lot of running and jumping at the daycare. We guessed it was just a bad day on his muscles and joints."

But as the evening progressed, Rory's complaints became more insistent. His parents looked closely for bruises or swelling—anything to indicate something other than normal wear and tear, but there was nothing. Then he couldn't sleep. "The pain started to get worse," says Rita, "and he couldn't turn on his own in bed. We had to turn him."

Orest: "Every half-hour he'd be moaning and crying, and we'd come in to turn him and try to relax him. We were up most of the night."

By dawn, it was apparent that Rory was in more pain than any amount of jumping and tumbling could explain, so they bundled him up as gently as they could and took him downtown to The Hospital for Sick Children. "Just trying to pick him up, he'd start screaming and crying," Orest remembers, "but we had to carry him to the car to get him there."

It was a good decision. The Sydijs had no way of knowing, but speed was of the essence. "The stakes are very high with septic arthritis," says Toronto rheumatologist Robert Inman. "There are many rheumatic diseases where watchful expectancy is appropriate in the early course of an undifferentiated polyarthritis that might evolve into a rheumatoid arthritis or even osteoarthritis. There, time is on the clinician's side. That's not the case in septic arthritis. It's a medical emergency, in which appropriate antibiotic therapy should be started as quickly as possible to avoid irreversible joint damage."

How quickly? In anywhere from twenty-four to forty-eight hours, SA can start damaging the cartilage in a joint. Had the Sydijs gone to their family doctor, Rory might not be bouncing around today. SA isn't a condition doctors see a lot, and it's easy to assume the swollen and tender joint is the result of overuse or an accident or mistake it for any one of a number of syndromes associated with JA. The patient may be given an antibiotic and something for the pain and told to rest the affected limb for a few days. The result is often permanent damage.

In fact, at Sick Children's, the first doctors couldn't identify Rory's problem. "They took blood, moved his leg, took x-rays," says Rita. "And when they moved his leg—and doing x-rays, they move you every which way—he'd be in excruciating pain, screaming and crying." The doctors knew Rory had an infection, but why it was causing such distress was a mystery. Rather than simply administer antibiotics and painkillers, they waited for the orthopedic specialist. Within minutes of the specialist's arrival, SA was diagnosed.

"Basically what they told us," Rita explains, "is that it's bacteria that gets into the blood. It settles in the hip joint, because the blood flows slowest in the hip joint, so it has an opportunity to settle and fester, which is what happened to Rory. They told us they had to operate to clean out the infection, that if it isn't caught fast enough, the infection can actually eat away at the bone."

Dr. Peter Armstrong, chief of staff at the Shriner's Hospital for Crippled Children in Salt Lake City, Utah, used to be a pediatric orthopedic surgeon at Toronto's Hospital for Sick Children. He did all of Rory's post-op checkups. "The concern about septic arthritis," Armstrong says, "is that products released by bacteria in the pus destroy the cartilage in the joint, and it doesn't take very long. You need to pick it up and deal with it quickly. If you leave it, it will destroy all the cartilage, the nice smooth, gliding surfaces of the joints. Then what will happen would be the development of a secondary osteoarthritis."

The surgeons told the Sydijs they wouldn't know how bad the infection was until they opened up the hip, but once that decision was made, things moved swiftly. The surgery, especially on a child, is relatively simple. The joint is opened up through a small incision and the joint cavity washed out with a saline solution. Antibiotics quell any residual infection.

"The doctor came in afterward," says Rita, "and told us there was quite a bit of infection in there, but they'd cleared it out and were going to leave a tube in to allow the remainder to seep out. He said he didn't feel it had done any real damage to the joint because we'd gotten there so quickly. We were very fortunate."

There were checkups every two months afterward, with x-rays and rotation of the hip and joints to assess mobility. But after four checkups, Armstrong told them Rory didn't need to come back. There was no point exposing him to more x-rays; they were happy with the results.

Septic, or infectious, arthritis is caused by bacteria invading a joint cavity, most often by hematogenous seeding, that is, blood-borne bacteria (which originate in soft-tissue infections or infections in the genitourinary, respiratory, or gastrointestinal tracts). SA can also originate in an infection, such as cellulitis or osteomyelitis, in tissue adjacent to a joint; and, far more rarely, by implantation, such as a traumatic injury, intra-articular injections, or orthopedic surgery.

Severe joint pain is the most characteristic symptom, with the pain increasing dramatically if the joint is flexed or extended or forced to bear weight. There may also be swelling, tenderness, and warmth in the tissue surrounding the joint, and some patients develop a fever.

SA can happen at any age, though it's more common in children than adults. In either case, it's more likely in people whose resistance is already weakened by disease or treatment for another condition with drugs—such as corticosteroids and immunosuppressives—that dampen the immune system. A previous accident or penetration of a joint by another form of arthritis may also predispose the joint to SA.

In children, bacteria may infect a joint directly through the tiny blood vessels beneath synovial tissue, but more often they invade from an adjacent osteomyelitis (a bone infection, characteristically in rapidly growing bones). This "hematogenous osteomyelitis" may develop when a minor injury results in a tiny fracture, causing bleeding into the area. When that happens, Armstrong says, "the flow is not particularly rapid, so if there are bacteria in the blood, they'll accumulate and start to duplicate." Eventually the bacteria "almost overwhelm the body's ability to completely eradicate the infection, and the pressure causes some death of tissue. That's good material for bacteria to grow in, so the pressure increases and it grows in size."

The infection then tries to break out at the place of least resistance. It could burst through the fibrous covering on the bone and produce an abcess in the soft tissue surrounding it. But, says Armstrong, "it may be that some of these cases of septic arthritis in the hip start with a small area of osteomyelitis that ruptures through, only when they do, they rupture right into the hip joint, and that's what seeds it."

There's also a condition called transient synovitis, a non-infectious inflammation that commonly affects the hip joint, but that doesn't inflict permanent damage on the joint cartilage. It may present with symptoms very similar to SA, Armstrong says, "though maybe a little less dramatic. You may not have the child looking sick or with fever, but they're obviously having pain in the joint, they don't want to move it, and they don't want to walk on it."

This presents the doctor with a dilemma: Is it transient synovitis or SA? Blood tests—particularly with younger children or early in the disease—may be normal. It may come down to the clinical examination. "If you can calm the child down a bit, and you can very gently take the limb and slowly put it through a range of motion, then you may be dealing with something more like a transient synovitis," Armstrong suggests. "But if you go to move the joint and they're screaming with pain, more likely this child has something like SA."

The best way to tell is to put a needle into the joint, usually in the operating room with the child under anesthetic. "If you get frank pus back," says Armstrong, "well, there's your diagnosis. Then you just open up the hip joint, clean it out and put the child on antibiotics. And generally that solves the problem."

In most cases, spotting SA shouldn't be difficult, Armstrong says: "It's pretty dramatic." The immobility of the joint without excruciating pain is the major clue, but there may also be fever or evidence of a respiratory tract problem. "If they develop a significant joint problem, they've got a fever and they're looking sick and they don't want to weight-bear," says Armstrong, "then I think you have every indication to take that child to an emergency department. I'd also be very insistent that an orthopedic surgeon see the child. If the child presents with those findings, it's SA until proven otherwise.

"We're acutely conscious of the damage to a joint an infection can cause," Armstrong says. He prefers to err on the side of caution—which in this case means being "a little more aggressive. In other words, get a needle in or surgically open the joint if there's sufficient evidence to suggest that SA is possible. We want to get in and find out, because if it is in fact SA, the longer you leave it, the greater the risk to the cartilage."

Uveitis

Today, one out of four children with pauciarticular juvenile rheumatoid arthritis will develop an inflammatory eye disease called uveitis; 30 per cent of affected eyes will develop substantial visual impairment; 10 per cent will be permanently blinded in one or both eyes.

Those numbers—those children—provide Dr. Alan M. Rosenberg with a good deal of incentive for his work. Rosenberg is director of pediatric rheumatology at the University of Saskatchewan in Saskatoon, where he's working on what he calls one of the most distinctive problems in pediatric rheumatology: the association of inflammation of the eye (uveitis) with inflammation of the joints (arthritis).

The uvea is the middle layer of the eye, a rich vascular tissue composed of the iris and the ciliary body in the front, or anterior, part of the eye, and the choroid in the back, or posterior. Inflammation may affect all or part of the uveal tract and its adjacent structures and is variously known as iritis, iridocyclitis (inflammation of the iris and ciliary body), choroiditis, retino-choroiditis, and panuveitis (inflammation throughout the uveal tract).

Different varieties of uveitis are closely associated with certain forms of arthritis—HLA-B27-positive uveitis, for example, with ankylosing spondylitis and related diseases. Patients may develop an acute form of the condition usually characterized by brief episodes associated with eye redness and pain or, in extreme cases, loss of vision, which requires immediate attention. It usually responds to therapy—in severe inflammation, a local steroid injection or even oral steroids would be considered—especially if therapy is initiated promptly.

Rosenberg, though, is concentrating on JRA-associated uveitis, which is four times less common: "It's asymptomatic and chronic. That is, the children don't complain of any symptoms at all, and it's only on looking microscopically into the eye that one detects the inflammation, so it's quite different and is unassociated with HLA-B27."

Why some children develop uveitis in association with arthritis isn't clear. Some form of genetic predisposition may be involved; it's also possible that some children are exposed to an agent, such as a bacterial or viral infection, that triggers the disease.

Rosenberg and his colleagues believe there may be a close link between uveitis and arthritis that could be explained by the presence of certain antibodies (immune-system proteins that help defend the body against infection). They're studying blood samples from children with uveitis to determine how many react to a key amino-acid sequence (amino acids are the "building blocks" of proteins). As Rosenberg points out, some children initially present with arthritis without any sign of uveitis, though it may develop later. He wants to focus on children who have arthritis without uveitis, but who test positive for a protein called antinuclear antibody (ANA): "If we can find in those children that they react to the amino-acid sequence, and eventually all of them develop uveitis, then we basically have a test that will allow us to predict which children are going to develop the uveitis and which are not."

They also want to gain "a clear understanding of why eye disease and joint disease and nothing else should coexist in these children. It seems a curious association and one we hope to explain." And, finally, they'd like to come up with ideas about the cause of the disease: "Once we have a cause, then we can consider specific treatment, and perhaps prevention, which is the ultimate goal."

Juvenile Arthritis and School

As the parent of a child with JA, you have some tough decisions ahead. Not the least of them is whether your school-age child should be enrolled in a regular school. Perhaps a special treatment facility would be better. For that matter, you might want your child to skip school altogether, and stay home. Obviously you want to do what's best for your child; you want to make a decision that will best meet your child's needs and provide him or her with everything needed to meet the special challenges that life with a chronic illness entails—in addition to preparing your child to take advantage of the opportunities that make anyone's life fulfilling.

There are any number of factors that will influence your decision, of course, and unfortunately some of them may be in conflict. Is your child physically *able* to go to school (every day or even occasionally)? Are there insurmountable barriers—either at the school or because of his condition—that would prevent his going? If she's in a wheelchair, is the school wheelchair-accessible? Can the school staff meet any special needs he might have? If she has to stay home, can you or someone you trust be there with her? If not, can you afford to pay someone to come in? Are there appropriate treatment facilities near where you live? For that matter, does your child want to go to school—or a treatment facility? Is he capable of handling the impositions of his disease, the pressures of socialization, *and* the ordinary challenges of school?

That's a lot of questions, just for openers, and there may not be easy answers to any of them. By all means, get some advice. Consult your family physician and whatever other health professionals your child has been seeing. Ask for their judgment on your child's ability to handle the physical and emotional stress of school.

Every child with JA is different, the extent of each child's disease is different, and the way it affects him or her will be different, too, but children with JA don't necessarily conform to the stereotypes of disability. They may not be confined to a wheelchair or restricted by sensory or motor impairment. They may walk and run slower than their peers, but they usually *can* walk and run. Their learning and social skills are also on a par with their peer group, though missed classes because of illness may present an added challenge. And, because JA imposes unpredictable cycles of flare-ups and remissions, children with the disease may suffer pain and physical limitations that will require them to maintain a regimen of joint protection and energy conservation. Again, it comes down to your child and her overall condition, but in all likelihood it won't prevent her from taking part in most activities, though she may have to make some adjustments.

Every child desperately wants to be normal, to be accepted. Most kids *want* to grow up with their peers and take part in their society, and socialization is one of the things school provides—it doesn't just provide formal education. That's part of the theory that underlies arguments for integration, or "destreaming," as it's more often called these days. (Either term refers to putting a youngster, regardless of disability or exceptionality, in a regular classroom with age-appropriate peers.) Whenever possible, children should be in the mainstream, educators say. They maintain that it's psychologically unhealthy for people, especially children in their formative years, to live in "ghettos" of experience—to be marginalized.

You don't have to agree with such theories; in any case they may not be relevant to your child. Every child reacts differently to the kind of socialization schools impart. Some thrive on it; others don't. And every school is different. Some children suffer more from being immersed in an inappropriate school environment than they'd gain from any benefits of socialization.

Something to keep in mind is that a child with a chronic illness may already feel different, and keeping him at home may heighten the alienation he's already feeling. In some childhood-education studies, a positive correlation has been demonstrated between a child's self-worth, academic achievement, and the ability to get along with other people. In a good school, in other words, teachers pass on more than the three Rs; they also teach children about cooperation, collaboration, teamwork, and social interaction. If you're going to keep your child *out* of school (when his physical condition is good enough that he *could* go), be prepared to offer him at least as much.

As the parent of a youngster with JA, you have a special role to play. Your basic tool is your knowledge of your child and her special needs and abilities. Check out the school in advance. Knowing what challenges your child faces in the course of an ordinary day will better prepare you to help her to maintain a positive attitude. Your understanding, involvement, and communication are crucial, so get involved: Communicate your knowledge and understanding to your child's teachers and the "team" you develop to support her. By making that kind of an effort, you'll go a long way toward ensuring that she has as normal a childhood as possible. And, in large part, you'll determine what the rewards from meeting the challenge will be. For you *and* your child.

Making School a Grade A Success

So, you've decided to enroll your child in school. You've received medical assurance he'll be physically capable. What next? Contact the school you've chosen and arrange an appointment with the principal. Explain your child's condition, abilities, and symptoms; the principal may not have encountered a child with JA. And don't wait till the last moment. Your first school of choice may not have the kind of facilities your child will need, or there may be barriers, such as impassable stairs, that your child's condition will prevent him from overcoming.

Ask the principal what government-sponsored services are available in your province, and your area. Your child may be eligible for a home-care program, for example, or special transportation. Ask about special-ed experts, who do a great job helping to integrate a child with special needs into the system. If they're not based at the school itself, they may be available through the local board of education. They can often clear up situations that can't be handled by the principal or your child's teacher. (If the principal has only limited knowledge of available programs, consult your local chapter of The Arthritis Society or phone the provincial Ministry of Health.)

Another good reason for starting early is to prepare your child's educational team. Ask the principal if you can spend an hour with your child's teacher. Better still, try to arrange a time when you can sit down with the entire "team": the principal, your child's teacher, the gym teacher, a school nurse if there is one, office staff, guidance counsellors, and any other staff members who are available.

Educate the teachers. There are publications about JA available through your local Arthritis Society office; distribute them amongst the school staff. If they have a firm understanding of the disease, they'll be quicker to spot a problem, be it a door that's too heavy or a behaviour problem linked to fatigue after a bad day of joint stiffness and pain. JA fluctuates, and there'll be days when your child is physically able to do things, and days when she's not. Unless teachers are told, they won't know that your child gets up early for therapy before class, or that she woke up with unusually stiff joints and it's taken her longer than usual to get rolling. It's a lot easier on your child if the occasional lateness is met with understanding instead of a reprimand.

Remember, the way the disease fluctuates, an uninformed teacher may think your child is two different people. One day he's able to do almost everything his classmates can do; the next day he's not. For those who have never encountered JA, the transient nature of the disease is difficult to accept. Some days the JA child will look as visibly normal as any of her peers but complain of fatigue or discomfort. Even more misleading, she may not complain at all but appear to be disinterested or apathetic. If teachers haven't been informed about the disease, they can't be blamed if they suspect the child is lazy or has "an attitude problem." When teachers are educated and prepared, they feel less apprehensive and more comfortable with your child *and* her individual needs.

One of the best ways to introduce school staff to JA, of course, is to call in an expert: The Arthritis Society. It may be possible to book a Society representative from your local division to talk to the school about JA—with your help, naturally. And, depending on his age and maturity, you may wish to have your child attend, too. Either way, be prepared to answer a flurry of questions.

Turn the teacher's "aides"—your child's classmates—to your advantage. Teach them about arthritis; even kindergarten-age children can learn about it, perhaps from a parent who feels comfortable with the discussion or from an Arthritis Society speaker you've invited.

Talking to the entire class is important. That way, all your child's classmates are informed about the disease without any misunderstanding, and they have an opportunity to ask questions of their own. Young children are naturally curious about anyone who's "different," which can occasionally lead to unintended cruelty. "Letting them in on the secret" may save your child avoidable suffering. Your child's limited finger strength and flexibility may mean, for example, that a teacher has to help her with her boots, zippers, buckles, and coat. Children who don't understand your child's condition might make cruel comments because they're jealous of the special attention.

Keeping other kids informed is also a good way of grooming a troop of loyal companions. It could be other children that help your child with buckles and boots, heavy doors, or a load of books. In the higher grades, other children may be recruited to take notes if your child has difficulty writing.

There are also physical and procedural aids that may help, such as a wheelchair (and, of course, ramps). For some older children, a tape recorder may be the best way to take notes. And writing with a typewriter or laptop computer may be easier than trying to hold even an oversize pencil (though that may be sufficient for younger children), while a backpack may make carrying heavy books possible.

Make sure in all of your preparations that your child's sense of independence isn't weakened. A child who isn't given a chance to test himself isn't going to grow. He needs to learn he can do things for himself, that he isn't totally dependent on others. In other words, the child should be helped when necessary, but not to the extent that he's made to feel helpless.

Be factual and forthright about the child's arthritis, so that she learns to adopt your attitude toward it. Some people have no idea how to react to a child with arthritis; if your—and her—attitude puts them at ease, they're far more likely to treat her normally.

Learning to live with arthritis is a task shared, in different ways, by you, your child, and everyone else in your family. That's not always easy. It's hard to accept that at present there's no cure for arthritis, and it's hard to live with the uncertainty about how long a child's arthritis will last. Family members need to adapt to that situation as best they can by maintaining open communication. Don't overprotect your child; try to place emphasis on as normal a social development as possible, in terms of family environment, schooling, and extracurricular activities.

A positive self-image is an important asset for a growing child with arthritis, and attitude, or spirit, may be more important than academic ability. Certainly not every child will be totally self-reliant, but for every child it's a worthwhile goal.

Mind Over Modem

To: All
From: Jason
Hi there, my name is Jason. I am 11 years old and I am sending this message from Sick Kids Hospital. I just found out that I *might* have Lupus and would like to know if there's any other boy with Lupus.

To: Jason
From: Kyle

…You probably feel pretty scared and lonely. I did too when I first found out I had [dermato-myositis]….I felt like I wanted to kick and punch everything….Three years have passed now, and I've learned to deal with it. But sometimes, I still get really mad and frustrated, so I go stomping off to my room and start crying because I just can't take it. It really helps if you talk to someone and explain everything that's going on. Well, I hope some of this might help. Bye-bye for now…

Jason and Kyle are just two of the more than three thousand kids and adults, able and disabled, who exchange reassurance and sympathy, hope and encouragement, information and enthusiastic "conversation" on a unique telecommunications network called Ability OnLine (see Recommended Resources for access information). AO was formed in 1991 by Dr. Arlette Lefebvre, a staff psychiatrist and consultant to the rheumatology team at Toronto's Hospital for Sick Children (HSC).

It began in the fall of 1990, when Lefebvre got a modem—a device that connects computers via phone lines—and discovered "this wonderful world of instant information." She suddenly had access to a wealth of medical databanks and could "talk" directly to people from all walks of life. After six months on-line, she discovered that two of the leaders of the computer conferences she'd wired into, people renowned for their expertise, were disabled. One was blind; the other was in a wheelchair. "That," she says, "was the 'ah-ha' moment." Wouldn't it be great, she thought, if she could put some of her patients, many of whom were severely disabled and sorely isolated, in touch with people who could act as mentors?

Lefebvre's brainchild began as a pilot project at HSC after a chance meeting of minds—electronically, of course—between Lefebvre and Brian D. Hillis, a firefighter turned computer consultant. It was Hillis who showed Lefebvre how to set up the network and who volunteered to act as its manager. He'd taken an early retirement from fighting fires, planning, he says, "to sit around for the next twenty-odd years and maybe do a little consulting to pay the bills and relax with my feet up and go to Florida for the winter."

Instead, he met Lefebvre. "We had two areas of expertise," Hillis notes, "mine in computers and hers in the clinical side of dealing with disabled kids. I hate to use the word, but it was almost like fate. I had all this time on my hands, and this idea materialized. I said, I think I know the best way to do this, and that's to set up a system we can run and maintain that the kids can call into."

The electronic-mail systems accessible by modem are the fast lane in the new "information superhighway." What probably no one imagined when they were laying down these remarkable data routes was that they'd be wheelchair-accessible: Anyone, young or old, able or disabled, can leap right into the fast lane with equal ease.

That capability is exactly what piqued Lefebvre's interest. Her patients have every imaginable chronic illness, from arthritis and facial-cranial injuries to cerebral palsy, quadriplegia, diabetes, and spinal bifida. She saw e-mail as a chance for them to lead real social lives, make friends, develop some self-esteem and, not incidentally, learn from other disabled teens and adults who've "been there" and can share their experiences and provide support and information. The system also provides access to information from all over the world on disabilities, education programs, vocations, etc., so kids can get what Lefebvre calls "a shortcut to empowerment, before they get discouraged in the teen years and before they feel alienated and drop out of school."

Some of Lefebvre's kids are nonverbal; many are in wheelchairs or otherwise severely restricted by their illnesses, but once they're hooked into the network, they exchange typed messages with uncontainable enthusiasm. Suddenly even quadriplegic children can "reach out and touch someone." It's given many a whole new lease on life.

— —

Central to Lefebvre's treatment philosophy is her faith in "the magic of peer support, the feeling that you belong." That philosophy rests in turn on her belief—psychiatric credentials notwithstanding—that one good role model is worth a thousand shrinks. ("Arlette's a psychiatrist," says Hillis, "but on-line she's not Dr. Lefebvre, child psychiatrist—she's Dr. Froggie, kids' pal.")

Lefebvre began working with children with physical disabilities more than twenty years ago. "Many of our kids," she says, "particularly with lupus, were spending several weeks or months in hospital." For teens, especially, that can be devastating, she says, "because it's a time when fitting in and looking like everybody else matters a lot. It seems like the end of the world if something sets you apart, and losing touch with friends can cause a precious loss of friendships and alliances."

And that can have serious consequences. Lefebvre cites a long-term study of JA patients that examined the effects of physical impact, family stresses, missing school, being in the hospital, and so on. The study concluded that the single most important association with prognosis ten years down the road was the amount of time children missed at school. "That would seem to suggest that it's not so much the acuteness of the illness or the number of joints involved or this or that; it's just the very fact of being away from your friends," Lefebvre observes. "That lack of peer contact in itself does something to make children outsiders—strangers to their peer groups—and that in turn must affect their physical condition.

"It's bad enough that you have a chronic illness and you don't know what's going to happen to you medically, but if on top of that you feel your whole social world is on quicksand, that makes it very difficult to feel in control and be optimistic about your future."

It's crucial that these children be taught certain skills, says Lefebvre, so that "they can go back to school and explain what happened to them, because there are a lot of fears out there." It can be especially difficult for peers to empathize with something like arthritis, which is usually thought of as a disease of older folks. "They don't see it as something likely to happen to them, and the tendency is to distance yourself from things you don't really think will happen to you."

Ability OnLine provides a bridge across that gap. It's a forum, says Hillis, "in which disabled kids have an opportunity to interact with regular kids, and regular kids have an opportunity to find out more about disabilities." The children don't *have* to talk about their disability; "if they just want to talk about regular kid things or teen things, like rock shows or TV programs, that's OK," says Hillis. "And if you don't want someone saying, 'Well, we've got to be nice to him because he's got a disability,' you don't have to have that happen. You can build a little bit of self-esteem by having a dialogue and a relationship with other kids and adults based on what you say and what you know, not based on whether you're in a wheelchair or using crutches."

Carlos Costa is the perfect example. "He joined the conference," says Lefebvre, "as a regular teen. You never ask anyone when they join whether they're disabled or not, and he was one of our most active communicators." Lefebvre had posted a "believe in yourself" message, and Costa replied, "I believe in myself, and by the way, I'm going to swim across Lake Ontario." Costa had come across as a bit of a showoff on-line, so everyone took it with a grain of salt. Then he said, "Oh, by the way, Vicki Keith is my coach, and I was born without legs."

"It was the first time he'd revealed he had a disability on-line," says Lefebvre. "It was fascinating. Within two days there were about eighteen messages from kids and adults—'Oh, Carlos, I came across too strong. I'm sorry, I shouldn't have said that,' and he said, 'On the contrary. This is the first time in my life I've been treated like everyone else.' " (Costa did swim the lake—the youngest male and the first disabled person to accomplish the feat.)

"It's sort of a big family that develops with people of all ages and backgrounds," Lefebvre says, "from Ph.D.s to taxi drivers. But we all have one thing in common: We all believe that the computer can be the great equalizer for kids who are isolated and feel different." It's the ultimate in barrier-free design. As one of the network kids puts it, "you get to know people from the inside out."

"We have the best health-care and education system in the world as far as integration," says Lefebvre, "yet only six per cent of disabled kids get to university. Why? Sixty-three per cent of disabled Canadians are underemployed or unemployed. Why? Why do so few disabled kids finish high school? There are all the services, but they don't feel part of the mainstream. We may think we treat them the same, but the Carlos Costas of this world aren't treated the same as everybody else."

Lefebvre wants to see that imbalance corrected. She wants to see children with disabilities of any kind and any degree given an opportunity to be treated just like everybody else, and taught to compete in the mainstream. That's where mentors—great mentors—come in, she says, "people who have been there and can be an example that, yes, it's your ability, not your disability that counts."

Parents with Arthritis and Children

Vera Chouinard would appear to have it all: Her husband, Ed, is a physician, she has a fulfilling career as an associate professor in the geography department at McMaster University in Hamilton, Ontario, and she has two healthy children, Alexandre and Renée. But it isn't Easy Street: Some nights when Alexandre was younger he'd cry himself to sleep because his mother looked so ill.

Chouinard *is* often ill. She has severe rheumatoid arthritis (RA), and can only walk short distances with two canes; otherwise, she's in a wheelchair or rides a motorized scooter. The effect on her family has been traumatic. "Chronic diseases like these hurt families and the personal side of people's lives," she says. "Both my children have been angels to me, supporting me and working hard to cheer me up, but they've been hurt from the tremendous effort this takes. It was hard for them to have a mother who was very ill at only thirty-six."

Juggling family responsibilities with household duties and work outside the home is a test for any parent, healthy or not. There are times when energy runs low and patience is stretched thin, and it can be a challenge finding quality time to spend with the children. But add to ordinary demands the pain and discomfort of a chronic disease such as arthritis, and you have stresses that can tear a family apart. When Chouinard's health was especially bad, when it "deteriorated," she admits it was hard to be patient with "normal kid squabbling."

The emotional side of arthritis is often as devastating, sometimes more devastating, than the physical side. Parents and children alike are frustrated when arthritis gets in the way of everyday activities and special events, but it's usually the children who suffer disappointment most intensely. Young children, particularly, can't be expected to fully understand what their parents are going through, and even if they do, they can't help how they feel about how *they're* affected. Most children feel let down, even angry, after repeated disappointments, though they may not express their anger openly—it may only come out indirectly. Chouinard, for example, found that her children had a heightened sensitivity to criticism. They'd be quicker to become tearful, and try as she might to be tactful, there were inevitably times when that was simply beyond her. In the aftermath of situations that got out of hand, she'd try to assure the children that their anger or disappointment was normal, "that it's OK to feel that way."

"Children need to get in touch with their anger and fear," says Janet Goodhoofd, a social worker with The Arthritis Society in London, Ontario. Goodhoofd encourages all members of a family to express their negative feelings, then she helps them think through what they can do with them: "You have a choice, to let those bad feelings stay inside, or do something about it."

That means communicating, even if it's not always immediately: Sometimes, when an arthritic parent is too tired or in too much pain to talk, Goodhoofd suggests children think up other ways to channel their frustration—hitting a punching bag, going for a bike ride, or drawing a picture. But hurt feelings shouldn't be postponed indefinitely—eventually they have to be discussed and dealt with.

Not everyone possesses the kind of communications skills a chronic illness requires, which is where a social worker can help. Goodhoofd has parents begin at the beginning, explaining why they hurt and why they're tired. Small children need to be reassured that "it's not their fault," something they may unconsciously infer from the way parents express themselves. Goodhoofd teaches them to use "I" statements instead of "you" statements, saying, "I am tired" or "I need help," rather than "You make me feel..." or "You should do this..."

Parents can offer a model of coping with their communication—not just in the words they use, but also in what they reveal about what they're actually feeling: "If parents express the disappointment they feel when they have to cancel an activity, they make it OK for children to express their feelings," says Goodhoofd. Then it's the parent's job to listen and try to understand what the child is thinking and feeling—not just what he or she is saying.

Sometimes it's easier said than done. Some kids don't even like to *talk* about arthritis, and it may not be because they're denying it, just that they find it hard to accept. Underlying much of their anger and resentment is fear, fear that you're going to become deformed or crippled by the disease—or that it will kill you.

Children may also be frightened for themselves. Every ache they feel in a joint, every time they fall and hurt themselves leaves them wondering if they, too, will develop arthritis. Parents need to address those concerns in a relaxed, realistic manner. Children should be told that just because parents have arthritis, it doesn't mean their children will develop it; they should also make a point of reassuring kids that arthritis is rarely fatal. And while it's important, says Chouinard, "to teach our children that some kinds of diseases are not always mild— that arthritis can be severe and debilitating—it shouldn't be a message of despair. Severely ill people can enjoy a reasonable quality of life."

Irene Morel, who lives in Parry Sound, Ontario, is a mother and grandmother who also has severe RA. Children shouldn't be kept in the dark, she says. "I'm not suggesting crying sessions, but be realistic. Anticipate that everyone will have a hard time dealing with the disease."

Sometimes it helps if the explanations come from an outsider, if a physiotherapist or social worker explains why Mom or Dad can't scrub floors or pick up toys. A social worker can help to explain to children what it's like "when Mommy has arthritis." That's often the kind of information kids need, not only to understand what Mom or Dad is going through, but how to explain the disease to their friends, whose misconceptions can burden children with unnecessary and misplaced anxieties. Children need the tools to deal with arthritis in a positive way.

Many families manage just fine, thank you, without outside help. Others, though, shy away from even asking because they assume social workers' only role is in the legal and financial departments, to help guide people through the red tape of bureaucratic procedures. But social workers can help families cope emotionally, teaching the whole family to focus on family goals that help put arthritis into perspective.

Family misunderstanding, even disbelief, is a common experience, especially where there are few visible signs of the disease, a phenomenon people with lupus or fibromyalgia find all too common. Most people simply find it difficult to empathize in the absence of evidence—all they *can* see is that Mom or Dad is often cranky, depressed, tired, and withdrawn. A social worker can help put them in the picture with information about the condition and by explaining just what the person with the disease is going through. Sometimes that's enough to turn things around, to get them talking. Kids have to know they can talk things out if a parent's got arthritis, and parents have to be prepared to listen. Social workers can help make it happen.

Irene Morel's RA was diagnosed when her children were in their early twenties. Even though they were old enough to understand, they couldn't help expressing their resentment and disbelief. It didn't help that the family was athletic and fond of the great outdoors. "Maybe if you did more sports and exercise or lost weight," they'd suggest, "it wouldn't be so bad. Maybe it's because you did this or did that..."

The first time Morel was admitted to the Orthopaedic and Arthritic Hospital in Toronto, she was given a crash course in arthritis. She dearly wished her whole family could have sat in on the class. She watched enviously as other families had round-table discussions with an Arthritis Society physiotherapist, but the logistics of getting her whole family in from Parry Sound, more than 200 kilometres north of Toronto, were insurmountable.

Indirectly, though, they did end up profiting from their mother's experience. Morel's daughter Susan was later diagnosed with fibromyalgia. Having heard from her mom how The Arthritis Society could help, she immediately got in touch, asking for information. She was given a videotape, which she sat down and watched with her own eight- and ten-year-old children. It helped to answer their questions and dispel their fears.

"It's a matter of constant re-education," says Goodhoofd. "With each new stage a child goes through, new learning is possible." That doesn't mean talking about the disease constantly. Parents get tired of complaining, and children develop deaf ears. A simple technique that works for some families is to post a pain thermometer on the refrigerator. On a scale of one to ten, the parent indicates whether it's a good day or a bad day, leaving children to adapt their behaviour accordingly.

At the same time, parents need to be sensitive to their children's reactions. All teens, for example, are occasionally embarrassed by their parents, and in families with arthritis, the disease may become the focus. Some teens may not want their friends to see a parent's misshapen hands or shuffling gait. It's not abnormal for them to say something like, "You needn't bother coming to the parent-teacher night."

Children shouldn't be allowed to deny their parents in this way, says Goodhoofd, but parents can make it easier for the child to handle the situation, by asking, for example, "Is there something you'd like me to wear?"

It doesn't do anyone any good to try to avoid the problems arthritis imposes. "A person in pain tends to withdraw," Goodhoofd observes, "and that hurts families." Even if the family can't go out together, they need to be together. Don't hide in your bedroom. Plan a family night with rented movies, and invite the kids to cosy up with Mom or Dad on the bed or the living room couch to watch.

Chouinard rarely has the energy to attend evening school activities, so she makes a point of listening closely to the children's descriptions the next day, and when she's up to it, she takes them out on her own for lunch and a shopping expedition, phoning ahead to make sure there's someone at their destination who can help get the wheelchair out of the car. If not, she takes her canes and arranges to sit down while the children bring her what they're interested in buying.

The Morels have learned to adapt their camping expeditions, using a trailer instead of a tent, so Irene can join the fun. Do what you can, she advises, to minimize the guilt children may feel: "Let them live their lives and continue to enjoy activities you can no longer participate in."

Pace yourself: Lack of energy means parents with arthritis have to decide what's really important and what they can let go. Chouinard enjoys preparing special dishes and sauces, but she's learned to simplify menus, and the family doesn't seem to mind. They'll often overcook on weekends, so that they have planned leftovers during the week, or Chouinard will ask homecare workers to make casseroles she can pack away in the freezer.

Chores and family responsibilities can be another problem area. Children may resent the fact that it seems more responsibilities fall on their young shoulders, and it doesn't help if parents focus their requests for help on the disease. If you say, "Help Mommy do this because her arms are sore," the kids are likely to resent it; they might well assume that if Mom wasn't ill, they wouldn't have to do as much. Goodhoofd suggests letting children choose their own chores; they respond better to requests when they have some sense of control. Reward their efforts with positive reinforcement: Tell them how much their help means to you.

And don't be a martyr. Don't try to clean the entire house in a day;

do it in bits and pieces, whenever you have the energy, and get the kids to help, even if it's only in small ways. If you can spare yourself a bit of bending, or pushing, or pulling, you'll have a little more energy to spend with them, and they'll feel useful and helpful. Make it a trade-off: If they help you with chores around the house, maybe you can ease up on them a little when it comes to *their* bedrooms.

Learn to ask for help. For some people, that's hard, but trying to do too much is a form of denial. If you have arthritis, there are all kinds of things that can leave you too tired to really *be* with your children. Maybe your spouse or the kids can pitch in a little more; if you can afford it, consider hiring a babysitter now and again, just to give you a break, or someone to help with the household chores.

If you've got a big event coming up that you desperately want to attend, plan for it. Get some rest, so you'll have enough energy to go out or play host later. If you let your arthritis cut you off from every social activity, you'll only make matters worse: You need to take part in special events so you don't feel left out. That's demoralizing for you *and* your family.

"I probably should have hired sitters more often, even when I was home, but needing to rest," says Chouinard. She says she still needs to bring herself to call on friends more. When she does, she tries to minimize the inconvenience by fitting her request into her helper's routine—having a neighbour pick up extra groceries when she's shopping, for instance, or delivering a parcel that's on her way.

Above all, celebrate the joy of children: Goodhoofd organized a support group for young parents with arthritis. At the first meeting, the conversation quickly found a kind of lowest common denominator—hardships and coping strategies—until Goodhoofd suggested to them that all their experiences with children seemed to be uniformly discouraging. Immediately the parents started talking about how much joy and fulfillment their children brought to their lives, and how being able to share in their curiosity and excitement provided an important distraction from the pain of illness.

In the long run, children probably benefit from a close exposure to illness. Living with someone who has arthritis can be a harrowing experience, but it can also teach children valuable lessons in compassion. And, in the end, says Morel, "if you're coping, they'll cope."

5

I Hurt, Therefore I Am
Pain and Pain Management

It is not learning, grace nor gear,
Nor easy meat and drink,
But bitter pinch of pain and fear
That makes creation think.
                    —*Kipling*, The Conundrum of the Workshops

However unwelcome, pain—acute pain, at least—has an obvious function: survival. It's a reflex that makes us withdraw a finger from a flame, faster than thought, an irresistible impulse to massage a stubbed toe or the urge to rest an injured limb. Pain, especially chronic pain, will never win a popularity prize, but it *can* protect us. What's not so clear is how it does its work.

The Nervous System

At bottom, pain (all sensation for that matter) is a product of the nervous system. More complex than the most advanced electronic circuitry, it's the most baffling of all the body's systems, yet our basic understanding of it is thousands of years old. The Egyptians had a nodding acquaintance with the nervous system, thanks to embalming procedures, but the foundations of neurological understanding were laid by a pair of third-century B.C. Greeks, Herophilus and Erasistratos. Between them, they described the peripheral nerves, sensory and motor, that run to and from the spinal cord and brain.

In the centuries that followed, scientists and surgeons made only incremental advances in identifying and mapping the complex of nerves. Then, in 1664, French philosopher and scientist René Descartes suggested that pain travels specific pathways from extremities in the skin to the brain. With certain modifications, and within certain limits, that understanding has been corroborated down to the present day.

The nervous system consists of three interconnected parts: afferent nerve fibres and their receptors, efferent fibres with their muscles and glands, and the central nervous system—the spinal cord and brain. Like all living tissue, the entire network is made up of cell matter, in its case primarily nerve cells, or neurons. (We're actually born with the cells of the central nervous system; unlike all other cells in the body, they're irreplaceable.)

Nerve cells are akin to other body cells, except that at one end they have a number of rootlike projections called "dendrites"; at the other end, each cell has a long, whiplike tail called an "axon." Grouped in bundles like the fibres of a rope, nerve cells may be the merest part of an inch long or run three feet or more from the tip of the toe to the base of the spine. It's their fantastic interconnectedness—a large neuron, for example, may be in contact with the dendrites of as many as 200,000 cells—that gives us such a rich sensory apparatus.

The afferent and efferent fibres, which comprise the peripheral nervous system, are essentially one-way transmission lines. The afferent nerves conduct messages *to* the spinal cord and brain; the efferent nerves conduct signals *away* from the brain, to the muscles and glands. The kind of messages efferent fibres carry to their end organs are generally command signals. If the destination is a muscle, it may be a command to contract; if an organ is the goal—the stomach, say—it may be an order to release digestive enzymes.

The afferent fibres' messages, on the other hand, convey sensory information—sensations such as heat, cold, touch and, unfortunately, pain, from bumps, bruises, and other failings of the flesh.

Be they via afferent or efferent fibres, messages are sent in a sort of Morse code—series of sequential dots grouped in volleys of electrochemical nerve impulses, racing along at anywhere from 2 to 120 metres per second. As fast as that sounds, pain is hardly instantaneous: Stub your toe, and you know you *will* feel pain before you actually *do* (the scientific name for this awareness is nociception). And in the case of chronic pain, the signal from the nerve endings seems instantaneous, but only because it never really stops.

All of this wealth of detail, however complicated, makes neural structure sound somehow... simple. And it makes the Cartesian model of pain (remember Descartes?) seem perfectly sound: You stub your toe, and the mass of bruised tissue releases chemicals, such as the neuro-peptide transmitter Substance P, to sensitize the adjacent nerve endings (peptides are organic chemicals a step up from the simple amino acids that are the building blocks of proteins). Once stimulated, these send electrochemical nerve impulses to the spinal cord via afferent fibres; in turn, the spinal cord passes on the signals to the brain, which deciphers them as "pain." It then emits secondary instructions, via the efferent pathways, to various muscle groups and glands, which initiate a series of motor activities (you lift your foot, reach down and massage the toe, while the vocal chords produce a resounding "Ow!")—not to mention the usual blood-borne "healing cascade" of immune cells and inter-cellular messengers. What could be more straightforward?

Pain and the Gate-Control Theory

The problem is that pain is anything *but* straightforward. How is it, for example, that almost identical injuries can produce widely varying experiences of pain? In *The Mind,* Richard M. Restak recalls the British Army's landing at Anzio in Italy in 1943. Hundreds of soldiers were severely wounded, but "according to the surgeon in command, three-quarters of them refused morphine...He later questioned a group of civilians with similar, though far less severe, wounds and found that 80 per cent requested the analgesic. The surgeon concluded that pain is not a state of the body, but a state of mind."

Ronald Melzack and Patrick D. Wall cite another example in *The Challenge of Pain*—the "hook-swinging ritual" practised in parts of India. At a certain time of year, a man is chosen to represent the power of the gods to bless the children and the crops: "What is remarkable about the ritual is that steel hooks, which are attached by strong ropes to the top of a special cart, are shoved under his skin and muscles on both sides of the back. The cart is then moved from village to village...at the climax of the ceremony in each village, he swings free, hanging only from the hooks embedded in his back, to bless the children and crops. Astonishingly, there is no evidence that the man is in pain during the ritual; rather, he appears to be in a 'state of exaltation.'"

And what of pain *felt*, for which there is not even any flesh in which to experience it? Melzack recalls a seminal encounter in his career, with a patient named Mrs. Hull, who had lost a leg but still complained of severe pain in the missing limb. "It's one thing to read about phantom-limb pain," says Melzack, "but when you actually talk to someone who describes how a red-hot poker is being driven through her toes—and there's nothing there—it's a shock."

It also makes the Cartesian model of pain look woefully inadequate. Melzack studied sensory experience in animals for his Ph.D. in psychology at McGill University and had already concluded that no Cartesian "I hurt, therefore I am" formulation would do justice to the complexity of pain. In 1959, he met a British physiologist, Patrick Wall, at the Massachusetts Institute of Technology, where both were working. It was a meeting of minds. They became friends and co-researchers and, in 1965, published a paper in *Science* magazine that outlined what became known as "the gate-control theory of pain."

It proposed a neural mechanism in the spinal cord that acts as a kind of gate, shutting down or opening up the flow of signals from the periphery to the brain. Whether the gate is open, closed, or partially closed depends on what sort of signal it receives from the brain. Emotions, expectations, memories—even cultural attitudes—could play a part. Thus, soldiers wounded at Anzio might have been so thrilled to survive that their elation "closed the gate" to any sensation of pain. Likewise, the Indian celebrant chosen to bless the children and crops would have "the gate shut to pain" on the strength of his cultural preconditioning.

The theory created a minor revolution in scientific circles and launched an avalanche of new and invaluable research into pain and related questions. "The gate theory offered a tremendous integration of all sorts of different types of evidence into one coherent potential understanding of the topic," says Dr. Harold Merskey, a psychiatrist at Ontario's London Psychiatric Hospital and president of the Canadian Pain Society, the local branch of an international interdisciplinary association. "Some of the details of the physiology were not right, but that's not important now. There's been an abundance of work, much of it by

Patrick Wall, showing that there are all sorts of mechanisms in the spinal cord to which the idea of gating is relevant."

More than two decades later, Melzack believes the theory has stood the test of time. There have been new discoveries, of course, things that don't fit, but, he says, "you can expand the theory to include observations people weren't aware of before.

"The gate-control theory as we proposed it dealt mostly with the mechanism of gating in the spinal cord. It says that signals from injured tissue undergo some kind of modulation in the spinal cord. It's that simple—your attention can open or close the gate. If you're busy attending to something else, the gate closes, meaning nerve impulses are inhibited from passing further up toward the brain. Or if your brain wants to know more about what's going on in your body, it can open the gate, by which we mean the information is facilitated. There are fibres that excite and facilitate the transmission to the brain."

The gate-control theory opened up a whole new way of looking at pain, says rheumatologist Dr. Glenn McCain, a fibromyalgia (FMS) specialist formerly at the University Hospital in London, Ontario, now director of a fibromyalgia treatment program in Charlotte, North Carolina. "They also opened up whole new ways of *treating* pain." From the idea of modulating the pain signal, Wall developed transcutaneous electrical nerve stimulation, or TENS (described below).

The treatment helps some of McCain's patients, who characteristically complain of generalized chronic muscular aching, along with fatigue. But the hallmark physical finding, says McCain, "is the presence of fibrositic tender points in specific anatomical locations that don't vary from patient to patient. There's something very important about these points, but we don't yet understand it."

Investigators are only beginning to understand the syndrome, but there are many theories. One concerns the way people experience pain. "Just the circuitry of how pain impulses are transmitted through the body is very complex," says McCain. "One theory is that FMS is simply disregulation of the normal pain pathway."

Scientists still know very little about how pain signals are transmitted to the brain, and how the brain decodes those signals, interpreting them as pain. What Melzack and Wall's pain theory suggests is the idea that our experience of pain is the result of complex interactions between different nerve cells, which "communicate" via chemical messengers they secrete called neurotransmitters. Nor is it clear whether all nerve cells communicate using the same or different neurotransmitters.

In that sense, the nervous system may be as complex as the immune system. If certain cells in the immune system go awry, you end up with an immune disease like rheumatoid arthritis. Something similar happens with pain, McCain says: "You could have an abnormal regulation of those neuronal networks, and that could lead to an augmented painful state."

Melzack readily admits the gate-control theory only went so far. He's since been looking at the "pathways" that convey information to the brain. The rapidly conducting pathways tell the brain where an injury has occurred and how severe it is. The brain can then make adjustments to manage it—as in reflexes that draw an injured extremity away from the source of the injury, the finger from the flame.

The slowly conducting systems, on the other hand, "give rise to *affect* and emotion. They're the ones involved in chronic pain, and what's predominantly involved in arthritic pain. It's a continual input that goes along the slowly conducting pathways. The pain is poorly localized—you may feel your arthritic pain somewhere in the region of your knee or shoulder, but you don't locate it as precisely as stepping on a tack or burning your finger."

"Fast," or phasic, pain, carries a great deal of what scientists call "sensory-discriminative" information. The perception and experience of pain involve a number of dimensions, one of which would be sensory-discriminative information, described as pulsing, pounding, throbbing, or hot, burning, searing—sensory qualities of pain. "Then there's this other dimension," Melzack says, "that emotional or affective dimension of pain that drives you crazy, that makes you get into bed or call the doctor, take pills or jump off a bridge. It's what persists to make you utterly miserable, and that's the affective component of pain."

Surprisingly there's still a good deal of confusion about just what constitutes *chronic* pain. At one time, it might have been defined as pain that persisted for more than three months. Another favourite criterion, says Merskey, "was that it should be present after the normal time of healing. But what's the normal time of healing for rheumatoid arthritis?

"What we tend to do now," he says, "is group three different sets of phenomena under chronic pain: One is pain that has persisted past the expected time of healing. Another is associated with a chronic disorder, such as arthritis. The third is pain that's recurrent and troublesome but not there all the time, as in bouts of migraine."

Wrestling with Angels
Approaches to Pain Management

Arthritis pain can be so intense and constant it dominates your every waking moment and many a sleepless night. It has a purpose, as we've just seen: All those overexcited nerve cells are racing to inform the brain that harm is being done to your joints. In response, the brain signals muscles in the affected area to contract as a form of protection. The resulting spasms prevent you from using the joint normally, while the body makes its mostly futile attempts to effect repairs.

If the source of pain isn't tended to by a doctor, there's a heavy price to pay: Studies show that muscle tissue starts wasting away after only three to six days of inactivity—followed by a corresponding loss of strength and flexibility, which of course leads to more pain. Unchecked, the underlying disease process continues its dogged work, which only increases the pain further.

Persistent, severe pain from arthritis requires combination therapy. No single medication or management technique is enough to provide nonstop, safe relief. You need to discover what works for you, dovetailing different approaches to prolong pain relief.

So, start with your doctor. He or she can diagnose the reason for the pain and determine whether there are symptoms of inflammation. If there are, you'll be prescribed an anti-inflammatory medication, probably a non-steroidal anti-inflammatory drug, or NSAID. You'll also be prescribed medication for immediate pain relief, but let's be perfectly clear: "Relief" doesn't mean a complete absence of pain. The goal is to reduce your pain levels so that you can start moving again.

Your doctor might also refer you to a physiotherapist, who can devise an exercise program to help prevent muscle wastage and reduce pain by strengthening and increasing the joint's range of motion. Your physiotherapist is a key member of your treatment team.

An occupational therapist can also help, especially if you have an inflammatory form of arthritis. Occupational therapists can have custom splints and orthotics made to help keep affected joints properly aligned and protected from further injury. They're also an excellent resource for all kinds of practical strategies for avoiding injury and reducing pain.

Chronic pain is the universal constant with arthritis, its hallmark, the sine qua non. To some extent, everybody who has arthritis is going to suffer pain. There's no getting around it, but you can learn to cope with it. How you meet "the challenge of pain" will in large part determine not only how well you cope with your illness but how much pain you experience. It's a matter of pain management, says Dr. McCain. He teaches patients to regain a measure of control over their bodies so that they can achieve some mastery of their medical condition, and thus don't feel so much that the pain is controlling *them*.

"Different people react differently to pain and illness," he says. "Some become paralyzed. They sit at home, don't go out, become more and more alienated, depressed. Other people say, 'I can't let this pain get to me,' and they go out and do all kinds of things, trying to prove to themselves that they *can* do it, and finally they crash. We try to bring everybody toward the middle, and utilize their good strategies and minimize their maladaptive strategies."

The first step, as we'll say more than once in these pages, is the tough one: learning to understand and accept the pain. Only then can you begin to deal with it, establishing priorities and setting goals— taking responsibility for yourself. There are skills you can learn that will help you to maximize your level of everyday functioning, but you have to help yourself first. You have to be willing to take a close look at your- self and your lifestyle and learn to accept your own limitations.

In other words, you're going to have to learn to accept that there are certain things you can't do any longer. Activities that increase your pain will have to be modified or eliminated, and you may have to adopt prac- tices that will maximize your ability to do the everyday things you *have* to do to maintain your altered self-image and self-respect. Painkillers are a partial answer at best; they only mask the pain, and they can cause real harm by allowing you to do things that cause damage to arthritic joints, activities that pain would "tell" you to avoid. No one expects someone in chronic pain to stop taking medication, but there *are* complements to drug therapy that help people take repossession of their lives.

- One of the simplest isn't always easy, but it is effective: **Relax.**
  Pain, it should come as no surprise, causes stress and tension,
  and not just psychological tension. Taking a relaxation training
  session teaches you to enter a more relaxed physical state that
  lowers blood pressure, respiratory rate, and adrenalin flow.
  You'll be taught to lie down and find a comfortable breathing
  rhythm. Close your eyes, focus on your body's different muscle groups, starting with your calf muscles. Slowly relax your
  muscles, moving progressively up your body to your neck and
  shoulders. As the muscles relax, there's a concomitant release
  of the body's natural opiates, called endorphins, pain-relieving
  hormones that are related to synthetic opiates like morphine.

- **Humour** helps. Endorphins can be released by any number of
  stimuli, including laughter. A good belly laugh relaxes stomach
  muscles, and that may be one reason why it works; releasing muscle tension is a relief from an unconscious source of pain and discomfort: The heart speeds up, blood pressure rises and, when res-
  piration accelerates, there's an increase in oxygen exchange. A
  good belly laugh while watching a TV sitcom not only exercises
  your diaphragm and abdomen, but the muscles of your face and
  shoulders and sometimes even the muscles of your legs and arms.
  By the time your laughter subsides at the commercial break,
  you've had a short aerobic workout—what Norman Cousins
  called "internal jogging" in his book *Anatomy of an Illness, As
  Perceived By the Patient.*

- After an exhausting "laugh-out," don't underestimate the value
  of **rest, energy conservation,** and **sleep.**

- **Biofeedback** can help those who have trouble learning deep
  relaxation techniques (many people do). It consists of sensitive
  electronic equipment that measures biological activities, such
  as heart rate or muscle tension, through an electrode taped to
  the skin. You're "fed back" the electronic reproduction of your
  own bodily process so that you know, for example, that certain
  muscles are tense; you're then taught to relax them.

- An approach similar to biofeedback was developed by Dr. Wall in the wake of the gate-control theory, called transcutaneous electrical nerve stimulation, or **TENS**. Electrodes taped to the skin near a painful area are wired to a battery-operated stimulator, which produces a series of electrical pulses that "close the gate" on the nerve cells that transmit pain signals to the brain. You adjust the strength of the pulses until you feel a slight tingling. "What it does," says McCain, "is bombard the peripheral sensory afferents with electrical stimuli and probably changes the input going into the dorsal horn [part of the spinal cord]—in a good way, so that it actually ends up closing the gate and turning off the pain."

  TENS' effectiveness in treating chronic pain is no longer in doubt, Melzack and Wall say in *The Challenge of Pain*, but perhaps its most exciting feature is "that it produces relief in patients who received little or no relief by other methods, including neurosurgical procedures, anesthetic blocks, and so forth." The next generation of electrical stimulation—called inferential treatment—is even more effective, its manufacturers claim, because it works at a cellular level to reduce inflammation.

- **Acupuncture**—like a number of less successful and more radical procedures, such as scarification, cauterization, and so on—is an ancient technique. The procedure is intended to provide symptomatic relief from any number of conditions, including chronic pain, via extremely fine needles, which are inserted through the skin at specific points on the body. The acupuncturist then twirls the needles for some time at a slow rate. Although the technique hasn't been widely accepted in Canada, a number of studies confirm what many people claim: that acupuncture works. How isn't clear, though it may work by releasing endorphins.

- **Massage** is widely used for pain relief, not least because anyone can perform it on himself or others, but its results are open to question. At best, massage may relieve muscle ache or tension, and its results are relatively short-lived.

- **Heat** is another common treatment method (though it shouldn't be used on already inflamed joints). From hot springs and spas to Finnish saunas, relief is most likely due to general relaxation and a sense of well-being. As such, the results are fleeting. Local applications, using everything from heated bricks in olden days to ultrasound in ours, produce a more significant vasodilation of the blood vessels in the skin and a consequent warmth. Electric heating pads aren't recommended, because they involve a risk of burning the skin; more important, they produce a dry heat—what a muscle in spasm really needs is moist heat, as in a water bottle.

- **Diathermy** uses small paddles taped to the skin to direct electromagnetic radiation (as against the pressure waves of **ultrasound**) to heat a part of the body or a limb from the middle outward.

- **Cold,** not heat, is the proper treatment for inflamed joints. Ice packs, even a bag of frozen vegetables wrapped in a towel, can provide temporary relief, penetrating deeply into the joint structure and surrounding muscles. Frequent icing of an inflamed joint constricts blood vessels to the area, slowing down the inflammatory process and reducing swelling. The drawback is that numbing with ice or frozen peas is time-consuming (ten to twenty minutes, five or six times a day) and requires that you stay still—a real inconvenience when you're sitting behind the wheel of a car. That's the time to use one of the alcohol-based mentholated gels that cool the skin's surface instantly. They're a good temporary solution, even if they don't measure up to real ice in terms of relief.

- **Splint the pain.** If you have inflammatory arthritis, splints and other custom orthotics protect fragile joints from injury and keep them properly aligned, thus reducing pain and deformity.

- **Counterirritants,** which include liniments, vapocoolant spray and poultices, work by pitting one pain against another, inducing the body to lower its sensitivity. Applied to a painful joint, they produce a temporary local reaction that may cause skin irritation, mild swelling, or a temperature change—and a lessening of pain. Most counterirritants "distract" the brain from recognizing the signal from the pain source, a gate-theory effect.

  A more effective compound would interrupt the flow of the neurons sending the signals in the first place. That's what a Substance P "antagonist" like capsaicin does. (Substance P is a neurotransmitter implicated in the body's pain response.) Capsaicin's the alkaloid that puts the *Ai chihuahua!* in chili peppers. Prescription salves or lotions, such as Zostrix, Capzasin-P, and Capsin, containing as little as 0.025 to 0.25 per cent capsaicin, not only produce a feeling of warmth on the skin, they actually reach beyond the surface level of pain to the molecular level of neurons and Substance P. According to research into the pepper's punch, capsaicin first stimulates neurons to release Substance P, then prevents them from producing more. For some patients, rubbing one of these salves on an arthritic joint is as effective as the pain relief they experience from non-steroidal anti-inflammatory drugs (NSAIDs) and, beyond a brief burning sensation, there are none of the side effects that often accompany NSAID use, such as gastric upset or bleeding. Capsaicin can even be used as an adjunct to ongoing NSAID treatment.

According to the November 1995 issue of the *University of California at Berkeley Wellness Letter,* clinical studies into capsaicin's use have been small and short-term, and not much is known about the effects of long-term use. Still, they note that many people find capsaicin helps. "As the package directions should say, you need to use the cream three or four times daily, and you may not notice much improvement... for a week or more... However, some people can't tolerate it—just as some people can't eat chili peppers. If your skin becomes irritated, you should stop using the cream. Never use the cream under a bandage, and don't get it in your eyes or an open cut."

- There are also psychological techniques for pain. **Hypnosis,** unfortunately, is only rarely effective. Melzack and Wall write that "despite a vast amount of research on the effects of hypnosis on experimentally induced pain, there is virtually no reliable evidence from controlled clinical studies to show that it is effective for any form of chronic pain."

Dr. Merskey agrees. Generally hypnosis doesn't really offer anything more than support for the patient, he says. **Psychotherapy** may be more appropriate in providing people with "assistance in planning their lives and thinking differently about things." Where hypnosis *does* show encouraging results is when it's combined with other treatments. Melzack and Wall report a case in which hypnotic training instructions were supplemented by biofeedback training. While neither treatment in itself had any measurable effect on the patient's pain, together they produced "a statistically significant reduction in pain." It's safe to predict, they say, "that the panacea for pain will not be found. Instead, the future of pain therapy appears to be in the rational use of multiple therapies."

- **Imagery,** or **guided imagery,** is a form of self-hypnosis in which you build on a base of relaxation, then concentrate on images, places, or events that are completely absorbing. Anything will do: a painting, a game of chess, a phone conversation with a friend, music, the afternoon soap operas. Try taking a mental excursion to a favourite location (from your childhood, perhaps), reconstructing as much detail as you can. You'll be amazed at how much you can recall and how quickly pain fades from the picture. For variety, create a fantasy. Follow the yellow brick road.

- **Focusing** is a slightly different technique in which you concentrate on your pain, rather than on some imaginary destination or event. You're then taught how to reduce the concentrated image in your mind, which can actually reduce the experience of pain.

- **Meditation** and **prayer** are not to be underestimated, either.

- One last suggestion: *Avoid pain*. If there's something you really want to do—go shopping, have the in-laws over for dinner, take the kids on an outing—and you know it's going to cause your pain to flare up, try a little pain management. Schedule rest periods before and after the activity; reduce the tension that may be building up in your muscles by stretching before and after; try icing affected joints before and after; and take your pain medication so that it's at its peak level of effectiveness during the activity.

Losing Yourself in the Flow

A kissing cousin, so to speak, to both guided imagery and focusing, is distraction, a time-proven technique for altering the experience of pain—as in being "distracted by distraction," to borrow a phrase from

German philosopher Martin Heidegger. The modern exponent of the theory is an American psychology professor who has a slightly different take on the idea. He talks about "flow."

Professor Mihaly Csikszentmihalyi, a former chairperson of the University of Chicago's department of psychology, is the author or coauthor of a number of books, including, most recently, *The Evolving Self: A Psychology for the Third Millenium*. But it's his book *Flow: The Psychology of Optimal Experience* that people with arthritis may find most interesting. For more than two decades, Csikszentmihalyi (pronounced Chick-**sent**-me-hi) has been studying states of "optimal experience," those moments people call their most intensely concentrated and enjoyable. What his research has revealed is a state of consciousness he calls "flow," a state of concentration so focused "that it amounts to absolute absorption in an activity."

Most of us have experienced the feeling at one time or another. It's that blissfully extended moment during a favourite activity when time seems to stand still, when all our thoughts or actions flow effortlessly from impulse, when our activity swallows every other thought, even sense of self. "'Flow,'" he writes in his book, "is the way people describe their state of mind when consciousness is harmoniously ordered, and they want to pursue whatever they are doing for its own sake."

Artists, athletes, writers, and musicians all report the sensation. So do surgeons, rock climbers, gardeners, and chess players. But Csikszentmihalyi has deciphered the components of the experience to reveal how it can be attained and controlled by anyone. The concept can be applied to almost any activity, from home cooking to nuclear physics, that involves a degree of skill and challenge; in effect, flow is a technique for improving the quality of life. That makes it worth everyone's attention, but it should be of special interest to those with a chronic disease like arthritis, for whom control over quality of life is an ever-present concern. In fact, some people actually find relief from pain through their total absorption in an activity.

In explaining his theory, Csikszentmihalyi didn't try to write "a popular book that gives insider tips about how to be happy," he says. Nor is it a book that will work for everyone, but it *is* very accessible, and few readers will have trouble getting through it. The difficulty lies in learning to apply what you've read. As Carol Tavris, a social psychologist and editor of a book on emotional well-being, says, "Flow takes energy and effort. It's not the same as fun, the teenager's grail, nor one of those moments of pure joy that seem to spring from nowhere. It's not the same as the passive selflessness of 'going with the flow.'"

It's also more than an admonition to "buckle down and concentrate." If that's all it was, says Csikszentmihalyi, people would be performing activities "against the grain, not enjoying what they were doing. It would be work for them." Trying to sustain such an impulse would likely result in a feeling of compulsion. The trick is to make the transition to a form of control over the activity so that it can be enjoyed. Then it becomes "something we want to do and that we enjoy while we're doing it, instead of another one of those things we feel we have to do."

At the heart of his theory is the recognition that it's hard to change quality of life by altering external conditions. What we *can* do is change how we *experience* conditions. With that in mind, Csikszentmihalyi looked at the way people experience activities, through long interviews, questionnaires, and other data collected over a dozen years from several thousand respondents—rock climbers, musicians, chess players, doctors, dancers, and "ordinary" people. The results are what he sees as the most common "elements of enjoyment": a challenge requiring a specific balance of skills, the merging of action and awareness, clear goals and feedback, concentration on the task at hand, a sense of control, the loss of self-consciousness, and the transformation of time. An activity with those characteristics is an "optimal experience," one, that is, likely to produce the state Csikszentmihalyi calls "flow."

Even such simple physical activities as walking can be transformed into complex flow activities, Csikszentmihalyi believes, as long as you follow certain steps. Begin by setting realistic and measurable goals, which you then refine as you meet the challenges inherent in the activity. Use whatever opportunities the activity presents to develop increasingly complex skills, and keep raising the stakes if the activity becomes boring.

Csikszentmihalyi suggests ways of measuring progress and feedback and how to instill challenge and develop skills. If the activity is walking, for example, he suggests that you develop a way "to move the body easily or efficiently" or "an economy of motion that maximizes physical well-being." And there's no reason why an arthritis patient couldn't adopt a similar pattern to his or her joint therapy program. In fact, Csikszentmihalyi argues that there are few limits on who can tap into the flow experience—whether they're "healthy, rich, strong and powerful or sickly, poor, weak and oppressed."

The important thing, he says, is to pay attention to an interaction with a part of the world or your experience. It doesn't have to be highly cerebral, involve rare skills, or be something you have to prepare for in an intellectual, disciplined way: "What you have to do is pay attention, see what's going on, respond to it and get involved with that other reality."

But how can those who suffer from chronic pain achieve a state of flow? The problem with pain is that it prevents you from using your concentration freely, says Csikszentmihalyi, who suffers from gout, a form of arthritis. When he has an attack, he can't think of anything except the pain, which is what makes it difficult, he says: "It's not the pain itself, obviously. The problem is that it forces you to pay attention to it. If you could get distracted enough from the pain, then the pain would not be a problem."

Admittedly there are limits to what you can do in that sense, but it's true that at least at low levels of discomfort, getting involved in something is excellent therapy. Csikszentmihalyi has found with a variety of people "who really get concentrated, during their activities" that they forget about their pain and discomfort because there's not enough room in their consciousness for information about the pain. For all intents and purposes, they're free of it until the activity's over.

For some people, it's hard to imagine taking part in an activity that swallows so much of their conscious awareness. But as Csikszentmihalyi reiterates, "it could be anything." You don't have to develop a complicated interest to achieve flow. It could be gardening or games or simply learning to prepare a gourmet meal: "The trick is to try out what you're good at, what you're interested in, and then try to improve your skills in that area." If you make an honest attempt to adopt Csikszentmihalyi's theory and technique as he lays it out in his book, "Pretty soon you should get hooked."

His book isn't a game plan that can be digested overnight, he says; "There's a saying from Cicero: 'If you want to be free, you have to submit yourself to a set of laws.' I think that's true. You have to develop your own laws, your own rhythm, your own discipline, that make sense to you. And once you do that, you'll be much freer."

Mastering Wellness

Flow is the sort of book many readers will find inspirational. Some find it a call to action, the kind of encouragement they need to turn their hand to their own interests and lose themselves in them. Others—many others—can't imagine anything of the kind. For them, they say, it's too late: They've lost control of their lives to their arthritis and nothing can be done about it, so why bother?

That's pretty much the divide that Dr. Kate Lorig discovered back in the early 1980s. At the time, Lorig was a public health educator at the Stanford University Arthritis Centre in California who was developing a new concept of arthritis management associated with learning. The thrust of her approach was teaching people how to become health *self-managers*—not to replace a physician's care, but to help them gain confidence in their ability to personally control their health condition, their pain, and ultimately their sense of well-being.

She and her colleagues began with the assumption that if they taught people exercise and relaxation, they'd have less pain, less disability, and less depression. In fact, people did increase their exercise and relaxation enough to satisfy scientific measures: "Their pain decreased," Lorig says, "and their depression decreased marginally, as well. But we couldn't find a relationship between people's behaviour and changes in health status. So our assumption didn't appear to be valid."

Rather than second-guess themselves, they asked sixty of the people they'd been teaching—half whose pain had decreased and half whose pain had stayed the same or increased—to be interviewed by trained researchers, with a view to identifying differences. Those whose pain had decreased consistently reported feeling that they'd gained more *control* over their lives. Those whose pain stayed the same or increased were in the "nothing can be done, so why bother?" camp.

A *belief* that pain and depression could be controlled appeared to be the missing element in Lorig's original assumption and the difference in results between her two study groups. But what could be done to enhance people's belief in their power to control their pain and ultimately their wellness?

Continuing research had already led Lorig to psychological theories of control. Then, a chance meeting with renowned Stanford psychologist Dr. Albert Bandura brought a previously separate field of study into her search for answers. Bandura's work on people's sense of personal control could be applied to treating arthritis.

Bandura's control theories explore the significance of perceived self-efficacy, the belief or sense that someone has about his or her personal capacities in accomplishing everyday situations. Everyone's sense of efficacy is specific. An effective business manager might blanch at having to speak in public. Someone capable of persuading a large audience might be a chocoholic. No one's in total control of every situation. But, if people *believe* they can use their skills effectively to accomplish a set goal, not only are their chances of success increased but they gain a sense of personal power or "mastery." It's not just a matter of knowing *how* to do something, in other words, it's believing you *can*.

Bandura's theories have found a wide range of applications. One such is in predicting the extent that people will benefit from medical treatment. Findings show that people with a strong sense of their ability to exercise control over their health conditions are the ones who benefit most from treatment.

With that crucial insight, Lorig began to revamp her arthritis program, with a greater emphasis on strengthening and enhancing self-efficacy. "There are a lot of techniques you can use to enhance people's beliefs that they can do something," she says. "We have people write a contract to perform a certain behaviour, then we have feedback and problem-solving sessions about what they've actually done. We also do modelling: People who have arthritis teach others who have little experience of their real capacities. We put a high value on group work because peer pressure enhances efficacy."

People already felt better after taking Lorig's self-help course. They felt more in control of their lives, more confident that they could do what they wanted. They experienced less pain, less fatigue, and very little depression. Lorig adjusted her program to build in training that would not only teach people how to manage their arthritis but also how to enhance this feeling of self-confidence or belief in their ability to exert control—despite arthritis. The expanded concept became the Arthritis Self-Management Program (ASMP).

The program was an immediate success in the States and began as a pilot project in B.C. in 1989, then went nationwide in 1992, thanks in large part to a half-million-dollar Seniors Independence Program grant to The Arthritis Society (corporate donors have been underwriting it since then). The six-week course is open to people with all forms of arthritis, their spouses and families, and anyone else who may be interested. (Participants are charged a nominal fee to cover the price of a book and other incidental costs.) The ASMP acts as a complement to traditionally prescribed treatment, helping people to better understand their arthritis, cope more effectively with chronic pain and depression, and take a more responsible role in their arthritis care. People with arthritis are trained as group leaders, and group work is emphasized, because peer pressure has been shown to enhance efficacy.

Another factor people learn to deal with is "learned helplessness," the erosion of confidence a chronic disease can impose. If you learn that climbing stairs is always a painful experience, for example, you may stop dropping in on a basement-level shop or visiting a friend in a third-storey walk-up. You'll learn to be helpless in the face of those challenges. And, if every time you experience a change in symptoms you feel you have to consult your doctor, you become dependent. The ASMP teaches people how to avoid or get over such hurdles. It also "injects" them with a healthy dose of self-efficacy, by giving them a take-charge attitude about every aspect of their arthritis.

To date, taking part in the ASMP has taught thousands of people to "take charge" of their arthritis. They're more informed about their disease and better able to cope with it on a day-to-day basis than they were. And, because they're more informed, they're also prepared and confident in their dealings with medical professionals. They know what questions to ask, and they inevitably come away with more information about medications and their side effects, potential prognoses for their condition, and exercises than someone without the training.

Knowledge is power. The more you know, the more able you're to cope—and the better you're able to live—*with* arthritis. The next step is to educate yourself about medications. They're about to become a big part of your life.

6

The Apothecary's Art
Medications

The desire to take medicine is perhaps the greatest
feature which distinguishes man from animals.
—Sir William Osler

There's no point beating around the bush: If you have arthritis, you'll almost inevitably require some kind of medication. That could mean daily, and for the rest of your life. To minimize your risks and maximize your benefits, you're going to have to become an enlightened consumer and learn to work as part of a team with your doctor and your pharmacist.

Why? Consider this scenario: You haven't been feeling well for some time—persistent joint pain, flulike malaise and morning stiffness. You see your family physician who does a physical exam and orders some lab tests. At a follow-up appointment, your doctor announces that you may have rheumatoid arthritis (RA), and an appointment is being set up with a specialist. In the meantime, he says, have your pharmacist fill out this prescription and follow the instructions on the label. You're so stunned by the diagnosis you barely absorb anything the doctor has said.

You follow instructions blindly, not knowing what to expect, and, several months later—just as you're starting to feel better—you're totally unprepared when your RA flares up again. Or you throw away the pills and gradually get worse. Or you take the pills when you feel bad, and stop when you feel better. Of course, your doctor's confused. Although you're not getting worse, you're not really getting better, and she starts adjusting your drug regimen...again!

Here's an alternative: You seize the initiative. You learn everything you can about your condition, become an arthritis self-manager, someone who knows about "risk-to-benefit ratios," "optimum blood serum levels," and "indications and contraindications." Now you know what your medication's supposed to do, when, and why. You know what to do if it doesn't, and what side effects to watch for—which are serious and which can be easily dealt with, either by you or with a quick phone call to your doctor or pharmacist. You're not buffeted by every change in your condition. You're less anxious and far less fearful. You're in control. You've made yourself a key player on your health-care team.

The latter course of action takes effort and determination, but it does produce results—the best possible results under the circumstances. So, to get you started, here's a crash course in arthritis medication.

The first thing to understand is that currently available medications treat arthritis symptoms and some of the underlying disease mechanisms. That's it. No matter what anyone tells you, there's no such thing as a "magic bullet" that will cure your arthritis. Your doctor will try to identify which medication your arthritis responds to best, and what is the lowest daily dose that will achieve maximum benefit with a minimum risk of side effects.

Depending on what kind of arthritis you have, your doctor may have to change your prescription from time to time, perhaps many times over the course of years. There's a certain amount of experimentation that goes on, as your arthritis responds, or doesn't, to one medication or another. That's completely normal. Not every medication works the same way for everyone's arthritis.

In what follows, there are a few caveats to bear in mind:

- The information in this chapter isn't meant to replace proper diagnosis and treatment by an accredited physician.
- It applies to adults only.
- If you have one or more joints that are persistently painful or swollen for more than six weeks, consult your doctor.
- If you're allergic to a specific medication or you're taking medication for another long-term health problem, such as heart, liver, and kidney conditions, high blood pressure, ulcers, or asthma, make sure your doctor knows. Arthritis medications

can interact with medications for other conditions in a number of adverse ways.

- If you're pregnant, trying to become pregnant, or breastfeeding, inform your doctor, since certain medications can be passed through the placenta or mother's milk.
- Age is a key factor in medication usage. Generally if you're over sixty-five, your metabolic rate will be slowing down. Because of natural declines in liver and kidney function, your body won't process and eliminate medication as quickly or efficiently as it once did; not only will you usually require lower doses of any medication, but any drug you do take will have a longer "half-life" in your body, which means your doctor should monitor its effects more closely. Also, seniors are more vulnerable to stomach and digestive tract upset, because of a natural thinning of the lining that protects the stomach wall. Many arthritis medications are acidic in nature, so this is an important consideration.

For our purposes, we're broadly dividing arthritis into two categories: inflammatory arthritis (RA, psoriatic arthritis, lupus—any arthritis with persistent joint inflammation, including short-term problems, such as bursitis, tendonitis, etc.) and non-inflammatory, or degenerative, arthritis, such as osteoarthritis (OA). It's not a clean division, however, because cartilage erosion in OA sometimes causes loose part-icles and debris to irritate the synovial membrane in a joint, causing inflammation, in which case anti-inflammatory medications may be appropriate. One thing just about every form of arthritis has in common, though, is pain, which makes it a pretty good place to start. You've already examined the *non*-medicinal routes to pain relief; let's look at what medications can do to relieve your pain.

Relieving the Pain

If you have inflammatory arthritis or you're going through a periodic inflammatory phase of osteoarthritis, you're probably experiencing pain. Since it usually takes at least two to four weeks before any non-steroidal anti-inflammatory drug (NSAID) begins to reduce the inflammation—the source of your pain—you'll probably want something that will help in the interim. That's where straightforward analgesics— pain-relieving medications—come in. For minimal to moderate pain, there are a number of over-the-counter formulations; for more severe pain, you may require a prescription medication.

In the meantime, chart exactly how much pain you're experiencing. On a sheet of paper, draw a scale from 0 to 10, where 10 is the worst pain you've ever felt or can imagine, then mark where you feel your present pain is. This allows you to measure whether you're getting better or worse by giving you a baseline reference point, and it provides your doctor with valuable information when prescribing your pain medication. If you're in a lot of pain, don't be bashful about asking your physician for strong medicine.

Once you've established your pain reference point, you can determine whether nonprescription medication will provide enough relief or whether you need stronger, prescription medication from your doctor. If, for example, your pain level is at 3 or below, try a nonprescription analgesic, or even a nonmedicinal approach (such as an ice bag). If the pain persists for more than seventy-two hours or worsens, consult your doctor. But you be the judge; everybody experiences pain differently.

There are three major nonprescription pain relievers for arthritis— acetaminophen (Tylenol, Panadol, Exdol, etc.), ASA (Aspirin, Entrophen, Anacin, Novasen, etc.), and ibuprofen (Advil, Motrin IB, Medipren, etc.). They're all more or less equally effective and well tolerated, provided you're not already taking a prescription NSAID for your arthritis: ASA and ibuprofen are also anti-inflammatory medications and shouldn't be taken in addition to a prescription NSAID, because of a slightly higher risk of side effects. If you *are* taking an NSAID, acetaminophen is the preferred choice, because it can be safely combined with a prescription NSAID for increased pain relief or for headaches and fever.

Acetaminophen is safe and effective, but it does have limits: You can take regular-strength tablets (325 milligrams) every four hours to a maximum of 12 in a 24-hour period, or extra-strength tablets (500 milligrams) every six hours, to a maximum of 8 tablets in a 24-hour period. Be careful about exceeding those limits; a serious overdose can cause permanent liver damage. If you find yourself repeatedly taking acetaminophen more frequently than recommended, consult your doctor about a stronger pain medication.

One option is an acetaminophen formulation with codeine, which affects the central nervous system, reducing pain sensitivity. It's most often available in combination with 325 mg (milligrams) of acetaminophen and 32 mg of caffeine (the caffeine's to combat any drowsiness the codeine causes). Regardless of the brand, the amount of codeine in these preparations ranges from 8 mg per tablet in nonprescription formulations, such as Tylenol 1, Exdol-8, or Atasol-8, to 15 mg of codeine in Tylenol 2, Extol-15, and Atasol-15, and 30 mg per tablet in Tylenol 3, or Extol-30, and Atasol-30 (which require a prescription).

A common fear about pain relievers is addiction (and, yes, codeine is a narcotic, a class of drugs that are inherently addictive); even some doctors are wary about recommending or prescribing what some of their patients believe to be essential levels of pain-relieving medication. The important point is that pain medications only make pain more bearable—they don't treat the underlying cause. Make sure you also seek treatment for the real source of the pain. Certainly analgesics shouldn't be used simply to mask pain: If you feel no pain at all from an arthritic joint, you might be tempted to overuse it, causing irreparable damage. Again, the best approach to controlling pain involves medication with complementary therapies and coping strategies (though if you're in extreme pain, your doctor can prescribe a limited course of a stronger pain reliever).

That said, clinical research shows that people who take a narcotic at an appropriate dose for their level of pain are at very low risk of becoming addicted. Drug dependency is fuelled by psychological cravings for the euphoric effects of certain narcotics, such as the opiates. Although codeine is a narcotic, when it's used solely for pain relief it rarely produces the "high" that drug users seek—if anything, it tends to make life seem a little dull and colourless. Furthermore, codeine is the weakest of all the narcotic agents and can be taken for relatively long periods of time without fear of addiction—particularly if you decrease your daily dose as your pain decreases over time.

Still concerned? Then ask yourself these questions: If you're not in pain and you don't take the codeine, do you still feel a need for it? Do you require rapidly increasing doses to control the same level of pain? Do you get "high" when you take codeine? Chances are, you answered "no" to all these questions. If so, relax. You're not addicted to codeine.

The biggest problem with codeine is constipation (because it slows down the digestive tract). The best response is to increase your fibre and liquid intake. You can also try Metamucil, a nonabsorbed fibre, which may take a few days or a week to work but is an effective preventative (not a treatment) for most people. Psyllium, the active ingredient, is also available as Prodiem Plain, in chocolate mint; some people find it easier to tolerate. *Note*: Don't take Metamucil *with* your medications, because they may pass right through your system with it, losing their effectiveness.

For the most part, stimulant laxatives aren't advisable, because the bowel can become "addicted" to them—that is, it doesn't evacuate easily without them. Glycerin suppositories are an alternative: They hydrate the bowel, helping to soften stools. Mineral oils aren't a good idea: They deplete the body of vitamins A, D, E, and K.

Dismantling the Treatment Pyramid

Remember "pyramid power?" It was a seventies fad (the decade that gave us disco, let's not forget) based on vague interpretations of ancient mysteries, such as using crystals to "realign your aura." The mix of specious reasoning and hokey data was enough to convince students and athletes to sit under pyramids as a way of increasing their prowess in studies and sport. The practice, fortunately, has gone the way of the polyester suit, but the pyramid did have one serious application: as a symbol for rheumatoid arthritis management. The "pyramid approach to treatment" is a visual image for the administration of sequentially more powerful interventions: The base of the pyramid is rest, physical therapy, ASA, and other NSAIDs. Next up are progressively stronger disease-modifying anti-rheumatic drugs (DMARDs, also known as SAARDs, slow-acting anti-rheumatic drugs), capped, at the apex of the pyramid, by experimental drugs and procedures.

The pyramid approach has long been part of the fabric of rheumatology, certainly for as long as Dr. James F. Fries can remember. Fries is director of ARAMIS (Arthritis Rheumatism and Aging Medical Information Systems) at Stanford University Medical Center in Palo Alto, California, where, for the past twenty years or so, he and his colleagues have been building the biggest database on arthritis this side of Pluto. Their research has contributed to a new understanding of RA, and a recognition that the pyramid approach to treatment was based on some false notions about the disease.

The first was the view that RA is a relatively mild disease, following a leisurely course, that doesn't amount to much in most people, and often goes into remission all by itself. Then there was the belief, Fries says, "that ASA and NSAIDs were very benign drugs, and that disease-modifying drugs—like intramuscular gold and, even worse, methotrexate or azathioprine—were too dangerous to use in a benign disease." Wrong, and wrong again. On the basis of such false premises, says Fries, "we accepted the pyramid strategy."

In recent years, a number of studies—many of them drawing on the remarkable ARAMIS database—have led to very different conclusions. What they've learned has led to what Fries calls "a 180-degree change in the way we therapeutically approach RA," similar to the change in the way heart attack victims are treated: Years ago, heart patients were prescribed six weeks of absolute bed rest, which seemed logical at the time. But outcomes took a leap forward when cardiologists started hauling their patients out of bed and up onto treadmills and out running marathons. "Those of us who have seen both eras," Fries says, "realize we were just flatly wrong in the way we approached coronary artery disease—and we were flatly wrong in RA. So, we're at a time when we need to make a 180-degree shift, in this case with the treatment pyramid."

"Initially, the pyramid approach was useful because at the base of the pyramid you had one drug, ASA," says Dr. Bill Benson, a rheumatologist at St. Joseph's Hospital in Hamilton, Ontario. "And then, of course, you went very quickly from ASA to the disease-modifying drugs. Where things got complicated was in the '70s and '80s, when we had thirteen other NSAIDs come onto the market. It made the base of the pyramid so deep that many physicians started to go with the concept that you just keep trying these non-steroidals, which would give you two or three years' worth of alternatives before you move on to a stronger, slow-acting, anti-rheumatic drug. And that led to immense delay in the management of RA."

At the same time, it was clear that NSAIDs weren't stoppingthe disease in most people, while the slower-acting drugs showed greater potential to put the disease to rest, at least temporarily, sometimes permanently. In addition, doctors were becoming aware, from clinical experience if not academic studies, that DMARDs also worked best with early-stage RA—before it caused irreversible cartilage or bone damage.

As Dr. Paul Emery, a rheumatologist at the University of Birmingham, England, wrote in the *British Journal of Clinical Practice* in 1994, "There is now a great deal of evidence that inflammatory arthritis is at its most active soon after onset: The conventional delay in therapy until disease becomes severe is therefore a missed opportunity. The number of swollen and painful joints is maximal at onset and the rate of appearance of erosions [in cartilage and bone] also peaks early in disease. A further stimulus for early therapy has come from evidence that systemic disease is in itself harmful: For example, patients who maintain a high acute phase response over two years lose approximately 10 per cent of the bone from their hips."

"There was a feeling twenty years ago that you could sort of start anytime and these drugs would work and slow things down," says Benson, "so there was no particular rush. I think people appreciate now that, if you want to stop the disease, you have to treat early and slam the barn door before the horse gets out."

Since that realization, there have been a number of new ways of looking at RA management. Two researchers at the University of Washington in Seattle were among the first to suggest (in *The Journal of Rheumatology* in 1989) "remodelling the pyramid." In its place, they proposed a "step-down bridge" approach to RA, in which treatment is initiated "with a combination of rapid-acting anti-inflammatory medications and slower-acting second-line drugs. This provides early control of inflammation and a 'bridge' until slower-acting medications can take effect." Medications are then sequentially withdrawn, in contrast to the traditional pyramid, in which they're sequentially added.

A year later, Fries suggested a slightly different, "sawtooth" strategy. One of the problems with previous strategies, he said, was that patients didn't receive DMARDs before they had "substantial erosive disease and disability. Such drugs have most typically first been prescribed six to eight years into the disease course: too little, too late, for too few."

That course was based on the assumption that NSAIDs were

relatively harmless in terms of side effects compared to DMARDs. In fact, ARAMIS data showed that there's really little to choose between the two classes of drugs in that regard. The data also provided a new view of pain relief. It was always assumed that NSAIDs provided fast relief from pain, while DMARDs worked on the underlying disease. While that's essentially true, Fries noted that "pain in RA is a consequence of the inflammatory process and of prior destructive events in the joints." So, while NSAIDs provide day-to-day relief from pain, the ultimate pain reliever is the medication that best "reduces inflammation and retards bone and cartilage destruction and prevents future pain." An ARAMIS study that examined pain levels nine months after therapy began in some 10,000 courses of treatment with different agents found that pain relief from NSAIDs was "at best modest, while [treatments] with DMARDs were three times more substantial."

Fries also emphasizes that RA isn't as benign as people used to think. It does, in fact, increase mortality rates, a "long-established but neglected observation" that negates another frequent argument for the old therapeutic pyramid: "that drugs with the [extremely rare] potential for fatal reactions should not be used in a 'nonfatal' disease unless absolutely necessary."

Fries asserts that rheumatologists' dominant therapeutic strategy "has been an illogical one, based upon premises that can now be shown to be false, in which we treated patients symptomatically until their joints had sustained irreversible damage. Only then did we employ, slowly and fearfully, our most effective agents. We took a short-term view of analgesia in a long-term disease. We accepted rather uncritically the view that NSAIDs were safe and DMARDs were dangerous. We allowed slow month-to-month deterioration to pass unobserved until the best point to change therapy had long passed. We require a new strategy, rooted in the relevant clinical facts and dedicated to the improvement of long-term outcome."

The sawtooth strategy Fries initially proposed advocated the ser-ial use of DMARDs, introducing one or more as the therapeutic benefit of earlier drugs is lost, but that strategy has yet to prove more effective than the step-down approach. Since then, variations have been suggested, with clinicians employing different tactics to affect patient outcomes; rheumatologists no longer seem to talk about simply "reversing the pyramid," as they did only a couple of years ago.

Dr. Ed Keystone, director of the rheumatic disease unit at The Wellesley Hospital in Toronto, says that he and his colleagues are using more potent therapy earlier, and combining therapies. In contrast to Fries, who starts patients with the relatively mild hydroxychloroquine (an approach more common in the U.S. than here), Keystone generally starts RA patients on methotrexate: "It used to be you started with gold and then went to chloroquine, then you went maybe to azathioprine or sulfasalazine, and finally you'd think about an agent like methotrexate. Now, if you've got significant arthritis and you're really symptomatic, you go on methotrexate from Day One. That's quite a change."

Keystone calls methotrexate "one of the major breakthroughs in the treatment of RA. It's dramatically altered how we treat disease. Patients have more energy, they tend to have less swelling, and they tend to have less pain. Even if their joint swelling remains the same, people feel better, they're less symptomatic. And a proportion of people go into remission."

Keystone contends that Canadians "are more aggressive than Americans by far" in their treatment philosophy: "As soon as we make a diagnosis, we put patients on a DMARD. What's different is, we're using methotrexate earlier, and we're combining DMARDs earlier. So, in a sense, we *are* reversing the pyramid, because we're not waiting to get to the top, we're starting DMARDs from Day One."

Current strategy will alter according to research, of course. Recent genetic studies have shown that there are actually different subtypes of RA. "There's a mild disease that tends to be up and down, not really progressing," Benson says, "and it does respond to NSAIDs. The moderate disease is the disease the slow-acting drugs [DMARDs] work best in, and it's in those patients that, if you use the drugs early, you can usually stop the progression. Non-steroidals won't hold moderate disease. Severe disease isn't really held by the slow-acting drugs either."

Within five to ten years, Benson predicts, all those who present with what looks like RA will take a genetic subtype test to predict what group they fit into and what level of treatment they should start with. There's a lot of work underway to define subtypes and develop medications for the severe group, "as well as work into drugs that turn off the disease better," Benson says. Among those are drugs "that are going to become even more selective in hitting the anti-inflammatory process." Such drugs have the potential to become "a real bullet, because they hit the inflammation but not normal function. These drugs will be much safer." And, with them, pyramid power *and* arthritis may finally be relegated to the past—where they belong.

Anti-Inflammatory Medications

From the 1940s to the 1960s, the front-line medication for inflammatory arthritis was Aspirin (a name trademarked in Canada but used generically in the States to refer to ASA, or acetylsalicylic acid, the active ingredient in a number of different products). Although it's generally thought of as a kind of modern minor miracle drug, ASA actually hails from Hippocrates' time, about 400 B.C. The Father of Medicine is said to have concocted an elixir from the bark of the willow (the source of the natural form of ASA) that he administered to his patients for the relief of headaches and labour pains.

An effective analgesic for minor pains at the usual adult dose (two 325-mg, or 5-grain, tablets, every four hours), over-the-counter ASA becomes an anti-inflammatory medication at daily doses of twelve to twenty tablets, depending on your age and weight (to be effective, the amount of ASA in the blood has to be kept at a constant level).

While it's relatively safe, ASA does have drawbacks at those high doses: It can cause gastrointestinal (GI) upset, even—in a very small percentage of people—ulceration and bleeding. Many contemporary ASA formulations address these issues with enteric coatings and slow-release formulas. A more common complaint caused by too much ASA is buzzing or ringing in the ears (tinnitus), often in the early stages of medication, while you and your doctor are trying to find your ideal dosage. It can usually be stopped by reducing the daily dosage by one or two tablets. You might also try Disalcid, a non-acetylated salicylate that can cause tinnitus if the dosage is too high, but is easier on the GI tract in some people.

To maintain anti-inflammatory effectiveness, however, you should only reduce the dosage in consultation with your doctor, who can determine the amount of ASA in your blood with a simple test known as a salicylate level (there's no such test for other anti-inflammatories). This will confirm that you're getting enough medication from enteric-coated

ASA, which is poorly absorbed by some people. If you're on long-term ASA therapy and there appears to be a problem, your physician will probably recommend you have your blood levels checked regularly (every few days at first, then every few months or even once a year).

Establishing and maintaining an ideal balance between safety and effectiveness with ASA therapy can be a tricky business; be careful you don't disrupt a hard-won equilibrium by inadvertently adding to your salicylate intake. It's easily done: There's a host of over-the-counter pills, potions, and elixirs that contain ASA or salicylates, and using any one of them could be enough to push you over the fine edge you've established: Alka-Seltzer, Pepto-Bismol, Aspergum, Coricidin and Dristan cold tablets, 222s (and 282s, 292s, and 692s), Midol, Percodan, and T-R-C Preparations all contain forms of ASA. So do many topical skin creams and ointments, including A-535 Rub, Analgesic Balm, Ben-Gay, Heet, and Buckley's Stainless White Rub, and that doesn't begin to list them all. Check the ingredients list for "ASA," "acetylsalicylic acid," "salicylate," "salsalate" or "salsamide"; better still, ask your pharmacist or doctor.

Because decades of research have established optimum daily blood levels for salicylates, many arthritis specialists—despite the caveats—still consider ASA the safest of all anti-inflammatory medications. But it's no longer the only horse in the race, and it may not even be the pick of the field.

In the last twenty years, pharmaceutical research has produced an extensive array of competition in the growing class of non-steroidal anti-inflammatory drugs (technically, ASA formulations are also NSAIDs, though some health professionals put them in a class by themselves). All of these compounds reduce pain and inflammation (and fever) by inhibiting cyclooxygenase, an enzyme that triggers the production of prostaglandins, hormones that perform various regulatory functions, some helpful, some harmful. For example, prostaglandins are one of the immune system soldiers assigned to protect the lining of the stomach and intestines. They also dilate blood vessels, permitting increased blood flow to the site of a "normal" injury. The inflammation that results is part of the healing process. In arthritis, though, the inflammation gets out of hand; by inhibiting the production of prostaglandins, NSAIDs reduce the pain, swelling, and tenderness in an affected joint and slow down the disease process.

There's considerable evidence that the successive generations of NSAIDs are as safe as ASA. Their pain-relieving properties are fast-acting, usually within an hour or two, with the anti-inflammatory effect (which confers added pain relief) taking two to three weeks. They also offer one big advantage over ASA: ASA has a very short half-life (the time required by the body to metabolize or inactivate half the amount of a medication after ingestion), which is why you have to keep taking it (and remembering to take it) every four to six hours—to start to build an anti-inflammatory level in the blood at the start of therapy. NSAIDs can achieve and maintain therapeutic levels with fewer doses—often only one or two tablets a day.

Like ASA, even the most recent NSAID compounds have undesirable side effects, primarily in the GI tract: By inhibiting prostaglandin production, NSAIDs reduce inflammation, but inhibit prostaglandins' role in protecting the walls of the stomach and intestines. Such effects are especially common among the elderly and people with a prior history of GI problems. Some people find that ingesting the medication with food and taking antacids can offset these effects. More refined NSAIDs are released every few years. A recent example, Arthrotec, is the splicing of diclofenac, the world's most prescribed NSAID, with the synthetic prostaglandin misoprostol to reduce gastric problems.

NSAIDs (Non-Steroidal Anti-Inflammatory Drugs)

The number and frequency of tablets you take every day varies greatly with anti-inflammatories, which doesn't mean you can adjust the dosage yourself. Follow your doctor's instructions. More is not better—NSAIDs aren't like pain relievers that can be taken (within certain limits) as required. To be effective against inflammation, anti-inflammatories have to be taken on a continual basis and at the specific dose prescribed for you. Don't expect an immediate effect, as you would from an analgesic: NSAIDs provide some immediate pain relief, but it usually takes two to four weeks of continual use before you experience a noticeable reduction in inflammation.

Although most people (seven out of ten) respond well to the first NSAID they try, some people experience no benefit and suffer side effects.

Non-Steroidal Anti-Inflammatory Drugs

Product	Brand Name	Dosing Information / Range
ASA	Aspirin Entrophen Novasen	650 mg, 3 – 5 times daily
salsalate	Disalcid	750 mg, twice daily
ibuprofen	Motrin Apo-Ibuprofen Novo-Profen	400 – 600 mg, 3 – 5 times daily
fluribuprofen	Ansaid Froben	50 – 100 mg, twice daily
sulindac	Clinoril Novo-Sudac Apo-Sulin	150 – 200 mg, twice daily
diflunisal	Dolobid	250 – 500 mg, twice daily
piroxicam	Feldene Novo-Pirocam Apo-Piroxicam	10 – 20 mg, daily
indomethacin	Indocid Novo-Methacin Apo-Indomethacin	50 mg, 2 – 4 times daily / slow release: 75 mg, 1 – 2 times daily
fenoprofen	Nalfon	300 – 600 mg, 3 – 4 times daily
naproxen	Naprosyn Naxen Anaprox Apo-Naproxen Novo-Naprox	250 – 375 – 500 mg, 2 – 3 times daily / slow release: 750 mg, 1 – 2 times daily
ketoprophen	Orudis Oruvail Rhodis Novo-Profen Apo-Keto-E	50 – 100 mg, twice daily / slow release: 150 mg, daily slow release: 200 mg, daily
nabumetone	Relafen	1000 mg, twice daily

Non-Steroidal Anti-Inflammatory Drugs, cont.

Product	Brand Name	Dosing Information / Range
tolmetin	Tolectin	200 – 400 – 600 mg, 3 – 4 times daily
tiaprofenic acid	Surgam AlbertTiafen	200 – 300 mg, twice daily/ slow-release: 600 mg, once daily
tenoxicam	Mobiflex	20 mg, daily
diclofenac	Voltaren Novo-Difenac Apo-Diclo	25 – 50 mg, 2 – 4 times daily/ slow release: 75 – 100 mg, 1 – 2 times daily
diclofenac and misoprostol	Arthrotec	50 mg plus 200 mg; 2 – 3 times daily

Don't worry if it happens to you: Not every type of medication works the same way for everyone. You and your doctor will simply have to experiment a little to find the NSAID that works best for you—there are lots to choose from. How long you'll have to *keep* taking your NSAID is something you'll have to work out with your doctor; it depends on the degree of inflammation present and what kind of arthritis you have.

Constipation and indigestion are the most common side effects of NSAIDs, and there are others (see the chart below), but don't be too quick to attribute every failing of the flesh to them. If you have inflammatory arthritis, for example, there are a number of complaints (fatigue; flulike symptoms; weight loss; hair loss; dry eyes, mouth, or vagina; chest pain; jaw pain; or numbness or tingling in the hands and feet) that can be related to the underlying disease—and not the medication.

Note: Not only are most anti-inflammatories acidic in nature, they also promote acid production in the stomach, so it's a good idea to reduce your intake of other strong acid producers and, thus, stomach irritants. Some of the most obvious: caffeine (coffee, tea, cola, chocolate), alcohol, and nicotine. You can also reduce heartburn and indigestion by washing down an anti-inflammatory with a large glass of water, which helps dilute any acid the medication produces and helps dissolve the tablet. Taking it with food may also help you to tolerate the anti-inflammatory better. Any stomach pain, heartburn, or indigestion you do experience can be relieved with an antacid (such as Maalox, Mylanta, Gelusil, etc.). If symptoms persist, notify your doctor.

ASA and NSAIDs sometimes cause a kidney dysfunction that manifests itself in salt and fluid retention. If you find you're gaining weight or retaining fluid in the course of just a few days, consult your doctor. If the problem's caused by the anti-inflammatory, it's easily corrected by simply stopping the medication. Swelling of the legs and ankles can be caused by arthritis, other medical conditions, *and* by NSAIDs, though, so be sure your physician knows about the problem, especially if you have high blood pressure or congestive heart disease.

Side Effects Associated with NSAIDs

Symptom	Common/Rare	Call doctor?
nausea/heartburn	common	if severe or persistent
stomach pain/cramps	common	if severe or persistent
constipation	common	if severe or persistent
vomiting/diarrhea	rare	if severe or persistent
ringing ears/hearing loss	rare	always
skin rash all over body	rare	always
black/bloodstained stools	rare	always
wheezing/breathlessness	rare	always
fluid retention	rare	always
jaundice/brown urine	rare	always

FYI: More Tips about NSAIDs

- A number of rare nuisance complaints associated with anti-inflammatories are related to too high a daily dose. If you experience: ringing or buzzing in the ears, loss of hearing, dizziness, drowsiness, confusion, inability to concentrate (particularly if you're sixty-five or over), worse headaches than usual, or nightmares, consult your doctor about reducing your daily dose.

- Although rare and associated mainly with only two anti-inflammatories (piroxicam [Feldene] and tenoxicam [Mobiflex]), increased sun sensitivity has been reported by some people on

NSAID therapy. If you're heading south, don't forget that the tropical sun is many times stronger than it is here. Use a sun screen with an SPF rating of at least 15 and both UVA and UVB ray protection. A sun hat and long-sleeved beach shirt are also a good idea; for that matter, you might want to consider spending a little more time in the shade.

- Some people chew or crush their tablets. Don't: Many medications have special coatings to prolong their action or help them survive the trip through the stomach (they're then dissolved in the intestine, which reduces the risk of stomach upset).

- If you're supposed to take your medication at bedtime, take it a half-hour or so before bed, while you're still moving about. Time and activity help dissolve the medication, meaning it'll be less likely to send you scurrying for the Maalox in the wee hours.

Misoprostol: For Acid Relief

Your stomach is the only organ in your body capable of eating itself. Digestive juices contain enough enzymes and hydrochloric acid to cut right through the stomach wall. The reason they don't (usually) is a dense layer of mucous lining your stomach and intestines; under normal conditions, the mucous is renewed faster than it's eaten away by acids and enzymes.

If for some reason the rate of mucous renewal drops, however, that protective barrier slowly erodes, exposing the stomach wall to injury: an ulcer. If the ulcer occurs at the site of a major blood vessel, it can cause internal bleeding; if it perforates the stomach wall, the membrane

Side Effects Associated with Misoprostol

Symptom	Common/Rare	Call doctor?
gas/flatulence	common	if severe or persistent
abdominal cramps/diarrhea	common	if severe or persistent
nausea and vomiting	rare	always
menstrual cramps	rare	if severe or persistent
menstrual spotting	rare	always

lining the abdominal cavity (the peritoneum) can become inflamed. Both are serious conditions, requiring emergency medical attention.

One type of stomach ulcer can be traced directly to anti-inflammatory medications, specifically NSAIDs (they can also be caused by stress and bacteria, among other things). To understand why, you need to know about a family of hormones called prostaglandins. Different prostaglandins undertake different maintenance chores in our bodies, ranging from dilating blood vessels to regulating blood's clotting ability. One prostaglandin, called PE-1, helps keep the stomach's mucous barrier healthy; a close relative, PE-2, helps promote local inflammation.

NSAIDs inhibit PE-2 production, which is good for your inflammatory arthritis. Unfortunately, NSAIDs also reduce PE-1 levels, and that's not so good for the stomach's mucous lining: Less PE-1 means you're at higher risk of developing an ulcer. What's more, as we've already noted, most NSAIDs are acidic and stimulate the stomach's acid production.

So, does that mean the moment you swallow an NSAID, it's going to burn a hole in your stomach? No. NSAIDs are relatively safe, and the vast majority of people who take them never develop an ulcer. Still, there's always that chance, since NSAIDs have to be taken continually, and your risk of ulcers increases if you're over sixty or have a history of stomach problems. (Keep in mind that you might not *know* you've developed an ulcer. Ulcers caused by NSAIDs can be "silent," because the analgesic effects of NSAIDs may also mask the ulcer pain. Coughing up material that looks like old coffee grounds or passing black and tarlike stools could be signs of internal bleeding. Alert your doctor immediately.)

Even if your doctor thinks you may be at risk of developing ulcers, he or she may have decided that the benefits from continuing your NSAID therapy outweigh the risks of not treating your arthritis—*or* of your developing an ulcer—so, what you need is a little protection: misoprostol (Cytotec), a laboratory copy of PE-1, the prostaglandin that helps the mucous lining of your stomach and intestines stay healthy. Think of it as replacement therapy, replenishing depleted levels of PE-1 and thereby strengthening the mucous barrier against stomach acids. An added bonus: misoprostol decreases production of stomach acids.

Misoprostol is available in 200-mcg (microgram) tablets; one tablet is taken after breakfast and one after dinner. If you're taking misoprostol to *prevent* an ulcer, you may only need 400 mcg daily. (You can take up to four 200-mcg tablets daily, but abdominal cramps and diarrhea usually limit the daily dose.)

Misoprostol is also available combined with the prescription anti-inflammatory diclofenac, under the brand name Arthrotec—50 mg of diclofenac with 200 mcg of misoprostol. The usual dose is one tablet two to three times daily.

Misoprostol is usually effective after a few doses, but as your body adjusts to the medication you may experience cramps, diarrhea, or headache; taking it after food usually helps. These adverse effects usually correct themselves within a few days. If they persist for more than a week, consult your doctor. In the meantime, it's important to continue the misoprostol to get the proper benefit. Theoretically you'll need to continue it as long as you're taking an NSAID. Discuss the time-frame with your doctor.

Note: While misoprostol reduces acid levels, should you need an additional antacid, ask your pharmacist for one that combines magnesium and aluminum (Maalox, Gelusil, Gavascon, etc.): Antacids with magnesium only (such as Milk of Magnesia) can cause diarrhea, adding to the diarrhetic effect of misoprostol. Aluminum tends to constipate, offsetting the magnesium.

One last thing: If you're pregnant or planning to be, misoprostol is out. It's been implicated in stimulating false labour and provoking miscarriages. If you're of child-bearing age and you *are* going to take misoprostol, plan to use an effective form of birth control before starting.

Corticosteroids

Anyone who's benefited from corticosteroids—a cortisone injection, say, or prednisone therapy—can thank those women with RA who reported an improvement in their symptoms during pregnancy. That observation led to the discovery of cortisol and cortisone, powerful hormones secreted by the adrenal cortex, the outer portion of the adrenal glands, by American Dr. Phillip Hench and two other researchers. (They shared the 1950 Nobel Prize for Medicine for their work.) Their findings led to the development of corticosteroids, among the most potent anti-inflammatory drugs available.

In the body, cortisol and cortisone perform various "housekeeping tasks"; they play an important role in maintaining the body's salt and water balance, exert regulatory control over carbohydrate, fat, and protein metabolism, and control routine inflammation from cuts, bruises, and other minor injuries. They're a key part of the body's stress management system: Major physical (and emotional) traumas, including infection, broken bones, or surgery, spur the pituitary gland at the base of the brain to release a chemical called ACTH (adrenocorticotropic hormone) that stimulates the adrenals to produce even more cortical hormone as part of the body's emergency healing processes, though the demands of inflammatory arthritis are beyond the adrenal gland's powers.

Side Effects Associated with Corticosteroids

Symptom	Low/high dose	Call doctor?
increased appetite	low or high	if severe or persistent
weight gain/"moonface"	high	if severe or persistent
lower resistance to infection	high	if severe or persistent
cuts slow to heal	low or high	if severe or persistent
easy bruising/thin skin	low or high	long-term
muscle weakness	high	long-term
fluid retention	low or high	always
increased urination	low or high	if severe or persistent
excessive thirst and urination	high	always
emotional sensitivity	high	if severe or persistent
acne	high	if severe or persistent
hair growth ("peach fuzz")	high	if severe or persistent
insomnia/restlessness/ tremors	high	if severe or persistent
irregular menstruation	high	if severe or persistent
osteoporosis/bone fractures	high	long-term
cataracts	high	long-term

That's where Hench's discovery came in. The first corticosteroid was synthetic cortisone, an extremely powerful anti-inflammatory. (NSAIDs are called "non-steroidal" anti-inflammatory drugs to distinguish them from corticosteroids—which are *not* the same drugs as the anabolic steroids athletes use illegally to "bulk up.") Hailed at first as a medical breakthrough, cortisone began to reveal serious shortcomings within a decade. While it was safe and effective as a low-dose, short-term therapy against chronic inflammation, with prolonged use at high doses there was an increased risk of side effects, water retention, and osteoporosis among them.

It's now known that, because they dampen the immune system, corticosteroids in doses greater than 15 mg can increase susceptibility to infection by agents the immune system normally dispatches with off-hand efficiency. Used in the treatment of RA, lupus, polymyalgia rheumatica, and giant cell arteritis, corticosteroids require continual monitoring by a physician and careful explanations of risks and benefits. They come in oral and injectable formulations, and are even available as low-dose, over-the-counter topical creams and ointments for treating rashes.

Cortisone injections, also known as intra-articular therapy, are used to reduce severe, persistent inflammation in a specific joint (sometimes in a painful osteoarthritic joint), usually because other treatment methods haven't worked quickly or well enough. They can be done on an out-patient basis. To gain the most benefit from a cortisone injection, the affected joint should be rested: three full days for knees, ankles, and hips; two days for wrists, elbows, and shoulders. Complete rest helps keep the cortisone in the joint, allowing it to work most effectively. The joint usually recovers within one to four days; the cortisone takes two to three weeks to be eliminated from your body.

At its best, the anti-inflammatory effect is relatively long-lasting, though your doctor may want to repeat the injection to capitalize on the lowered level of inflammation. Most doctors will, however, limit the number of cortisone injections you can have in any one joint in a given period because of possible side effects. A small number of people are sensitive to one of the ingredients in a particular cortisone product, experiencing increased pain and discomfort within the first twenty-four to forty-eight hours. Fortunately there are a number of cortisone for-mulations available, and an adverse reaction is rarely repeated.

In inflammatory types of arthritis, prednisone (cortisone in tablet form, or another formulation, such as triamcinolone) is used to provide inter-im control of inflammation while waiting for one of the slower-acting disease-modifying agents (gold therapy, penicillamine, or anti-malari-als) to take effect. Prednisone also reduces inflammation when a num-ber of joints are affected simultaneously and your ability to perform daily activities is limited. And, if the membrane lining a major organ, such as the heart or lungs, becomes inflamed, prednisone is powerful enough to control the condition. In a very small number of serious cases of RA, lupus, and giant cell arteritis, high-dose corticosteroids are sometimes required to prevent irreversible damage to tissues. These "emergency" doses could be as high as 60 milligrams per day (some ten times a normal dosage), though it's usually tapered off as the patient's condition improves. If such a course of treatment is extended over weeks, or even months, there's a greatly increased risk of side effects, so your doctor may suggest complementary immunosuppressive drugs, such as Imuran or Cytoxan, to bring the inflammation under control and reduce your exposure.

There's a drawback to supplementing nature with any course of corticosteroids: After prolonged or high-dose therapy, the adrenal gland recognizes that its services in the anti-inflammatory department aren't really needed, and it begins to secrete less and less hormone. As a result, after three months or so of even low-dose corticosteroids, if your doctor decides reducing or stopping the medication is appropriate, it has to be decreased gradually to allow the adrenal gland to start producing again.

In any case, take exactly the amount prescribed by your doctor (usually three tablets or less per day). Most people find that prednisone works best when they take the complete daily dose in the morning. If the benefits don't seem to last a full twenty-four hours, try splitting the dosage; however, if you find a half-dose at dinner gives you an unwel-come "buzz" or causes insomnia, try taking it at lunchtime.

Prednisone works very quickly, usually within one to four days, providing the prescribed dose is adequate to your level of inflammation. How long you should continue taking it is a decision only your doctor can make, after assessing your condition.

Today, prednisone is the most commonly prescribed corticosteroid, especially as a mainstay treatment for moderate to severe lupus. For all its risks, prednisone can be credited with saving the lives of many women with lupus, as well as improving the quality of life for many others—because it's most often prescribed in low doses, it's generally well tolerated. There are side effects associated with all corticosteroids that you should be aware of, and prepared to deal with, though most are related to high-dose or long-term therapy (more than three months).

A couple of final tips: If you're on long-term prednisone therapy and suffer a major trauma, such as a car accident, your adrenal gland will be hard-pressed to meet the challenge. If you've been knocked unconscious, give attending physicians a hand: Wear a MedicAlert™ bracelet telling them to administer cortisone. And get used to wearing it—it can take up to a year for the adrenal gland to regain peak performance after prednisone therapy has been stopped.

Another possible consequence of long-term prednisone therapy is accelerated osteoporosis (weakening and thinning of the bone). If you're not drinking a litre of milk a day, your doctor may suggest you supplement your diet with 500-mg calcium tablets three times daily, as well as a daily multivitamin packed with 400 to 800 units of vitamin D (which helps the body absorb the calcium). Estrogen replacement therapy—a known osteoporosis preventative—is a good idea for most post-menopausal women.

Disease-Modifying Anti-Rheumatic Drugs (DMARDs)

So far as we know, no alchemist ever succeeded in transmuting base metal into gold, but their efforts weren't entirely fruitless. The alchemists—the first chemists—did valuable research and made discoveries about gold and other elements and compounds that countless other seekers, before and after, have built on and developed further. Many of their investigations and understanding culminated in one of the first discoveries of "modern" medicine, in the early nineteenth century, as professors André-Jean Chrestien and Pierre Figuier in France described the chemical formulation of gold chloride and advocated its use in the treatment of tuberculosis and syphilis. Then, in 1890,

German bacteriologist Dr. Robert Koch announced that he'd inhibited, *in vitro,* the tubercular bacilli with gold cyanide. From there, it was a short misstep to the treatment of arthritis: Dr. Jacques Forestier, a French physician, erroneously assumed that rheumatoid disease was an infectious ailment akin to tuberculosis. Acting on the assumption, he administered gold thiopropanol sodium sulphonate to fifteen of his patients, who experienced a marked improvement in their condition. Thus, from the alchemist's lab to modern clinical practice, did gold compounds—the first of the DMARDs—come to be used in the treatment of RA.

Severe, persistent inflammation in multiple joints for longer than six weeks requires strong medicine. That's where DMARDs—also known as second-line or remittive agents and slow-acting anti-rheumatic drugs—come into play. DMARDs' main target is RA, though hydroxychloroquine (Plaquenil) is now prescribed for people with lupus, and some of the other compounds in the category are useful in treating inflammatory conditions (never osteoarthritis), such as psoriatic arthritis and ankylosing spondylitis where there's peripheral joint involvement. The most commonly prescribed are methotrexate, oral or injectable gold, hydroxychloroquine/chloroquine, sulfasalazine, and azathioprine, an immunosuppressive agent.

Each DMARD has slightly different characteristics and works in a slightly different way, so your doctor will prescribe the one she thinks most appropriate to your condition, and you'll almost certainly take it in addition to your NSAID: As the NSAID reduces day-to-day inflammation in the joint, the DMARD slows down the biological processes driving the inflammation.

Sometimes finding the appropriate maintenance dosage—that is, the lowest effective daily dose—is a bit of a balancing act, with your physician adjusting your dose in relation to the latest results from laboratory tests and a physical examination. Don't expect overnight results: The fastest DMARD is methotrexate, which usually takes four to six weeks to kick in if the dosage is right for you. The rest of the DMARDs can take from three to six months before they begin to be effective, with the exception of oral gold capsules, which may take from six months to a year. Speed's not the essence here though; rather, it's

DMARDs' ability to control your symptoms and *your* ability to tolerate the medication over the long haul. The goal is to take the least amount of medication necessary to keep your arthritis under control. As your symptoms subside, your rheumatologist may gradually cut back the medication.

Keep in mind that much of the damage to joints caused by persistent inflammation tends to occur in the first two to three years if the process is left unchecked. As a result, DMARDs are generally prescribed much earlier than in the past, because the benefits of putting a brake on inflammation far outweigh the risks of side effects, which are usually reversible (though to minimize the risks, DMARDs have to be routinely monitored by your doctor). Because they really are "slow-acting drugs," it's a good idea to start treatment as early as possible.

DMARDs come as tablets, capsules and, in some cases, injections; doses can range from once or twice daily to once weekly. Side effects can range from the discomfiting to the alarming: nausea, diarrhea, mouth sores, vision problems and, very rarely, kidney, liver and white blood cell count problems.

Disease-Modifying Anti-Rheumatic Drugs

Product	Brand Name	Dosing Range	Benefits Begin
sodium aurothiomalate	Myochrisine	one weekly injection	3–6 months
sodium aurothioglucose	Solganol	one weekly injection	3–6 months
auranofin	Ridaura	1–3 tablets daily	6–12 months
methotrexate	Rheumatrex Amethopterin	2–3 tablets, once weekly	4–6 weeks
hydroxy-chloroquine	Plaquenil	1–2 tablets daily	3–6 months
chloroquine	Aralen	1 tablet daily	3–6 months
sulfasalazine	Salazopyrin SAS-500 PMS-Sulfasalazine	1–2 tablets, twice daily	3–6 months
azathioprine	Imuran	1–3 tablets daily	2–3 months

Note: Along with the greater benefits DMARDs confer comes an increased risk of side effects. The most serious are rare—and virtually all are reversible by adjusting the daily dose or switching DMARDs. Some side effects are common—flulike symptoms, mouth sores, diarrhea, and nausea—but they're a small price to pay compared to permanent disability or corrective surgery.

Don't be too quick to blame the medication for the misery, though: Many ill effects—such as fatigue; flulike malaise; weight loss; hair loss; dry eyes, mouth, or vagina; chest pain; jaw pain; or numbness or tingling in the hands and feet—are related to inflammatory arthritis, not the medication.

Gold Therapy

Ingesting minerals, especially heavy metals, which can be toxic, doesn't *sound* like a particularly robust idea. Gold therapy, though, is more like the minerals we take in a healthy, well-balanced diet, in which a small amount of iron, for example, is essential. While gold isn't an essential vitamin, it has proven effective against RA and psoriatic arthritis, among other things.

Of course, you can't just gnaw on a bar of gold; it has to be either injected or taken orally, usually in the form of a salt. Transforming gold into a salt requires a complex biochemical process, a kind of chemical cookery that binds gold to various oral or injectable compounds. The injectable versions—sodium aurothiomalate (Myochrisine) and sodium aurothioglucose (Solganol)—are the originals, dating back over fifty years in Canada; the oral form—auranofin (Ridaura)—which contains substantially less gold, has been on the market less than a decade. It's a little safer, though it does have one drawback—diarrhea—not often shared by its injectable counterpart that often limits the daily dose. As a result of the smaller daily dose, oral gold can take from six months to a year to achieve its effect.

With the injectable form, usually your doctor will start you on 10 mg or 25 mg weekly as a test, then increase the dose to 50 mg a week for five months. If you respond well, the injections will gradually be reduced to once every two weeks, every three weeks, and eventually once a month.

Some people can't tolerate oral gold, others can't handle injectable gold, but a reaction to one doesn't mean you'll have a reaction to the other. Which form you should take is something you'll have to determine with your doctor; there are side effects to both, and they're not to be taken lightly. They can be severe and they're unpredictable, though some problems are dose-related and can be relieved by reducing the dose. Common side effects (such as rashes) usually aren't severe, but gold compounds, in rare cases, can also affect the bone marrow's ability to produce new blood cells. That can be avoided in both forms of treatment with careful blood-count monitoring. If suppression of bone marrow is detected, the gold is simply discontinued (it can sometimes be restarted later at a lower dose without complications).

More common problems are such things as proteinuria, a loss of protein from the kidneys into the urine. Approximately 15 per cent of patients on injectable gold are affected, but it doesn't usually occur until from six to fifteen months into therapy. Mouth ulcers or canker sores are more likely to occur in the first six months of treatment. They affect 15 to 20 per cent of patients but aren't considered serious, since they can be

Side Effects Associated with Gold

Symptom	Common/Rare	Call doctor?
itching or mild rash	common	yes—stop or reduce dose
mouth sores	common	yes—stop or reduce dose
generalized skin rash	rare	yes—stop because of allergic response
metallic taste	rare	monitor for mouth sores
post-injection reaction (sweating, headache)	rare	yes—stop or reduce dose
low blood cell production	rare	monitored by blood tests
protein leakage in urine	rare	monitored by urine tests

treated by discontinuing the gold for a week or two while applying an oral steroid ointment.

Skin rashes affect approximately 30 per cent of patients. They're treated much the same way. Some patients may experience other minor, though irritating, side effects, such as diarrhea, stomach pain, nausea, and, in rare cases, inflammation of the eye.

There are few arthritis medications, of course, that *don't* involve some sort of side effects, and gold isn't the worst by far. In the long run, in fact, it's probably safer than cortisone; gold is often the treatment doctors turn to if cortisone hasn't proven effective, though more and more, gold is becoming a front-line soldier instead of a last-ditch effort. The tendency now is to use it and other DMARDs fairly early in the course of the disease, before irreversible changes take place.

Better than 70 per cent of patients respond favourably to gold treatment, many with improvement of symptoms after two or three months, and about one in ten will experience complete remission after eighteen months' to two years' treatment. If the disease was caught early enough, some of these people may suffer no deformity and return to the pleasures of the piano or a fast game of tennis.

Penicillamine (Cuprimine, Depen) is a DMARD developed in the 1970s that was sometimes used to treat gold overdoses and conditions caused by excess copper buildup (as its name suggests, it's distantly related to penicillin, though people who are allergic to penicillin aren't necessarily allergic to penicillamine). Although it's still used occasionally (with scleroderma patients, for example), it's prescribed less and less, because of its side-effects profile and unpredictable benefit. Many of those effects are similar to gold's—skin rashes, mouth sores, diarrhea, nausea and vomiting, etc.—but far more serious side effects are associated with its use, including kidney damage, precipitated by proteinuria and lowered white blood cell counts.

Methotrexate (MTX)

Methotrexate was originally used to suppress the immune system in cancer chemotherapy. One of the great contributions of Canadian arthritis research were the original clinical trials during the 1980s that established safe and effective dosages (a fraction of the dosages used in cancer therapy) for the treatment of RA. Today, MTX is a mainstay in the rheumatologist's medicinal arsenal against RA and psoriatic arthritis. Its advantages are low weekly doses and rapid beneficial response; it's often well tolerated, though a small number of people experience serious side effects. (If monitoring indicates that you aren't absorbing enough in tablet form, your doctor can give you a weekly muscle injection).

Choose the day of the week you're going to take your medication carefully—preferably the day that places the fewest demands on you—since many people experience flulike symptoms (increased fatigue and nausea, loss of appetite, headache, etc.) for twenty-four hours afterward.

- For methotrexate to be both safe and effective, it has to be taken once a week, exactly as prescribed. The once-weekly schedule gives the liver a rest and lowers the risk of cirrhosis of the liver, including scarring. Given its potential for damaging the liver (albeit rarely), MTX doesn't make a good drink mix: Alcohol should be used very sparingly. Talk to your doctor.

Side Effects Associated with Methotrexate

Symptom	Common/Rare	Call doctor?
flulike symptoms	common	if severe
increased sun sensitivity	common	no—wear SPF 15 sunscreen
vomiting and diarrhea	rare	yes—drink fluids
mouth sores	rare	yes, but can be reduced with folic acid
shortness of breath/ unproductive cough	rare	always
low blood cell production	rare	monitored by blood tests
liver problems	rare	monitored by blood tests

- Methotrexate also inhibits the body's absorption of folic acid (Vitamin B9), which is found in leafy green vegetables ("folic" is derived from the word "foliage"). You may need a daily folic-acid supplement to avoid nuisance complaints, such as nausea or mouth sores.
- For the same reason, you shouldn't take the antibiotic trimethoprim (Proloprim) with MTX therapy, since it lowers the amount of folic acid in the body and thus increases the risk of side effects. It's something you have to be especially vigilant about, because trimethoprim is often combined with sulfa medications, under the brand names Septra, Bactrim, Apo-Sulfatrim, Novo-Trimel, Co-Trimoxazole, or trimethoprim-sulfamethoxazale combination. Make sure that any doctor who treats you is aware of this restriction. If you do need an antibiotic for an infection, there are lots of others you can use safely.

Hydroxychloroquine and Chloroquine (HCQ and CQ)

Hydroxychloroquine is the latest refinement of a tea that sixteenth-century Jesuit missionaries observed South American natives brewing from the bark of the chinchona tree, which they used to calm the raging fevers of malaria. European doctors in the 1930s and '40s observed that the essential ingredient, synthesized as quinine, reduced the frequency of flare-ups in patients with inflammatory conditions. It was later found

Side Effects Associated with HCQ and CQ

Symptom	Common/Rare	Call doctor?
skin rash	rare	yes
nausea and upset stomach	rare	if severe or persistent
loss of appetite	rare	no—take at bedtime
increased skin pigmentation	rare	no—not harmful
increased sun sensitivity	rare	no—protect eyes and skin
blind spot	rare	yes—check with eye specialist

to improve RA symptoms in travellers to the tropics, who'd taken a synthetic form called chloroquine as an antimalarial.

Today, hydroxychloroquine and chloroquine are well-established agents for mild to moderate RA and mild lupus, with a good safety profile, though HCQ (marketed as Plaquenil) has largely supplanted the use of CQ: It has less potential to cause retinal toxicity, which can cause permanent eye damage. In the 1950s, a small number of people suffered irreversible damage before it was learned that the risk can be minimized simply by reducing the dosage. The maximum daily dosage recommended for HCQ is 6 to 6.5 mg per kilogram of ideal body weight (meaning lean body weight, not your actual body weight—ask your doctor for details). A common daily dosage is 400 mg; at recommended doses, retinopathy is now extremely rare. You can do home monitoring for blind spots (which indicate HCQ-related retinal problems) with a chart known as the Amsler Grid Visual Field Test, though it's no substitute for careful, semi-annual evaluations by an ophthalmologist.

Two potential, less serious side effects of HCQ are a tendency to sunburn more easily and photosensitivity—that is, your eyes may be sensitive to sunlight. Protect yourself by using sunscreen with an SPF factor of at least 15 and both UVA and UVB coverage; sunglasses and wide-brimmed sun hats offer some protection for the eyes. Less frequent side effects include skin rash, muscle weakness, nervousness, headache, dizziness, nausea, vomiting, or diarrhea; because of the rarity of those side effects, hydroxychloroquine is considered to be the least toxic and safest of the DMARDs.

Side Effects Associated with Sulfasalazine

Symptom	Common/Rare	Call doctor?
skin rash	common	yes—allergic reaction
nausea and upset stomach	common	if severe or persistent
loss of appetite	common	if severe or persistent
headache	common	if severe or persistent
sore throat, fever and flulike symptoms	rare	if severe or persistent

Sulfasalazine

Used for many years to treat inflammatory bowel disease, sulfasalazine has also found a niche as a DMARD, but it's a non-starter if you're allergic to sulfa medications. Sulfasalazine is best tolerated with meals; your regimen may start at one daily 500-mg tablet, then one tablet twice daily (breakfast and dinner), then two tablets twice daily. Your doctor will look for benefits after about three months and, depending on results, may increase your daily dose.

Drink 1.5 litres of fluid daily. You'll also notice that your urine may be a bright yellow or orange while you're on the medication.

Immunosuppressive and Cytotoxic Drugs

Immunosuppressive drugs, such as azathioprine (Imuran), are thought to interfere with immune cell division, and are also classed as DMARDs; cytotoxic drugs such as cyclophosphamide and cyclosporine destroy cells outright (*cyto* means cell; *toxic* means poison).

Azathioprine (Imuran) was developed to prevent kidney and heart transplant rejections. Because of its immunosuppressive effect, it was found to be useful in treating autoimmune disorders, such as RA and lupus, but its side-effects profile discourages its widespread use. Approximately 10 per cent of people taking azathioprine experience severe side effects, including GI problems and a greatly increased risk of infections. Doctors take the "go low, go slow" approach with azathioprine, starting with one or two tablets daily and gradually

Side Effects Associated with Azathioprine		
Symptom	**Common/Rare**	**Call doctor?**
nausea and vomiting	common	if severe or persistent
unusual fatigue or weakness	common	if severe or persistent
skin rash	rare	yes—allergic reaction
low blood cell production	rare	monitored by blood tests

increasing the dose to three tablets daily (either together or as a split dose). To reduce potential GI problems, take them with meals.

- Azathioprine can be taken with ASA and NSAIDs, but it interacts with allopurinol (Zyloprim), a medication prescribed for gout. Make sure your doctor knows if you're taking Zyloprim (or any other medication, for that matter).
- Cyclophosphamide (Cytotoxan) is used only in the most serious cases of immune-system disorders and with the most stringent monitoring because of its blanket destruction of cells, both healthy and harmful. It can suppress bone marrow production of blood cells, cause bleeding, and leave the patient open to infections. It's also associated with an increased risk of hemorrhagic cystitis (bleeding from the bladder) and, over time, increased risk of cancer and increased infertility.
- Cyclosporine, formerly known as cyclosporine A, is also an organ transplant rejection fighter. Its dampening effect on white blood cell production is more closely targeted to the inflammatory aspect of arthritis than cyclophosphamide, but it's still used only after other DMARDs have proven ineffective, and cautiously. Side effects include possible kidney damage, muscle tremors, problems with the gums, and hypertension.

Tenidap

Although it's already licensed for use in the treatment of RA in England and elsewhere in Europe, at press time tenidap (marketed as Enablex by the pharmaceutical giant Pfizer) was still awaiting approval in Canada. It's a new anti-rheumatic drug that studies have shown to be more effective in disease modification and symptom reduction for some people than NSAIDs alone and comparable in efficacy to NSAIDs in combination with second-line agents, such as gold and hydroxychloroquine. Its side-effects profile is also good, with a similar incidence of side effects to NSAIDs and fewer side effects than NSAID/DMARD combinations. Its effectiveness derives from its inhibitive properties on two of the main agents—cytokines and cyclooxygenase (see page 132)—implicated in the inflammatory process.

Lab Tests

Routine laboratory tests—there's a menu of hundreds to choose from—are an inevitable consequence of inflammatory arthritis and most DMARD therapy, beginning with a blood sample. Your arthritis specialist will use the information from several test categories to help diagnose your condition, check for side effects, and monitor your response to treatment.

Usually, there are five to seven tests per DMARD, but all can be done from one blood sample; if you switch DMARDs, you'll have to give another sample, since each medication is tested for different specifics. Blood tests don't have to be done by a rheumatologist. If there's a walk-in clinic or medical lab closer to home, have them done there: The results will be sent to your family doctor and rheumatologist—provided you make sure it's written that way on the requisition form.

Some DMARDs can lower the production of white blood cells, which are critical to the body's defence against infection and other health conditions. Others can affect how the liver or kidneys work. Lab tests can detect such changes long before you experience symptoms, giving your doctor a chance to adjust your dose or switch DMARDs. Without that critical information, DMARD therapy is definitely riskier, so whether it's weekly (for blood and urine tests, as with gold injections) or monthly (blood tests for methotrexate, sulfasalazine, and azathioprine) or semi-annual eye examinations (hydroxychloroquine), keep your lab appointments faithfully.

If you develop a severe or persistent infection (lasting longer than a week), some DMARDs, such as methotrexate and azathioprine, may be stopped until it clears up. If your family physician stops your DMARD for longer than a week, make sure your specialist knows, so that steps can be taken to prevent a flare-up, which can occur as the amount of medication in your body decreases.

Ask your specialist to explain what the different tests are for and how they're interpreted. Being in the know will reduce your anxiety about those mysterious results and help put adjustments to your medication regimen into perspective. That'll help make it easier for you to stick to it when the going gets a little bumpy—and "staying the course" can make a big difference in your health.

7

A New Kind of Compliance
Creating a Doctor-Patient Partnership

He that complies against his will
Is of his own opinion still.

—*Samuel Butler*

According to a major market-research survey of people with arthritis conducted for the Upjohn Company of Canada in 1989-90, "while on the whole patients are compliant, almost half claim to take medication only when they experience pain or inflammation," and "when [patients] deviate, it's almost always in a pattern entailing lower frequency of use."

Upjohn's inquiry didn't pretend to be highly scientific. It was a marketing survey, though one so large its statistical significance and conclusions can't be easily dismissed. Its findings also confirmed in the arthritis population what studies in the general population have found. A 1985 study in the U.S. journal Medical Care, for example, reported that 50 to 75 per cent of patients do not follow their physicians' prescribed therapy closely enough for the regimen to work.

Part of the problem, of course, is the too-brief time you actually have with your doctor; a patient has to be extremely well prepared to take full advantage of a ten-minute visit. Most people aren't, and don't. Studies have shown that patients forget as much as half of what physicians tell them immediately after an appointment. The visit is simply too stressful for many people, and they may not have clearly understood what the doctor was telling them.

The problem is especially acute with arthritis patients who only see their rheumatologist every three to six months. Many are so keyed up by the experience that they not only forget what the doctor said but what they wanted to ask about the medication they've been prescribed. The result is a communication gap that may leave patients without essential information.

Understanding Your Medications

Arthritis is a complicated and confusing disease, says Dr. Ian Chalmers, a rheumatologist from the University of Manitoba's Health Sciences Centre in Winnipeg. "We understand so little of it ourselves, it's hard to explain things in a way that makes a lot of sense to the patient, particularly in the time we have available." The situation generally improves with subsequent visits, but "on a single visit, and particularly on an initial visit, we rarely get a lot of information through to them, especially if they're faced with a diagnosis such as rheumatoid arthritis, which is pretty frightening. Often they just block out any information given to them."

The point is that compliance isn't simply a matter of choosing to take or not take your medication. There are any number of factors that come into play—communication failure, shortage of time, fear, ignorance, even, let's face it, how hard it is to stick to a strict regimen over a long period of time. "Maintenance is what we're all bad at, isn't it?" Dr. Arthur Bookman, a rheumatologist at The Toronto Hospital, asks rhetorically. "We're not very good at maintaining a diet or exercises, and the same thing applies to drugs. Doing things regularly, properly, is hard for all of us, and I think it's unrealistic to expect patients to take these drugs the way they're prescribed on a regular basis."

However, Bookman believes patients *do* comply if time is spent dealing with areas where there might be a problem: "I find it very helpful when a drug is prescribed to take time," he says—"not just give the prescription but really take time and tell them what to expect, be candid and leave the door open for them to contact me when there are side effects. Usually when I do that, I feel I'm getting very good compliance, at least initially."

You may not be so lucky. You might not have a doctor who's willing or able to take enough time to answer all your questions, so you've got to be prepared to take full advantage of the time available to you. Write down any questions you have beforehand, the most important queries at the top of the list. Deliberate on exactly what your problem is, medications you're taking, unusual symptoms you've noticed, and so on. If you don't do that, you may well forget the questions you wanted to ask or only get part of the information.

Some people *think* they're complying but have misunderstood what the doctor said. Marie Chambers, a rheumatological pharmacist with The Arthritis Program at York County Hospital in Newmarket, Ontario, had a patient who thought she was following her doctor's order to the letter. She'd been taking Entrophen, but her doctor recommended the prescription be changed to another NSAID. Unfortunately she failed to understand she was to stop taking the Entrophen, so she continued with both. "By the time she attended our program," Chambers says, "she'd become increasingly hard of hearing. Upon reassessment of her medications, the Entrophen was stopped, and her hearing returned to normal."

Another problem arises because people don't realize *why* they've been prescribed a medication. If they think they're taking an NSAID just for pain, they may stop taking it when they discover they get more effective pain relief from a straightforward analgesic, such as Tylenol 2. Unfortunately, the analgesic loses its effect over time, and before long they're up to six, eight, or more tablets a day—to get the same effect they once had with two. And, because they're no longer taking the prescribed NSAID, the disease management is lost. Chambers advises her patients to ask two key questions: "Why do I need this medication?" and "What could happen if I don't take it?"

Most anti-arthritis drugs, while they may have a pain-relieving component, are prescribed to control the disease. "Making patients feel better is obviously a major goal," Dr. Chalmers says, "but not the only one."

That's something few of us are likely to understand without coaching. To a greater or lesser extent, we're all victims of our conditioning, and we may expect "painkillers" to erase our pain more or less instantly, and preferably permanently. That's a partial truth at the best of times, and it's even less pertinent to most arthritic illnesses. If people expect arthritis medications to do for their disease what ASA does for a headache, they're in for a disappointment. Understandably, some of them are going to become frustrated. At some point in the long haul of their chronic disease, they ditch their doctor-prescribed regimen and try one of the many unproven remedies, either for pain relief or in search of "a cure." Chalmers doesn't really blame them: "I try to imagine what I'd do in the same circumstances, and I strongly suspect I'd be tempted to do the same thing."

At the same time, though, he urges patients to at least carry on with what he's prescribed, while he tries to "gently wean them away from the idea of looking for a complete cure." He encourages patients to let him know if they're experiencing pain that's not controlled by their other medications. If they are, he can prescribe things "that are often very effective at getting the pain under control."

People can do themselves real harm through noncompliance, Chalmers says, "especially if they're on a regimen of anti-inflammatories or a more particular regimen of disease-suppressive agents. If they allow the disease to break through by not sticking to their medication, then they do run the risk of increased joint damage and deformity over a longer period of time."

⸺ ⸺

"Compliance," Chambers admits, "sounds like a negative word, but patients can get themselves into a lot more trouble by deciding to stop taking something than if they talk to their physician and say, 'I've been great for some time now. What are the long-term goals with respect to my medication?' The medication can often be gradually reduced over time, but stopping it on your own is not an informed decision. The goal is to keep patients on the smallest long-term dosage that will control their disease."

Dr. Bill Benson, a rheumatologist at St. Joseph's Hospital in Hamilton, Ontario, believes some patients are confused by complex regimens, while others are alarmed by reports about side effects. "They fear these drugs," he says. It doesn't much matter that serious side effects are almost as rare as getting mugged on the way to the doctor's office. "Sometimes it paralyzes the fearful from making the better choice. They see them as little bombs that are going to go off in their stomachs, and they think that if they take half the dose, or two-thirds, that will cut their risk of adverse reaction. Unfortunately the nature of the drug is such that dropping even a little often completely wipes out the efficacy, while it doesn't substantially cut their risk of adverse reactions."

Not surprisingly, it can be an uphill climb explaining risk-to-benefit ratios to a skeptical patient, so Chambers turns the argument around: When people say they don't want to take a certain medication because of the potential side effects, she asks them, "'Well, have you thought about the side effects'—I use the same word—'that the *disease* could cause? Once the bone and cartilage begin to be eaten away, there's no going back.'"

"The biggest danger," says Bookman, "is when you list side effects but don't weight them. The patient only hears 'side effects'; he doesn't hear the frequency or chance of getting them. Even if it's one in a million, they don't want to touch the medication. It's really hard to convey the concept that the drug has been tested. Obviously it's safe to use in people, and the vast majority of people have no side effects whatsoever."

On the other hand, a physician can't guarantee his patient *won't* be one of those who experience side effects either, Chalmers says, "so you've got to watch out for it. As long as we do, we'll catch the side effects early, and there won't be any particular risk to you. We've got medications that can improve drug tolerance, particularly of NSAIDs."

That's not the royal "we" Chalmers is using, as though all responsibility for vigilance is the doctor's. You have a key role to play in your own medication management. It starts with self-education, becoming fully informed. Keep in mind that every form of arthritis is different, and the same form of arthritis will rarely affect two people in exactly the same way. Chambers often sees confusion and misunderstandings in the people who attend her health-care classes. In one, a man and his wife were baffled by their different energy levels—after all, they both had arthritis. It turned out he had RA; she had osteoarthritis (OA). It wasn't until Chambers explained that the man "feels like he has the flu all the time" that the woman realized why he wasn't able to simply "work through it," as she did. It's important to remember that not everything you hear about RA, for instance, and medications for the condition, will apply to you. Ask your doctor or pharmacist to help you put things into personal perspective.

To deal with apprehensions about medications, Chambers gives her patients a soup-to-nuts rundown of every medication they're prescribed or considering—not just when and how often to take it, but what it's meant to do, what the potential side effects are, and what patients should watch for. "Some people don't want *any* medication," she says, "but they may be making uninformed decisions if they change the medication because they don't like the number of tablets they take each day or how they feel that day. We want them to be part of the decision-making process, so they're comfortable with each medication and the schedule necessary for benefit. We teach them as much as we can," she says, "but what happens when they go home is *their* responsibility."

Taking Charge of Your Arthritis

Until recently, that would have been a revolutionary concept; many of us grew up believing our health care was our doctors' exclusive domain. Certainly in our grandparents' day, people pretty much took care of themselves, turning to doctors only in emergencies, but by 1940, as more medications became widely available and were dispensed with increasing frequency, the balance had shifted. Doctors began to take charge. Patients rarely even knew what drugs they were taking, because the name of the medication wasn't printed on the bottle, as it is now—a tiny mystery that only added to the physician's mystique and prestige.

It wasn't until the 1950s and '60s, as a deluge of still newer medications flooded the market, that the balance of care started to shift back to patients: For the first time, really, it was possible that people could be taking more than one medication at the same time, with the inherent dangers of drug interactions. For safety's sake, the names of medications had to be printed on pill bottles, "letting patients in on" the mystery of treatment.

New, specialized medications, of course, were only part of the changing scene. Concurrently there was an explosion of medical knowledge and a vast array of new technologies and treatment strategies, which in turn spawned an army of specialists. Whereas in the past people were often treated by one general practitioner, increasingly patients were finding themselves at the centre of a diverse web of medical professionals—rheumatologists, neurologists, dermatologists, ophthalmologists, gynecologists, orthopedic surgeons—a network whose only common link was the patient.

That process has only intensified since. If, in addition to your family doctor, you have two or more specialists all dealing with problems related to your arthritis, you'd better make sure they're all communicating; an interesting symptom to one doctor could very well be adiagnostic tipoff to another. To ensure everybody's in the picture, keep a full, accurate record of your health and treatment. Yours may be the only complete record that exists, and GPs and specialists may find it useful in plotting the course of your disease. Ask questions, learn as much as you can, and then utilize the system to your benefit. That's the best way to take responsibility for your health care. Your health care isn't just your doctor's responsibility. It's yours, too.

(To be sure, there are still doctors who refuse to relinquish responsibility to their patients, but they're becoming scarcer. A November 1995 *Maclean's/Medical Post/*Angus Reid survey found that 67 per cent of Canadian doctors "would rather deal with a semi-informed patient than one who relies wholly on them"—though in the same poll slightly more than half claimed that "patients who have done some reading on a condition are harder to treat than those who have done none.")

Taking responsibility for your own health care isn't as daunting as it may sound, and the benefits are significant. Certainly becoming more knowledgeable about your illness and treatment will leave you less anxious and better able to cope with an occasional setback. And getting actively involved will ensure you aren't overwhelmed by side effects from your medication. Merely knowing how to tell major from minor side effects—and what to do about both—strips them of their mystery and potential danger.

Calgary rheumatologist Dr. Steven Edworthy began a cross-Canada study (unpublished at press time) that measured the effects of education on compliance, though Edworthy and his colleagues didn't talk about compliance—they talked about "appropriate and inappropriate utilization." They put two groups of arthritis patients on one medication, Arthrotec, and intervened in one group with education—a computer program Edworthy and his colleagues developed, plus an audiotape and a booklet that each volunteer took home. They also told volunteers in the "education group" that if they had any questions, they could call the nurse co-ordinator.

The control group got the same medication but not the educational component. After eight weeks, the two groups were assessed as to whether they'd appropriately utilized the medication or not.

Inappropriate utilization might be someone who took the medication for two days, and when it didn't work for them stopped taking it, but equally inappropriate would be someone taking the medication for eight weeks, despite abdominal pain or diarrhea and no benefit. Edworthy would tell such a patient that they should have made a different decision, called their doctor to stop the drug or ameliorate the symptoms—something—rather than simply endure terrible side effects while enjoying no benefit.

That's a distinct break from the "traditional" approach, in which a physician would ask a patient to be compliant, meaning "'come hell or high water, you take this drug for as long as I prescribe it,'" Edworthy notes wryly—and most patients did as they were told. Nowadays, after a medication's been prescribed and recommendations given, patients make their own decisions, and some people choose not to comply. What Edworthy takes pains to point out, though, is that studies show that taking medication as prescribed—yes, being compliant—results in "less pain, more mobility, and a more active life."

One of the major reasons for patient noncompliance is the loss of control many people experience from constantly having someone else telling them what to do, Chambers says. The solution is to make patients part of the decision. "It's not as if someone simply told them to do something. A drug was offered, talked about—were they comfortable with it, did it work well, if they had to have monitoring could it be worked out so it was part of their lifestyle? Then it's not as if it's forced on them."

Chambers teaches her patients three key practices: Learning, making, and keeping. *Learn* as much as you can about your medications to get the most benefit and safety from them. Continue your education so that you can *make* informed decisions, not just about medications, but about general procedures, surgery, and other issues. And *keep* medication records as you move through the health-care system. To say you're taking a yellow or a pink tablet just doesn't cut it anymore; make sure you know the name of your medication, the dosage, and when and how often you're to take it.

It's not as simple as it sounds. A landmark study in the *Journal of the American Medical Association* asked sixty-seven people how they'd respond to a prescription label reading "Take one penicillin G tablet three times a day and at bedtime." Almost 90 per cent said they'd take it with meals and before bed. That sounds logical, but it's wrong. For optimum efficacy, penicillin G should be ingested at least an hour before or two hours after eating—in other words, on an empty stomach. In all, of ten prescription labels used in the study, not one was consistently or correctly interpreted by all respondents.

Patients rarely have any idea what they're up against, says Chambers, even those who keep medication records: "They'll say, for example, I'm on Inderal—but there are seven different strengths of Inderal." And patients may remember the name of the drug they're taking, but virtually every week, "there's a new medication put out [in fact, about 500 new medications are released every year in Canada]. There may be ten of them now that sound or look alike. The whole area is very difficult."

Taking responsibility for your health care doesn't mean you should make decisions independently of medical counsel, although many patients do, says Edworthy. He points to a study that followed RA patients over a thirty-month period. After about a year there was "tremendous attrition"—only about half of the patients were still taking their medication as prescribed, and by Month 30, the number had eroded to less than 40 per cent.

Lack of efficacy and perceived side effects were judged to be the primary reasons; again, medications were often stopped before the patients' doctors knew about it. If you *are* experiencing side effects, talk to your physician. Find out if it's a recognized side effect from the medication or something unusual that requires a change. Then appropriate action can be implemented.

Chambers' patients are taught to be businesslike. When they agree to take a medication, it's tantamount to signing a contract. And just as they wouldn't simply break a contract with anyone else, they're expected to go back to their doctor and renegotiate if they want to make a change.

In fact, a physician may agree that you *should* stop taking a medication, but if you interrupt a course of medication on your own months from your routine appointment—and then suffer a flare—it's going to be very difficult for the doctor to assess the efficacy of the medication.

The Doctor-Patient Relationship

At the heart of an ideal doctor-patient relationship is mutual trust, but it may be difficult to achieve without tearing down a few of the walls that traditionally separate the two. The first thing we have to do, Edworthy says, is take another look at this word "compliance": It needs redefinition. "That's an old, old word that shouldn't be applied in rheumatology," he says. "People with arthritis are the decision-makers. It's their pain, their disability, and their side effects they're experiencing that will decide whether a given drug is useful for them. It's not like tuberculosis, where compliance is critical for public health."

A good doctor-patient relationship goes well beyond prescribing medications. If they've formed a broader kind of relationship, the doctor should be able to provide encouragement and express real empathy and understanding for what the patient is going through—"absolutely essential" characteristics, Edworthy maintains, of a good relationship. And where the results of treatment are not as immediate as the patient hoped, usually that's offset "by the fact that the physician is still trying to help the patient at least come to grips with his or her rheumatic condition. I don't think the whole thing rests on whether the medication will make them better immediately. How they maintain a faith or trust is a big part of it."

It's a two-way street, of course: Patients have to take an active role in the management of their arthritis, in joint protection, medications, exercise, and therapy. They need to know as much as they can about their condition, and, once they have a clear understanding of what their condition entails, they have to learn about available medications in sufficient detail to ask the right questions.

Put yourself in the driver's seat. Get as much reliable information as you can, then work with your physician to find out what part of that information applies to you. Incorporate that into your lifestyle. Exploit your strengths and learn to cope with your weaknesses. In Chalmers' scenario, compliance means complying with the limitations your condition imposes on you, seeking help when you feel you need it, and trying not to do too many things on your own when things aren't going well. Patients tell him they didn't like to ask for help—they didn't want to bother him. "Those patients," he says, "must recognize that professionals are *there* to help them cope with their problems."

That said, there *are* constraints on a physician's availability, which is a major reason for self-education. No matter how well-meaning the doctor and how attentive you may be, a ten-minute interview—the standard GP's allotment for a patient visit—isn't enough for you to get a handle on all you need to know about your medications.

It helps if you can spell out your expectations ahead of time, so the doctor can address them—and eliminate disappointments caused by unrealistic expectations. Blindly following a doctor's orders may work well in acute-care hospitals, but with a chronic disease, you *have* to take an active role. Make sure you understand what the doctor is saying to you, and, says Chalmers, communicate your complaints to the doctor, "who by and large is not gifted with second sight. Two-way communication is very important, really the single most important factor."

What questions should you pose? Janet M. Maurer, M.D., is the author of a small book called *How to Talk to Your Doctor: The Questions to Ask*. Formerly director of Respirology Clinical Service at The Toronto Hospital, Maurer believes that good communication, through a relaxed and open relationship with your doctor, is the key to receiving the best medical care. Medicine, she points out, is often an inexact science. "Your doctor should know more about you than the *facts* of your illness."

Patients have rights, says Maurer, and they should know and understand them: "You have the right to know your diagnosis, prognosis, alternate forms of treatment, recommendations of your doctor and why. If a diagnosis has not been reached, you should have a clear explanation of why not. Also, if further studies or follow-up is indicated, this should be explained. It is, after all, your body and your health that are in the balance."

With the rights come responsibilities. Plan your visits. Ask questions. It's up to you, the patient, to "disclose all information relating to your illness to the physician," Maurer writes. "The doctor cannot be expected to make an accurate diagnosis and institute proper therapy if some information is withheld. In fact, withholding or misstating data requested by the physician may result in the use of improper, even potentially dangerous therapies or risky tests."

At the same time, doctors have rights and responsibilities, too. They have to tell patients not merely what the doctor feels they *need* to know, but what patients *want* to know. Sometimes the doctor may forget you need vital basic information or feel you don't want a lot of information. Don't be afraid to ask.

Maurer offers a set of fourteen questions referring to arthritis (what is it? is it contagious? is it fatal? etc.), as well as sample questions about hospitalization and understanding medication. Another section sets up a series of questions in five categories: certainty of diagnosis (is it correct?), cause and nature of the illness (what's the chance my children will inherit this illness?), course of the disease (will there be progressive damage? complications? what symptoms should I be alert for?), treatment (medications? is surgery an alternative? will diet changes help?), and implications for family, social, and work life (will I be able to continue my job, hobbies, and sports? will the disease or treatment be disfiguring?).

Like other medical professionals, Maurer recommends that patients take an active role in their health care. You can't afford to be timid about it; it's your health that's at stake: "If you feel your doctor has overlooked something," she says, "mention it. Do not assume it has been seen; doctors miss things, too." As a guideline, Maurer suggests some basic principles to help patients focus their questions:

- Make your questions clear and specific.
- Volunteer facts, and be ready to conquer your fear of the unknown (ignoring facts won't make them go away).
- Don't be afraid to ask for clarification or repeat explanations.
- Take notes and proceed in an organized way.
- Don't be overwhelmed or misled by statistics, and don't ask questions a doctor can't reasonably be expected to answer.

Ultimately patients have to remember that their role is at the heart of their own health care. All their concerns—whether about medication, procedures, or surgery—must be addressed. "Fear," says Marie Chambers, "is taken away by knowledge. Knowledge is power. It gives patients the power to go forward, to look ahead to a time when their illness won't be controlling them."

8

Up the Down Staircase
Overcoming Depression

Joy and Sorrow are inseparable. Together they come,
and when one sits alone with you at your board,
remember that the other is asleep upon your bed.
—Kahlil Gibran

Laugh, and the world laughs with you. Cry, and you cry alone.

Anyone who's ever suffered the grinding purgatory of severe depression knows the sad truth in the old adage. It's a cloud nothing can lift, a dark room light doesn't penetrate, a dry well, narrow and deep. It's a dissatisfaction so profound that food tastes bitter. Sleep is a storm-tossed sea that tosses you up on its waking shore wretched and spent. It's a listlessness that seeps into every act, every thought, every encounter. It's a mourning that won't go away.

Short of the death of a loved one, there's nothing so emotionally wrenching as being diagnosed with a chronic disease. Depression is almost inevitable—it's part of the grieving process. We grieve over any loss, and a chronic illness such as arthritis inevitably involves losses— the loss of health and the simple joy of feeling physically well; the loss of a job or self-respect or activities previously enjoyed—sports, recreation, even socializing. You grieve every time you discover something else your disease prevents you from doing. You grieve for hopes and dreams that seem to have withered and died. Or, just when your arthritis seems under control or miraculously in remission, it flares up again, and depression rolls over you like a dense, dark fog. All those mounting losses foster a depression that deepens with a sense of purposelessness, a shrivelling absence of meaning in life.

Barbara Brunton, who works for The Arthritis Society in Toronto, has seen that dark cloud again and again in the support groups she works with. She also has crushing first-hand experience. Brunton has "rupus," a nasty rheumatoid arthritis-lupus cocktail. More than a decade ago, when she was first diagnosed with RA, Brunton was so sick her doctor wasn't sure she'd pull through. She lost twenty-five pounds in twelve days and was so weak she couldn't lift a teacup. "I was very frightened," she says, "because RA is one form of arthritis that's potentially crippling. You go through the worst scenarios—I'm going to be in a wheelchair in no time—pity, pity, that kind of thing.

"I can remember sitting in a chair very much like this one," she says, swollen knuckles gripping the arms of her chair, "staring at the rug for five hours at a time. The tears would dribble down, and I'd just sit there. I didn't want to read or watch TV. I didn't turn on the radio. I didn't open the curtains. I was brain-dead."

At the heart of her depression was "an incredible feeling of hopelessness," a feeling that her life had spun out of her control. She couldn't feed herself, bring herself to get dressed, or accomplish any of the other minutiae of everyday life. "I had to quit work. I felt so ill I really didn't go beyond that, except to wonder what was going to happen to me. I was devastated."

Brunton was going through what doctors call reactive depression, an emotional backlash to her new state that's typical of people recently diagnosed with a chronic illness. Surprisingly, most people learn to cope with their disease *and* their depression, and most cope remarkably well, says Toronto rheumatologist Dr. Rachel Shupak. "Anybody who has to deal with the kind of pain and disability that people with severe forms of arthritis have to deal with, well, if they didn't go through some kind of depression, it would be very unusual. I give them a lot of credit that they're able to look within and find the inner strength to deal with it. And most patients do."

If you think coping with a verifiable illness is bad, try coming to terms with a disorder so amorphous its symptoms appear to have no explanation. Just ask Robin Saunders. After a serious car accident a dozen years ago, Saunders, now forty-eight, began to develop a series of apparently unrelated problems—a rash over most of his body, severe headaches, irritable bowel syndrome, light sensitivity, muscle spasms, sleep and cognitive disorders, and more—and no one could tell him what the problem was. His own doctor had seen him bounce back from skiing, motorcycle, and auto accidents over the years, but after two months of symptoms he couldn't pin down, he basically told Saunders to get his act together; there was nothing the matter with him.

The condition so distressingly difficult to diagnose proved to be fibromyalgia syndrome (FMS), a neuromuscular disorder characterized by chronic pain and sleep disorders, among a host of other unpleasantries. Getting that diagnosis, Saunders says, "was tough, but a lot of people with fibromyalgia have the same problem."

And if getting a diagnosis is tough, try living with the condition. Pain is a constant: "It never goes away. Sometimes it's your legs, sometimes your back, sometimes your arms or neck. It tends to move around. It keeps it interesting." Depressing? You bet: "I fight depression almost on a daily basis."

Not surprisingly, a lot of people with a chronic illness ask why *they* pulled the short straw. What did they do to deserve *this*? Brunton wondered if she were being punished: "I thought, 'Well, you wouldn't get this horrible disease if you hadn't been a bad person.'"

And a lot of people, says Saunders, who manned a hotline for people with FMS, never get past that point. "'Why me?' they ask. Well," he says, with a wry laugh, "there's no answer, guys. That's the way it is. Yes, it's unfair, but the fact is, you've got it, and that's that."

Saunders' FMS and Brunton's arthritis pretty much put a lid on their careers, Saunders' as a successful sales rep, Brunton's as a project manager for the Canadian Mental Health Association. Brunton retired her bicycle, stopped gardening, and gave up a full roster of recreational sports, yet, over time, she did learn to cope with her pain, her illness, and her distress. She reached a point, in fact, where she actually thought her life had improved—"in almost all respects"—but to reach that point she had to reprioritize her activities and develop a new set of values. In fact, she had to re-examine everything she'd previously held dear. In doing so—in coming to grips with the immutable fact of her arthritis—she developed a new perspective, and it gave her a serenity she simply didn't have before.

It came down to a simple question: If you can't do what you used to do, what *can* you do? As Brunton saw it, she could either address the question or stay mired in depression—and that was no option at all. She accepted the fact that arthritis demands a transition, from an "old me" to a "new me." If you can't do the things you used to do, the "old me" no longer exists. You then have to discover what you *can* do, what your "new me" will look like and what will give that new you meaning.

Yes, it's a difficult transition, Brunton admits, but you have to make it: "You have to find some sense of your worth, recognize that there are other things you can do. It may be an opportunity for people to realize they have gifts they've never seen or utilized."

Dr. Gerald Devins, associate professor of psychiatry at the Clarke Institute of Psychiatry in Toronto, has studied what he and his associates call "illness intrusiveness," the idea that, to the extent an illness becomes intrusive, interfering with activities and interests, people are more distressed and less happy. Any chronic disease affects people's behaviour, and they do less in general; therefore they have less opportunity to experience what Devins calls "response-contingent positive reinforcement." In other words, he says, "they have less opportunity to get the good things in life, because they're doing less."

Generally speaking, happiness and contentment are the product of an imbalance between positive and negative experiences: In order to feel really good, we not only need positive experiences, we need *more* positives than negatives; simply reducing negative experiences isn't enough. Thus, one of the most effective behavioural treatments for depression and emotional distress involves getting people more involved in valued activities. Unfortunately, if you have a passion for bowling and it hurts too much to play, "that's going to compromise your ability to benefit from treatment," Devins admits. When arthritis interferes, what's needed is "a more creative approach to what you're going to do to still get the zing out of life everybody needs."

An active response is certainly one of the best natural antidotes to depression. Get out and do something. Go to school. Join a club. If you're people-oriented, get out with other people. Do volunteer work if you can. At the absolute nadir of her depression, Brunton was encouraged by a friend to work with seniors. "Are you mad?" she responded. "I can hardly get dressed in the morning." No, the friend said, but you're going to go mad if you don't do something.

So, Brunton dropped into a daycare centre, where she met "a wonderful, wonderful gentleman," a former college dean who had Alzheimer's disease. "He never remembered who I was, didn't know his wife. We'd work on crossword puzzles every day, and I'd go home sometimes in tears, because I'd think, 'I did something. I didn't just wallow. I went out and did something.'"

Taking charge of her mental and emotional life gave Brunton back a sense of control, and a sense of hope. "You can't go anywhere if you don't have hope—about something. Make your disease this big," she says, squeezing a jot of empty space between forefinger and thumb, "and make yourself huge. It's hard, but it's salvation, too. You need to look for things in life that really have meaning. You have to find balance."

Finding Support

As she began to rediscover her own sense of balance, both mentally and physically, Brunton started a support group that met once a month. The idea was to bring people together who were "part of the same culture [that is, arthritis]."

That's an especially good idea in the first couple of years of a disease, says Dr. Shupak, when you may be feeling your frustration most intensely. What such services can provide, to begin with, is first-hand information. If professional counsellors are available, they can sit down with a group of people and lead them in airing their feelings and reactions to the disease. Social workers, psychologists, or psychiatrists can teach them different strategies for understanding and dealing with their illness. People benefit from just talking to other patients with similar problems, Shupak says: "They've been able to see that they're not alone, and that there are ways of dealing with their illness and their depression. I think that's important."

For some people with arthritis, support group participants are the first people who not only understand how they feel, they're the first who *believe* how they feel. One of the ironies of arthritis is that many people don't look as sick as they feel. No matter how sympathetic friends and family are, they can't share the pain or truly empathize with the degree of suffering someone with lupus or RA or FMS may be experiencing, and that can be deeply frustrating—and depressing.

It's not just friends and family. For Mary Yee, former president of the B.C. Lupus Association, getting a diagnosis was like banging her head against a wall. It took three years before she even knew what she had. By that time, she was in her mid-twenties, she'd lost her laboratory job, and was on disability insurance. She struggled with the not-so-veiled implication from doctors that "maybe what you have is all in your mind." They couldn't really tell there was anything wrong, and she had a hard time convincing them she had such severe pain that she was having difficulty walking or even writing, let alone working: "I was so relieved to hear there was actually something I could put a name to, and everybody started believing me."

Support groups can be especially helpful for young people, who may be fighting other people's misconceptions of arthritis as an "old person's disease"—why do *they* have it? Discovering there are other young people going through the same experience is a kind of validation that lifts a weight off their shoulders, and gives them a jolt of motivation."

Mapping the Emotional Landscape

Motivation is key, because there's a mountain to be scaled—acceptance —and that's not going to happen overnight: It isn't easy to accept something as big as arthritis. But, says Robin Saunders, "when you start going through it, you start viewing life very differently. I think you do become a better human being, because now you have to face the truth every day."

Along the way, though, there are traps, like feeling sorry for yourself, that you can't afford to fall into. You can avoid some of the pitfalls by becoming aware of the emotional cycles your illness imposes on you. Saunders doesn't argue anymore, for example, and if he does get angry, he blows it off quickly. Time has become too valuable. "I don't worry about things over which I have no control," he says, "and I used to. I view it very simply. If I can't control something, then worrying about it is a waste of energy, and my energies are a valuable commodity. My life is a lot simpler and I'm a lot happier for facing the truth about a lot of things, about life. Once you do the acceptance bit—that you have a chronic disease, and it's not going to go away—you start carrying that skill into everything, and you become a better person for it."

Understand that depression is going to be part of the disease. You can't expect to undergo extreme physical changes without some kind of emotional upheaval. To be sure, staying positive in the face of everything arthritis can impose is hard work, but in doing your best to stay positive, you minimize stress factors and are better able to cope.

Don't look too far ahead, Saunders advises. "That's something that gets a lot of people down, but if you start looking at the future and thinking, 'Where am I going to be in ten years?', you're in trouble, real trouble." Instead, focus on the here and now—one minute at a time, if you have to. Focus on the things you know you like, and try to do them. And remind yourself that you survived yesterday, you're surviving today—and you *will* survive tomorrow.

Getting arthritis is a bit like being pushed out of a comfortable home and into a run-down shack: Your "new" body, the "house" you live in, isn't so comfortable anymore, and nothing you can do will ever make it the way it was. It's going to need constant attention, and you've got to learn to live with (and in) it. At first, it may seem that everything your life has consisted of till now is in jeopardy—if not completely destroyed. And suddenly your emotional, physical, and perhaps even financial resources are pressed to the limit. And you've got to accept it? Who wouldn't be depressed?

Yet depression isn't usually a first reaction to arthritis. After diagnosis, most people actually go through a series of emotions: shock and fear, denial perhaps, anger, and only then depression. As psychologist Elizabeth Kübler-Ross pointed out in *On Death and Dying*, not everyone will experience every reaction, nor in the same order, but the majority of their emotions will be perfectly natural. Most may even be helpful.

Take denial: "This can't be happening," people protest. Some may even do their best to find a doctor who can provide a different diagnosis. If denial gets in the way of accepting the implications of the disease or prompt treatment, it can be a serious problem. For most people, though, denial is—again—a natural reaction, a psychological buffer against the shock of diagnosis.

The next stage is usually anger. Finding you have a chronic illness for which there's no real explanation and no cure might well make you ask, "Why me? What on God's green earth have I done to deserve this?" Anger, too, is normal and, if it can be expressed, healthy. Get it out in the open. Find someone—a friend, family member, or professional counsellor—who can help you sort out your feelings, rather than trying to suppress your anger. That can lead to other problems, such as channelling your resentment into resistance to treatment. Instead, try turning the energy of your anger into motivation: Refuse to be beaten. Don't let arthritis rule your life.

After anger may come bargaining. That's when you find yourself saying such things as "If only I don't have to give up golf or gardening or playing the piano..." Sure, or playing starting quarterback for the L.A. Rams. You may compare yourself to others ("I'm not as badly off as so-and-so. I should be grateful"), which is not such a bad thing, so long as you don't get stuck there: It's usually from this point that real acceptance begins, but you're not out of the woods. Depression can overwhelm you at any stage of your psychic journey. It's the most troublesome, recurring, emotional aspect of arthritis, but it's simply an instinctive response to feelings of loss and emotional upheaval. It's a form of withdrawal, a time to marshall resources and reorganize inner responses to drastically changed circumstances.

"It's an on-going battle," says Mary Yee. "After coming through depression, you may get depressed again. You may occasionally have to take a few steps back before going forward again. You go through cycles from anger to acceptance, then maybe back down to bargaining. It's not like it's Step One, Two, Three, Four, you're accepting and that's it." She laughs. "It's not the way it's always written up."

With no outside diversions, Brunton did some serious introspection before she came to that realization. Believing that mind, body and soul, or spirit, "have to work in concert to be a healthy person," Brunton began "a lot of internal housecleaning. It was a time of real inner growth for me. When I look back now, what I'm doing today [as an Arthritis Society counsellor] is far more satisfying than anything I'd ever done before I got this. It's really done a lot for me." Her life, says Brunton, is better "in almost all respects."

"You have to make certain changes to your life," says Yee, "so that you can avoid the depression, in that, OK, I can't go out and do this all day, but I *can* do this for an hour. It's learning to change your attitude and your expectations of yourself, so that you don't sit at home and say I can't do anything. Try to find your limits. Many of us try to push ourselves harder than regular people to try to remain active."

For many people, a dose of motivation is just what the doctor ordered. "We don't cure their arthritis," Shupak says. "We control it if we're lucky." Most people come to accept their arthritis, "and in that sense they cope within the context of the disease." The people who give up right at the beginning are the difficult ones, she says, "because I think attitude toward the disease in some ways influences its outcome—perhaps in a small way, but in some people it may be in a big way." The majority of her patients are fighters, Shupak says. In essence, "they conquer their disease because they learn to live with it. They really do learn to fight."

A Survivor's Story

The lesson isn't always easily learned. Scott MacLean, thirty-two, began to cope when he learned to accept RA, he says, as "a part of me. It's not entirely me, and I'll never be free of it." But instead of "dissociating" when he has a lot of pain, instead of seeing his body as an enemy he wants only to escape, MacLean learned to stop tuning out. He's come to understand his limitations and gain some control over his life again.

"I used to think I was just this person stuck in a crippled body," MacLean says. "I'd try to disconnect myself from the neck up, all the time. I lived in a daydream world, and the only time I was actually alive was when I was daydreaming. I'd crawl into my own head, where I could run and play ball and do all those things I couldn't do in the real world. And that's where I liked to stay." The rest of the time, he endured a depression so black that it came very near to being what a philosopher once called a "sickness unto death."

MacLean sits angled uncomfortably into one end of the living-room couch. His neck is painfully stiff; he doesn't turn his head if he can avoid it. There are scars visible on his left elbow and knee, below shirt-sleeves and shorts, evidence of two of the five operations that have left him with artificial hips and a plastic knee. When he walks, his stride is laboured and out of step with his age. His hands, the knuckles deformed by disease, rest quietly in his lap as he brings back the years.

Recalling the past is a descent into darkness, and at times MacLean's voice falters and his eyes mist. He agrees to talk about this only after much soul-searching. The thought of exposing his pain—especially now that he hopes and believes the worst of it lies behind him—wasn't easy. But MacLean feels a kind of obligation to speak. He believes that talking about his own experience of illness and depression might help other people get through theirs.

His story isn't unique, though it is wrenching. For more than twenty years, he's been taking a beating from arthritis and, emotionally, he's been down for the count more than once. What's important, though, is that he's gotten back on his feet. He knows he's never going to lick his arthritis, but he's learning to hold his own—with the RA *and* depression. And after everything he's been through, that feels like winning.

MacLean was born in a Nova Scotia mining village called Donkin. It was there his ordeal began, with a minor skiing accident, followed by the flu. In a way, he never recovered. In the next months, most of his joints became inflamed, and he was initiated into the harsh world of front-line anti-arthritis drugs. He was eleven. Over the next few years, he went through "pure hell," a mental and physical anguish sometimes intensified by others' lack of understanding. During an argument one day, another boy slapped MacLean in the face. "It snapped my neck," he says, "and I blacked out. At that instant I realized how fragile I'd become. It hurt my neck, but it broke my heart. The whole illness just hit me."

The disease went into remission for a few months after knee surgery, and MacLean thought he had it beat. Then it came back. This time he understood what was happening to him, and he just totally gave up: "I lost almost all desire to live. Most of my prayers, for a whole year, were that I would die. The pain was excruciating. "This," he thought, "is how I'm going to spend the rest of my life."

At sixteen, both hips were replaced. Within months, the pain returned, and MacLean drifted into alcohol and drug abuse. "I felt like I was walking alone and looking in the window," he recalls, "like I never really belonged anywhere because I never had anyone my age to communicate with. No one at school was sick."

MacLean turned eighteen. One day in early fall, he was home alone, reading in front of the fireplace. "To this day," he says, "I don't know why this happened, but I got up to go to the kitchen. It'd just gotten dark, and I walked out to the porch and grabbed a bucket. The next thing I know, I'm sitting in front of the fireplace again with my wrists split wide open and my hands in the bucket. When it dawned on me what I was looking at, it was like it wasn't even me that was there—I was just sitting there looking at my wrists with big gaping slashes in them and blood pouring into the bucket.

"I don't know where the knife came from. I phoned my brother, who lived next door, and told him, 'You've got to come over. I did something really stupid. I slashed my wrists.' When the reality of it started sinking in, I began to lose it. I couldn't believe I'd actually done it. The scary part was not realizing I *had* done it till after the fact. I still don't recall actually doing it."

MacLean spiralled through most of the classic symptoms of depression—feelings of helplessness and isolation, lack of meaning and prolonged despondency, mood swings and emotional outbursts, sleep disorders and lack of appetite, significant weight loss. Fuelled by alcohol and drugs, he developed a poor self-image and lost all will to live. His suicide attempt "was the climax to a steady decline in who I thought I was. From the time I got sick until that point, the disease not only ate away at me physically but mentally as well. The only time I wasn't depressed was when I was drunk or stoned."

After the suicide attempt—a desperate cry for help—MacLean was assigned a psychiatrist and admitted to hospital. It would be years filled with more suicidal thoughts, more despair and physical suffering before he learned to accept the *fact* of his arthritis and how to deal with depression in a real and lasting way.

MacLean's arthritis didn't go away, but he got it under control. He got his weight up, got into better physical shape, and began training for a career in computers. He took up some of the responsibility for his sister's children and developed a special relationship with an understanding woman. Most of the changes he was able to attribute to having "actually accepted the disease as a part of my life." Depression didn't vanish from his life, but he learned to handle it, rather than letting *it* handle *him*.

Everybody Gets the Blues—Don't They?

Barbara Brunton, Robin Saunders, Mary Yee, Scott MacLean—all have terrible stories to tell, each exemplary in its special misery, yet people with arthritis don't have a corner on the market: Everybody gets the blues. Depression is an absolutely normal part of emotional experience, says Dr. Devins. Everyone feels "down" occasionally. It becomes a problem, though, if your distress is interfering with the general business of living, with what psychologists call "your functioning." If you're really unhappy and you can't tolerate it or don't want to tolerate it, Devins says, "and you've tried to change things and you can't, then it's worthwhile seeking help." (See page 295 for a list of resources.)

Unfortunately a lot of people *don't* seek help—some studies number the reluctant as high as 50 per cent of all those who suffer from depression. Their reasons may be as simple as believing their depression isn't serious, or that they can't be helped. Some people are ashamed to admit they're suffering from depression—whether they have arthritis or not. "There's a tremendous stigma attached to all kinds of psychological and emotional problems," Devins observes. "A lot of people feel guilty about it. It's bad enough they feel depressed, but then they feel there's something wrong with them, that they're worthless or valueless or, even worse—somehow deviant."

Even without arthritis, depression can be a serious, debilitating disease, says Dr. Martin Katzman, a senior resident at The Clarke's Mood Disorder Clinic. "It can affect a person's social life, marriage, family, job, career, goals, aspirations. It can be so difficult for the individual to function that it can limit every aspect of their life, and there's a serious risk of suicide. People think of depression as, 'Well, they should pick up their socks'—as against, say, a 'serious' illness like heart disease. But there are people who die from depression. One should not think of depression as something that doesn't have risks. It's something that needs to be treated."

(To put this in perspective, it's been estimated that one in four Canadians will suffer a bout of depression sometime in their lives that's sufficiently serious to require treatment, and as many as 15 per cent of all cases of serious depression lead to suicide attempts. Beyond the damage it does to the quality of life and the number of lives lost, depression has been estimated to cost the Canadian workforce more than five million workdays every month, and all of us as much as five billion dollars annually in direct and indirect costs.)

Not everyone who has arthritis suffers from debilitating depression. There are any number of theories why some people become depressed, while others—given similar experiences—don't. Heredity may play a role, though that's not at all certain; there may be biochemical factors that predispose some people to depression. It may be that certain people, due to a combination of environmental, experiential, and biochemical factors, tend to interpret their experience differently. Psychologists used to think that people who were depressed demonstrated a bias to be pessimistic, that they felt helpless and under-recognized the amount of control they had over events in their lives. What research from the early 1980s seems to show, says Devins, "is that it's not so much that depressed people underestimate or discount the control they have— they seem to report fairly accurately how much control they have in a number of situations—it's that people who are not depressed *overestimate* how much control they have."

In other words, rose-coloured glasses may be useful for mental health. If you lose those rose-coloured glasses, "well," says Devins, "it's a cruel world. If you see it for what it is, you may get depressed."

Can family and friends help? Yes, they can, first of all by recognizing that someone suffering from depression may need professional help. One of the common mistakes that people make, says Ottawa geriatrician Dr. William Dalziel, is to urge someone who's depressed to just "snap out of it. Pull yourself together." The idea that people can be talked out of a severe depression he says "comes from the misconception that depression is just a psychological illness. Physical, chemical, neurotransmitter changes in the brain make it a physical illness as well. You can try as hard as you want, and you're not going to *try* yourself out of a serious depression without help."

"We tend to think each person has to take responsibility for his situation," Devins says. "Many people who are depressed know what they need to do. It's not that they don't feel like it—they just can't bring themselves to do it. Very often, they'll criticize themselves for not being able to, and then they become even more distressed."

In other words, family and friends have to walk a fine line. Activity can exert a beneficial influence, but you can't browbeat people who are depressed into doing something they don't want to do, especially if they're already struggling to come to grips with their arthritis. That might only make their depression worse.

At the same time, Devins says, "the more people are able to maintain their involvement in valued activities and interests, the more it's going to help lift their depression. They can go for treatment if they're really feeling distressed. They can see their family doctor, they can try to get referred to a psychologist or psychiatrist or another mental-health professional, and those people are trained to help. But again, relying on friends and social relationships is very important. They can help with physical activities that need to be done—doctors' appointments, paying bills, grocery shopping, etc. They also can help in bolstering your sense of self-esteem, by expressing interest in what you have to say, by being curious. These are all nonverbal but very powerful cues that you're a good person. And everybody needs that kind of communication."

Simply feeling blue is an "endogenous" depression, an inner storm usually as ephemeral as the weather—it might even be "caused" by the weather, or by "waking up on the wrong side of the bed." The other type, "reactive" depression, is caused by some definable outside event, such as arthritis.

"We see a lot of reactive depression," says Toronto rheumatologist Dr. Rachel Shupak. People with arthritis, she says, "have a lot to deal with." But in a dozen years of practice, the number of patients Shupak has referred to a psychiatrist for depression is "not many, perhaps ten to twenty."

Shupak does her best to prepare her patients, right from the shock of the initial diagnosis. "In the beginning, I try to be very honest with patients, because I don't want them to have unrealistic expectations." This is the tough-love approach. She tells RA patients, for example, that they have a chronic illness they'll have to deal with for the rest of their lives, but there are drugs to control the disease: "What we attempt to do is keep their lives as normal as possible."

Shupak gives patients "a bit of a hard sell in the beginning," but she also tries to paint as reasonable or optimistic a picture as she can. She explains that the initial treatment for their arthritis is going to be no walk in the park, but there's a good reason for taking an aggressive approach: If they can reverse even a part of the inflammation at the outset, not only will the patient feel better more quickly, but there's less chance of sustaining irreversible damage later on.

A lot of people with arthritis keep harking back to when they were well and use that as a benchmark. No wonder they're depressed, Saunders says. Don't look back, he advises. A former competitive skier, he "hardly ever" thinks of when he was well. "If I think about skiing, I think, well, that was when I was skiing. I don't think, that's when I was well. It's the past. It's gone. This is the life I lead now, and in many ways it's not a bad life. There are still things I can do. There's still beauty in the world; there's still food to be eaten, music to be listened to..."

Things that make you happy you *have* to do, Saunders says: "Do things that bring you joy, things you truly love. That starts to build up, and you begin to feel better about yourself. Don't do things you don't like if you can possibly get away from it. Sally Jean wants to come over for tea and you hate her, and it's agony sitting there for two hours— why do it? People *do* do these things, right? I mean, they spend their time on stupid things they don't want to do. Take control of your life. Do things you want to do, and be damned about the rest. Either people will like you and accept you or they won't, so start living your life properly. That carries you through a lot of garbage."

Understand your disease and how it works. If it helps, keep a daily log to track pain, fatigue, sleep, and activity. If you can figure out what causes fluctuations, you may learn what keeps the pain down, and thus be more in control of your life. Some people let their pain and illness become their whole lives. Look at every aspect of your life—your physical side, your social side, your work, your spiritual life, your self-esteem—and try to determine what you can do in each area that will leave you with a balanced lifestyle.

Other people can help get you through (or better still, out of) a depression, but "only if you do it with them—if you participate," says Saunders. "It's a 'self' thing. You get yourself out of depression or you ain't going to get there. Other people can help, if you're chronically depressed, for example, and you get a psychiatrist, but you're still the one who ultimately has to cross the line."

9

Caveat Emptor
Diet, Nutrition, and Alternative Remedies

You are what you eat.

Some people with arthritis may have special dietary needs, because of a medication program or because certain foods seem to cause flare-ups or simply because they're physically unable to shop for and prepare three meals a day. (People with gout, for example, are advised to maintain a diet low in purines and alcohol.) If you're in that situation, ask your doctor for a referral to a dietician. And don't take dietary advice from someone who isn't a registered professional dietician: Anyone can call him- or herself a nutritionist, but only a dietician has met strict educational requirements (a four-year university course, followed by a one-year internship and perhaps further specialization). Asking for important dietary advice from anyone but a fully accredited dietician is a bit like asking the gas jockey at the local pumps to give your Ferrari a tune-up.

Dieticians have certain advantages even over doctors, starting with the fact that *all* their training has gone into nutrition, whereas a doctor's studies in nutrition may have been buried in biochemistry or some of the other disciplines of disease treatment. On top of that, doctors generally have a lot of patients and only a few minutes for each. With a dietician, says Eleanor Brownridge, a registered professional dietician and former president of the Ontario Dietetic Association, many initial consultations will be an hour long.

There are special considerations for arthritis sufferers. First of all, says Lucie Asselin, a London, Ontario dietician, many people with arthritis take medications that might impair their ability to tolerate food, such as non-steroidal drugs, which can be extremely irritating to the gastrointestinal tract. Fearing stomach upsets, many people avoid certain foods that contain important nutrients for maintaining health.

But don't worry that a dietician is going to insist on a diet of carob and cooked cabbage, even though you hate both. A dietician starts where you're at now, says Brownridge. "She'll say, 'OK, you're doing some great things. We can incorporate this and this and that from your favourite foods in a menu pattern; you'll just have to cut back on this, say.' Many people come in thinking that a dietician will tell them what they *shouldn't* do and leave knowing there are lots of things they *can* do. We try to give them a positive orientation and try to provide new ideas and things they can do to make their lives easier."

This includes a few surprises. TV dinners, for example—a real no-no, right? Not necessarily, says Asselin. "TV dinners are a good source of nutrients, because they contain all sorts of proteins, fat, and carbohydrates; the variety is fine. But, because they're commercially processed, they contain lots of salt, so they might not be compatible with the treatment we want to provide. If a patient needs a sodium restriction to prevent fluid retention, due to the use of corticosteroids—that's one of the drug's side effects—we'd definitely not recommend TV dinners. But we would provide cooking tips: how to prepare a meal that's easy to make, that won't drain all your energy, for example, and we keep in mind what's available on the market already prepared."

Tell a dietician what you like, Asselin advises. "If you like sandwiches, I'll tell you what to combine with them to get the variety of nutrients you need, so you'll get the benefits of this as a slow-release energy meal that will carry you on to the next meal. A lot of arthritis patients can't eat much at one sitting. We'll suggest that calories and vitamins be spread out through the day. Instead of planning three large meals you can't eat, we'll determine how much you *are* able to eat. From there, we'll say, 'Well, you should adjust this, or that isn't right. Perhaps you have to take this out because it's going to elevate your blood sugar or it's not dense in terms of calories and nutrients.'"

Dieticians look at quality as well, Asselin says, "what people are willing to buy or adjust, based on their ability to cook and do their shopping—and their budget." Dieticians can even help you to plan menus you're able to cook, based on your physical limitations, sometimes in consultation with an occupational therapist, who can teach you how to move around the stove or use specially designed cooking utensils. "If a patient can't prepare the food or buy it or afford it, you've done nothing," Brownridge says. "Our advice would cover the whole gamut: from purchasing food, storing it and preparing it, to being able to swallow it—and enjoy it. It's a pretty complete approach."

Most people won't need that much help, but it's there if you do. Remember: If you have arthritis, basic good nutrition is vitally important to keep you strong in mind and body. It's a fighting chance you owe to yourself to provide and maintain.

Eating for Weight Reduction

Most of us need to be reminded now and again that getting regular exercise and maintaining an ideal body weight are good for us—and that goes double for people with osteoarthritis (OA). For people with OA, there's a special reason, in addition to staying fit, in addition to reducing their risk of heart attack, in addition to all the benefits of increased lung potential and the undeniable advantage of simply being healthy: For people with arthritis, keeping their weight down is a way of fighting the disease that's lodged in their weight-bearing joints.

That understanding was confirmed and amplified by the results of a long-term study done on a substantial portion of the adult population of Framingham, Massachusetts. Begun in 1948, the original study set out to determine risk factors in heart disease, but data was also collected on OA. The results from the project were published in 1991 in the American journal *Annals of Medicine*.

"We've known for a while that people who are overweight are at increased risk of knee osteoarthritis," says Dr. David Felson, a rheumatologist with the Boston University Arthritis Center and one of the project's principal researchers. "This is the first study that looks at whether they can prevent the disease by losing weight." Felson and his colleagues compared sixty-four women who had OA of the knee with another group who did not, taking into account previous knee injuries, physical activity, educational status, smoking, and weight.

Analysis of all the collected information showed that weight loss over a ten-year period enabled overweight women, middle-aged or older, to cut their chances of developing OA of the knee in half. They also found that recent weight gain had a substantial impact on the disease's progress, suggesting that the development of knee OA not only depends on current weight, but also on how long someone has been carrying the excess weight.

The good news, according to Dr. John Lefebvre, a Toronto nutritionist and media commentator, is that you don't have to shed a lot of pounds to make a difference. The reason is that every pound of body weight adds six times the amount of force across your knees and three times the amount across your hips in normal weight-bearing. So, he says, "if you put on ten pounds of extra weight, you're carrying an extra sixty pounds across your knees every time you walk. Twenty pounds isn't a lot of weight, but that translates into one hundred and twenty pounds of force every time you take a step."

If you drop ten pounds, you actually decrease your risk of developing OA by about 50 per cent. So, if you're at risk—if you're over fifty, if you have a family history of OA, if you've had previous trauma to a joint or you're involved in some type of repetitive activity of those joints—keeping your weight down is a good idea. It even helps if you already have OA, Lefebvre says. "A study showed that if people [with OA] lost weight, the amount of pain and discomfort they experienced decreased dramatically." In fact, overweight people suffer more rapid disease progression in OA, and they're also more likely to develop OA in the other knee. On top of that, if you're overweight, you may not be a candidate for a prosthetic replacement.

The most important aspect of weight control is the amount of fat we eat as we get older, and not just for people with OA. Fat is implicated in heart disease; stroke; breast, prostate, and colon cancer; diabetes; and it's right at the heart, so to speak, of putting on the pounds. It's not just because fat is, well, fat, but because of the way the body takes it in. On a gram for gram basis, there are twice the calories in fat as in carbohydrates and protein. In itself that doesn't explain fat's precocious ability to turn us into butterballs. The key is that 90 per cent of all the fat we eat gets stored on our bodies. So, if it goes in, it goes on.

Fat's different from anything else you ingest. It's nature's way of preparing you for the next famine. When you eat fruits or vegetables, Lefebvre says, "your metabolism turns on and breaks them down. If you eat a slice of bread, your metabolism breaks it down. When you eat fat, your metabolism doesn't do anything. It just gets stored."

One approach to slimming down is to count your daily calories, figure out how many of those calories are derived from fat, then decide you're only going to consume 30 per cent of those calories (or less) in fat. Naturally that can get complicated fast; Lefebvre suggests tackling it on a gram-for-gram basis—for women, 50 to 70 grams of fat per day, for males, 70 to 90. It's even easier, he says, "to look at each food. If you eat a lot of foods that tend to be low-fat, it can be less than 30 per cent, so, instead of looking at all the foods you eat, try to eat lots of low-fat foods. The idea is it's going to balance out with occasionally eating some of those high-fat foods."

To determine how many calories you require daily to maintain your current body weight, multiply your "activity factor" by your weight in pounds. Activity factors range from 10, for extremely inactive people, and 12, for people who get only occasional activity, to 14, for people who are active every day. Let's say you're in the "active" category, and you weigh 150 pounds. That means you need 2100 calories a day to keep your weight constant. To lose a pound a week, you'll have to cut 500 calories a day from your diet, although exercise can help burn off the calories faster. If you're thinking of going on a diet, draft a plan with your nutritionist to ensure you get all the nutrition you need.

Caveat Emptor!

Dietary Fads and Alternative Remedies

If a healthy diet promotes healthy living—you are what you eat—does that mean that altering what you eat changes who you are? After all, if certain foods promote health, doesn't it make sense that others could make you sick? If you retool your diet can you prevent or cure arthritis, or reduce its symptoms?

These are the apparently logical questions underlying most dietary claims for arthritis, claims, to be fair, that are often made in good conscience. There's plenty of anecdotal evidence: Aunt Betsy stopped eating red meat and threw away her canes; the mail-carrier's sister started sipping devil's claw herbal tea, and she's never had a painful joint since; or an author claims that eating tomatoes and green peppers is bad for your arthritis because they're related to deadly nightshade...

Unfortunately, from the perspective of arthritis specialists, most theories about food causing, curing, or affecting arthritis are just that—theories that remain to be proven. Reading strictly from the book, the medical community has repeatedly noted there's no connection between diet and arthritis until scientific evidence proves otherwise—particularly when other safe and effective treatment options are available.

In recent years, though, changes have opened a chink in the previously unassailable armour of science. In the first place, doctors are no longer held in the same regard they once were. Their patients have begun to recognize what doctors themselves are slowly coming to accept: that they can't possibly know it all. There's simply too much science being done for any one person to assimilate, and medical specialties, with their constantly increasing databanks of knowledge, are pushing the limits of understanding available to any one physician further and further out of reach.

Thus, some doctors are opening their minds to the possibility that some long-held beliefs have to be re-examined in the light of new knowledge, and with the recognition that certain things—food and its potential role in arthritis, for instance—may not be as easily dismissed as they once were. They're starting to accept that there may be exceptions to the established rules: There are simply too many people claiming that this or that has an effect on how they feel to be ignored.

The key, though, is the word "exceptions." Becoming more open-minded doesn't mean a scientist can ignore what facts there *are*, and the central fact is, no study has ever shown that there's anything like a universal dietary influence on arthritis, even if some people's arthritis may be affected in as yet unaccountable ways by foodstuffs they ingest. In fact, beyond any purported benefit from ginseng or carrots or charcoal-broiled beef, there are at least two well-known reasons why some people experience an improvement in their symptoms after engaging in a particular dietary experiment. The first is the cyclical nature of arthritis; the second is the placebo effect.

"For reasons still poorly understood," says Dr. Andrew Chalmers, director of the rheumatic disease unit at the University of British Columbia, "many types of arthritis go through periods of spontaneous remission and flare-up of symptoms, independently of treatment." These periods can last days, weeks or months and are entirely unpredictable. So, if someone were independently to begin a new treatment, such as dietary modification, at the same time a remission began, it's easy to see how he or she would attribute the improvement to the new treatment. And even if that person's symptoms never returned, Chalmers says, "it would still be impossible to say unequivocally that it was a result of a particular treatment. By contrast, in controlled scientific experiments, arthritis researchers do their utmost to take into account this variable, so that it won't distort the results."

Then there's the power of mind over body. Medicines are tested against a placebo (an inert substance) because studies have shown that the symptoms of up to 30 per cent of clinical test subjects improve, simply because they *believe* they're doing something positive for their condition. The literal translation of the Latin *placebo* is, "I please," and embedded in that simple phrase is the powerful phenomenon of positive thinking: I believe my treatment is good for me; therefore, I will get better. In the hard-nosed arena of bringing pharmaceutical compounds to market, a medication must, at the very least, significantly outperform the placebo to be considered effective.

"If you have arthritis, the downside of the placebo effect is that nothing is actually being done for your arthritis," says Chalmers, "and the absence of symptoms does not mean the disease is cured. Regrettably, for most people with arthritis, the placebo effect is short-lived, and the illness returns with increased severity."

Still, there are ways in which food might be connected with arthritis. First, some people are allergic to certain foods, and it's conceivable that they may have a type of allergic reaction in their joints. Second, certain types of diets—with particular amounts of calories, protein, and fatty acids—may affect the inflammation that occurs with arthritis.

Dr. Richard S. Panush, an immunologist at Saint Barnabas Medical Center in Livingston, New Jersey, is one of the leading scientific experts in North America on food and arthritis. In the late 1980s, Panush conducted rigorously controlled food-challenge studies to test the theory of food-induced arthritis. He selected thirty people with inflammatory arthritis whose claims that their symptoms were related to foods were sufficiently compelling to warrant further studies. The results were then published in 1990 in the highly respected *Journal of Rheumatology*.

Although he's the first to admit that his observations aren't conclusive and need confirmation in larger scale studies, Panush found that "most patients alleging food-induced rheumatic symptoms did not show these on blinded challenge [a form of test in which subjects don't know what they're ingesting], but some did. Probably not more than five per cent of rheumatic disease patients have immunologic sensitivity to food(s). Such patients have only been identified by controlled challenge studies. These observations suggest a role for food allergy in at least some patients with rheumatic disease."

If Panush's observations hold true when projected over a general population, then people who develop inflammatory arthritis resulting from an allergic reaction to specific foods are fairly rare.

OK, so food may not *cause* arthritis in most cases. But can altering the nutritional intake of your diet—either by ingesting supplements or eliminating certain foods—alter the course of the illness? Maybe.

In September 1993, arthritis researchers in Boston reported startling results from a three-month study involving sixty people with RA. The people in the study were taken off their regular arthritis medications: half were given a placebo, an inactive substance; the other half were given oral doses of type II collagen, a major component in joint cartilage—from chickens. The researchers reported that the chicken collagen group experienced a measurable decrease in swollen and tender joints, with no side effects.

Although the Boston researchers were quick to downplay the significance of the results, citing a need for further and more in-depth study, less cautious (and far less scientific) observers were quick to see a kind of validation by association for every arthritis remedy ever proposed—including chicken soup.

The idea of a link between diet and arthritis just won't go away, and scientific "discoveries" like the chicken collagen study only add fuel to the fire. In fact, there are numerous such studies: One done on an isolated group of Greenland Inuit suggested that omega-3 fatty acids, found in cold-water fish oils, may alleviate inflammation in some people. However, there was no proof that the oils actually altered the course of anyone's RA; the best that could be said for them is that they may be useful as complementary therapy to current medication. The fact is, you'd probably derive more benefit—nutritional and otherwise—from tucking into a platter of fish than you would from popping capsules of fish oil. And there's something else to consider: Fish oils used in research are highly refined, with the naturally occurring vitamins largely removed. By comparison, fish oils sold in health-food stores are crudely rendered; anyone tempted to mega-dose on them runs the risk of ingesting toxic levels of vitamins A and D.

OK, then, what about fasting? Yes, over short periods fasting can be beneficial: Malnutrition suppresses the immune system, reducing disease activity in inflammatory arthritis. Eventually, though, you have to eat, and symptoms flare up again—and there are two important qualifiers. Fasting and a strict vegetarian diet require the supervision of a physician and a registered dietician to ensure proper nutrition, and you should continue to take your medication. No dietary regimen can replace a prescribed treatment plan.

No end of dietary supplements are touted as alternative therapies for arthritis—from vitamins and minerals to such herbal extracts as kelp, yucca, and ginseng to the decidedly exotic New Zealand green-lipped mussel extract. If you have chronic arthritis, if you've suffered through years of regularly changing medications whose effects are less than you may have hoped, it's only natural that you may have considered some of these "alternative remedies" (let's not forget that ASA was first derived from the bark of the willow).

So, what about some of these other herbal "remedies" touted for the relief of arthritis symptoms that line the shelves of your local health-food store? Should you try devil's claw or the exotic essential oil of anise? Never mind that the label tells you practically nothing: no list of active ingredients (well, it's pure, isn't it?), no information on how to take it (do you let the tea brew for thirty seconds or thirty minutes?), no information on how much you can take safely (four cups or four litres daily?), no information on possible side effects or interactions with other medications—nothing. Never mind. It's worth a try—isn't it?

Well, that depends. Do you feel lucky? After all, there must be *some* reason for the conspicuous absence of consumer information on the package. There *is*—the law (up to a point). It's illegal for manufacturers of herbal remedies to claim their products have any power to modulate the disease process, but they *can* claim certain products provide "symptomatic relief for arthritis," because government regulatory agencies classify herbal remedies as foodstuffs, thus exempting them from the stringent regulations reserved for pharmaceutical products. (That may change very soon, though, as new federal regulations are introduced to deal with herbal treatments.) Promoters exploit the legal loophole. No one can guarantee that a given herbal "remedy" is safe.

And why would they? A lot of herbal remedies *aren't* safe. In 1986, the consumer watchdog magazine *Protect Yourself!* selected twenty-seven preparations recommended by vendors as arthritis treatments. Pharmaceutical researchers at the poison control centre at Laval University in Quebec were asked to determine whether the products were safe and effective. Of the twenty-seven products tested, sixteen were "not recommended" (because of a variety of side effects, including stomach irritation, nausea, vomiting, and rashes) and ten were rated "advise against use" (because of even more serious potential side effects). Only a topical cream was judged "acceptable"—and then only if used less than four times daily.

In each case, any anti-inflammatory properties the tested product had were judged insufficient to be effective against arthritis, unless the product were swallowed in industrial quantities (which greatly increased the risk of side effects). One arthritis "remedy"—essential oil of anise—had no safety warnings or indication of therapeutic effect, yet ingestion of 1 to 5 ml can cause nausea, vomiting, convulsions, and fluid in the lungs. *Protect Yourself!* rated it "advise against use."

As enticing as herbal remedies might be—many are cheap, compared to most prescription medications, and herbal remedies don't require a prescription—the evidence is hard to deny: Some of these strange brews can be dangerous.

Questions about diet and arthritis come thick and fast, but answers come very slowly. They're hard-won only after years of painstaking study, and many apparently excellent studies have produced results that are confusing, contradictory, or not reproducible.

Still, times are changing. Small groups of researchers have been doggedly following leads in this area for years, and in the past decade or so, the field has really taken off. The quality of study design has improved dramatically, and the results researchers are now getting are beginning to raise some interesting questions. During the next decade, some experts believe, research in this area could yield some of the greatest insights into our knowledge of rheumatic diseases.

But, until those studies have been done, employing unimpeachable scientific methods, people with arthritis will be best served by following balanced and healthy diets and adhering to their doctors' prescriptions. In other words, be skeptical of "miraculous" claims and avoid fad nutritional practices. Snake oil may work wonders for your brother's wife's second cousin, but until it's been proven effective—and safe—your best bet is to stick to the facts.

Strange Devices and Miracle Cures

At the risk of repeating a too-familiar and not particularly pleasant refrain, there are—so far—no known cures for most kinds of arthritis. There is treatment—prescribed medications, physiotherapy, early diagnosis, careful monitoring of the arthritis in all its stages and symptoms—that can lead to permanent remission of the symptoms of the disease, but ditching the program your doctor has devised may mean abandoning the best thing going for you.

Which brings us to all those *other* solutions for your arthritis. For every dollar spent in legitimate arthritis research each year, North Americans shell out twenty-five dollars on quack and unproven remedies—to the tune of several billion dollars. Why? "Frustration. Desperation," says Dr. Panush. "Many rheumatologic diseases are chronic, and in many instances, we can't provide patients with the kind of symptomatic relief they'd like to achieve. I think in many instances, out of frustration and, in a sense, desperation, they'll look elsewhere, outside conventional medicine, for relief.

"Some of the things they hear about are very simplistic and in many instances very seductive; fortunately some of them are also benign, so they're not going to hurt patients. But for somebody who hurts all the time, who's having bad reactions to medication or the medications are not working for him, if someone says, 'Follow my diet and I'll make you well,' it's only human nature to want to try it."

The major concern rheumatologists have, Panush says, "and the reason why we place so much emphasis on the risks involved in unorthodox remedies, is that there are enormous things we can do for patients. The concern is, in a patient trying Dr. X's Magic Cure, we lose the chance to do those things we *can* do for him or her."

In fact, if you have a relatively minor form of arthritis, there's a good chance it will go into remission by itself, after a period of time and a doctor's care, so don't waste your money on questionable remedies. If you have a serious form of the disease, getting a correct diagnosis—as early as possible—and taking the proper, scientifically proven treatment could protect you from escalating pain and chronic disability. If someone else says he can cure your arthritis, he's mistaken. At best, he may provide temporary symptomatic relief; worse, he might be lying— there are all sorts of people with no compunctions whatsoever about making money from your misery. What's more, some so-called remedies are downright dangerous.

And remember: In almost all alternative treatments, short- and long-term safety has not been established. Why? "Well," says Dr. Panush, "most of these remedies escape scientific scrutiny. Unless somebody's very interested or there's a compelling theoretical rationale for thinking something may be useful, who's going to invest time and energy in trying to dispel every ridiculous claim that's made?"

As it happens, natural remedies are probably the least of an arthritis sufferer's problems in dealing with unorthodox treatments; there seem to be an almost infinite number of claims for everything from copper bracelets to mussel extract and insect venoms. The trouble is, says Panush, the advocates of some of these unproven remedies "cloak it all in pseudo-science that doesn't conform to what we consider good established conventions of modern-day science, and they sell it to gullible patients. The patients are in no position to make that distinction."

Herbal-based topical creams, for example, have been around since Babylonian times, five or six thousand years ago, but even when they're jazzed up with pharmacological additives like triethanolamine salicylate (a mild anti-inflammatory agent absorbed through the skin), recent studies show no clinical benefit from treatment.

Not all alternative remedies and treatments should be foresworn. Acupuncture, for example, was at first dismissed by the medical community (and still *is* dismissed by a good many of its members), but many people with a wide range of arthritic conditions have found that it works to relieve some of their pain and discomfort.

Biofeedback techniques, which involve the control of end-organ responses through passive concentration and the attainment of a relaxed mental state, have been used successfully for a range of illnesses, including migraine headaches and hypertension. A 1981 scientific study concluded that biofeedback improved the symptoms of RA patients and that favourable objective responses were observed when biofeedback techniques were compared with more traditional physiotherapy.

Animal venoms have also shown promise at various times. Snake venoms, for one, have been promoted for treating arthritis, but no clinically relevant scientific data are available to support such claims. And high-dose, purified honeybee extract—though it has shown some initial experimental promise—has been placed on the scientific back burner: The cost of a single effective injection in humans has been estimated at more than $11,000.

Other claimants from the natural world have not shown as much promise. New Zealand green-lipped mussel extract, for example, showed no noticeable difference in the treatment of RA in tests; cocaine does nothing to arrest the development of your arthritis, but it may get you arrested; and no reputable doctor would prescribe a Chinese herbal remedy known as *chuifong toukuwan*. The promotional material circulated with *chuifong toukuwan*, when it first appeared several years ago, listed twenty-three ingredients; laboratory analysis found several other highly dangerous drugs as well—including cortisone, a potent anti-inflammatory drug that's used more widely than it once was, but only very judiciously. "The real danger lies in people using [cortisone] unbeknownst to anybody, even themselves [as in *chuifong toukuwan*]," says Dr. Panush, "and therefore—potentially—there's a very great risk, because there's no way of monitoring it."

At the other end of the spectrum are antimicrobial drugs known as imidazoles and their derivatives, such as nitroimidazole and clotrimazole. The late Dr. Wyburn-Mason in England claimed to have found protozoa in the joints of RA patients, which he treated with clotrimazole. Unfortunately, protozoa have never been demonstrated by any other researcher, even with electron microscopy.

An even more radical medication is DMSO (dimethyl sulfoxide), which is applied as a topical anti-inflammatory. It's received widespread publicity on the basis of only partially successful results—

and in the face of often dangerous side effects—leading some frustrated patients to go to great lengths to seek it, despite their physicians' reluctance or disapproval.

— —

The fact is, the number of potential—and unproven—remedies for arthritis is limited only by the imaginations of the hucksters trying to sell them. "Claims of efficacy have been made for many remedies," says Panush, "usually in the lay or popular literature or by word of mouth—but not in peer-reviewed, scientific literature."

Some of the "remedies" are indeed inventive, including burial in horse manure, the ingestion of yucca tablets, buckeyes, horse chestnuts, potatoes, immune milk, topical oils (snake, cod liver, olive, and peanut), topical applications of brake fluid, gasoline, lighter fluid, corncob particles, and aloe vera. Gin-soaked raisins are the latest (forget 'em).

On the hardware side, things get even stranger: "inductoscopes" (allegedly of magnetic induction), "solarama boards" (to align mixed-up electrons), "earthboards" or "vitalators" (to produce rejuvenating electrons), "oxydonors" (to "reverse the death process into the life process") and, oh yes, copper bracelets. Don't waste your money: None is effective in treating arthritis and relieving its pain.

And if you're planning a trip down a "radon health mine" (radon is a radioactive gas formed, together with alpha rays, as a first product in the atomic disintegration of radium), cancel your plans. Despite extravagant claims in its behalf, radon therapy is totally unsubstantiated by scientific studies.

"I guess the message is that people shouldn't feel guilty about being curious about these things," Panush says. "That kind of reaction is understandable. They need to be skeptical; they need to beware of simplistic solutions, and I wish patients would be wary of acting on them without discussing them with their physician. *Caveat emptor!* as the ancient Romans said: 'Let the buyer beware!'

"Some remedies—even though we think they won't help—probably won't hurt. It's probably not going to harm anybody, if they don't eat red meat or pork." Experimenting with something like *chuifong toukuwan* or DMSO, though—"that's dangerous," Panush says. "Their physicians should be consulted before they do that. At the very least, they can avoid possible catastrophes."

10

Use It or Lose It
Activity: The Key to Maintaining Mobility

The cure for this ill is not to sit still,
Or frowst with a book by the fire;
But to take a large hoe and a shovel also,
And dig till you gently perspire.
                    —*Rudyard Kipling,* Just-So Stories

Not so very long ago, exercise wasn't on your doctor's prescription pad if you had arthritis. Then again, it wasn't prescribed for people with heart problems, either, yet now it's seen as not only one of the best treatments in many cases, but as one of the best preventative medicines. The same kind of rethinking has transformed approaches to arthritis and exercise: Now it's understood that staying active, within certain limits, is one of the most important parts of your treatment plan.

It starts with the recognition that regular exercise is a key determinant of overall health. People who exercise (and that includes people with arthritis) look better, feel better, sleep better, have more energy and endurance, and enjoy all the benefits of improved circulation and lung capacity—*and* they reduce their chances of having a heart attack. As researchers at New York's Columbia University reported in 1995, people with arthritis have a one-third higher risk of heart attack than others their own age, probably because people with arthritis are less likely to exercise and more likely to be overweight.

The answer (in addition to proper diet and nutrition) is to be active. It will even give your self-esteem and sense of accomplishment a boost, and, if you get your exercise as part of a group, it'll give you a chance to socialize, something arthritis often inhibits. That in turn can work wonders on depression and stress.

As if all that isn't reason enough to get out and kick up your heels, there's an even more important reason for exercise and activity. If you have arthritis, your aching joints encourage you to slow down to a complete halt; when you do, your joints become stiff and your muscles weak, and that makes it even harder to get moving. It's a vicious cycle: The less you move, the harder and more painful it is *to* move. If you keep a painful joint in a bent position for too long, it can lock—what's known as a contracture, which means the muscles and connective tissues are shortening through disuse. Over time, that can lead to loss of function and deformity.

Activity and exercise are also part of a joint and surrounding tissues' normal health processes. To begin with, the cartilage that covers the bone ends in a joint is mostly avascular, that is, it's not infiltrated with the network of blood vessels that enrich most other tissues, carrying nourishing oxygen to every part of the body. Instead, cartilage absorbs what it needs from synovial fluid: Each time you bend a joint or put weight on it, waste products are pressed out of the cartilage; as you relax, it fills like a sponge with oxygen and nutrients from the fluid filling the joint cavity. Thus, moving a joint is essential to keep cartilage healthy—and not just cartilage: Keeping a joint active also strengthens and helps maintain the flexibility and elasticity of the soft tissues surrounding the joint—the skin, muscles, tendons, ligaments, and bursae.

Arthritis and Exercise

The trouble is, for a lot of people, exercise and arthritis are mutually exclusive terms. It's especially tough for people with rheumatoid arthritis (RA) or other forms of inflammatory arthritis, in which the swelling and inflammation in a joint may make moving prohibitively painful. Even mild to moderate osteoarthritis (OA) can make exercise a daunting prospect.

"Arthritis takes you from being an active to an inactive person very quickly," says Dr. Marion Minor, a physical therapist, or physiotherapist, at the University of Missouri in Columbia. "The pain, stiffness, the fear of doing damage...Very often therapists and physicians caution you not to do too much."

Minor has a Ph.D. in human performance, a field she describes as "a combination of exercise, physiology, biomechanics and aging, so it kind of takes in most everything that's happening to all of us as we go through our lives." In North America, she says, "the major reason people report less physical activity than they'd like is because of arthritis. It has more of an effect than heart disease, diabetes, and lung problems."

Inactivity can cause illness all by itself: "You don't have to have anything else wrong with you when you sat down, but if you sit there for a week, you'll have lots wrong with you when you try to get up. Prolonged inactivity can make us sick and less able, and if we have arthritis to deal with, adding inactivity to the arthritis is really a bad combination."

One of the first problems physiotherapists see in their arthritis patients is muscle weakness: They can't climb stairs as well as they used to. They aren't as flexible. They're stiffer, it hurts to move their joints, and they tire faster than otherwise healthy people. Patients' cardiovascular fitness and overall health are also poorer after they've had arthritis for a long time, and they often suffer from fatigue and depression.

It used to be thought that such problems were simply the result of having arthritis, Minor says, but researchers found that those same problems developed in otherwise healthy people who were inactive for a long period of time: "Things do happen to our bodies as we get older and we lose some of our elasticity and flexibility. But, the more we learn about aging, and the more we learn about inactivity, the more we're also beginning to think it's the inactivity that makes us old faster than just getting more years."

We can't cure arthritis or aging but we *can* cure inactivity—simply by exercising. Minor used to tell people they needed to exercise twice a day for the rest of their lives, but she came to realize that there wasn't much *she'd* do twice a day—outside of brushing her teeth, perhaps—for the rest of her life. Not because of arthritis, anyway.

Instead, she began to encourage patients to be more active and exercise for fitness and health, a much more positive idea. The trick then became how to do that in spite of arthritis: "We can't let arthritis in our hips and knees and feet put our hearts and blood vessels to bed," she says, "because if we let that happen, we're going to have problems over and above our arthritis. If we can get more active and more fit, we get all the general benefits that everybody else gets when they're more active. Your heart's better, your lungs are better, you're able to maintain your weight and keep your calorie expenditure up so weight doesn't get to be a big problem, and you get more stamina and energy. You actually just feel better, more emotionally in control and can handle your stress."

Becoming Active

Minor's new approach was especially pertinent to people with OA. She began with aerobic exercise. "'Aerobic' just means doing exercise that uses your whole body," she explains, "and you keep at it for a little while. If you have arthritis, doing that kind of exercise and keeping up your flexibility and strength actually makes your cartilage healthier. It keeps your bones stronger and your joints stronger and more flexible. If you can move from being a sedentary person, a person who sits most all the time and doesn't have a regular activity pattern—you'll have made important strides to put yourself in a much healthier category of people."

And it doesn't take much. Minor doesn't recommend lung-busting, gut-wrenching athletics: She's talking about "the kind of exercise that's comfortable and enjoyable for you and that you can continue doing without getting too tired or too out of breath." You're not training for the Olympics; this is strictly low-key exercise for better health, and you should be able to have a conversation while you're walking. If you're alone, sing a song, recite a poem, or count—without getting breathless. "If you can do that," Minor says, "then you're exercising at a good moderate, healthy intensity. If you can't, you're working unnecessarily hard, you won't like the way you feel the next day, and you might as well just slow it down so you can keep on going."

Make your exercise regimen, whatever it happens to be, as interesting as you can. It may be general calisthenics in a group, walking, a stationary bike. If you prefer exercising alone, fine, but if you'd rather have the social interaction of a group, join one—take an aerobics class for people with arthritis, take up swimming, or join an Aquabics class (a pool program offered by The Arthritis Society). "If you don't like the word 'exercise,'" she says, "just think physical activity. Dance is a wonderful way: line dancing, square dancing, ballroom dancing—I have some people in our classes who do belly dancing as a form of aerobic exercise."

One advantage of exercising in a group is that you can ask questions of the leader or the other people in the group. Don't forget, if you haven't been using those joints and muscles, they're likely to complain, and it helps to have somebody around to tell you if those twinges you're feeling are normal or a sign you should slow down. It's also a good idea, if you can find the energy, to try more than one activity; that way, if one doesn't suit you, you'll still have the other activity to keep you going.

If there's something you enjoy doing but it exacerbates your arthritis, should you give it up? Probably not, but you may have to modify some activities so that you can keep doing them comfortably, and without doing harm to your joints. If you love bowling, for example, try playing fewer games or use a lighter ball. Rest up beforehand, and do range-of-motion exercises before you start. Whatever the activity you enjoy, look for ways to modify it so you don't have to give it up. Too often people become inactive because they've given up the recreational activities they love, which robs them of a treasured social activity. Find ways you can participate, even if it's only keeping score.

Minor has a favourite quote she uses to put things in perspective. It comes from an eighty-five-year-old rheumatologist who started running marathons when he was sixty-five. "He's got arthritis, and this is what he says about exercise and activity," Minor recounts: "'The weakest and oldest among us can become some kind of athlete, but only the strongest can survive as spectators.' He's talking about the dangers of inertia, inactivity, and immobility. As we get older and have other things happen to our health, it's more important than ever to try to keep our activity at a level that helps support our health, and if we let ourselves sit, then we add to our problems."

Therapeutic and Recreational Exercise

It's dismayingly easy to injure a joint already weakened or stiff from arthritis, so any physical activity should be entered into with a certain degree of caution. Check with your doctor or physiotherapist before joining a calisthenics class, but don't let your arthritis stop you altogether; you need exercise for that weakened joint, and you need it for your overall health.

Exercise can be divided into two general categories, therapeutic and recreational. Therapeutic exercise is prescribed by your physician, physiotherapist, or occupational therapist with specific goals in mind, such as increasing strength or flexibility or improving the function of a joint. Recreational exercise is more like play. It may include activities that are used in therapeutic exercise, such as swimming or walking, but its name says it all: It's designed to amuse and relax, as in games, sports, and some exercise classes. Because many types of recreational exercises help to improve muscle strength, improve joint range of motion, and increase stamina, they may complement a therapeutic program, but they can't replace it.

Therapeutic programs consist of strengthening and range-of-motion exercises, the former to maintain or increase muscle strength around a joint, the latter to maintain or improve joint movement, relieve stiffness, and restore flexibility. Both are designed to accomplish very specific goals. Strengthening exercises are either isometric or isotonic resistance. Isometric exercises are excellent for people who have especially painful joints (such as those with inflammatory arthritis), because you move the joint very little or not at all. In fact, you can do most of them without getting out of your chair: They simply involve tightening, or flexing, the muscles around a joint. Isotonic resistance exercises strengthen muscles by using light weights or other forms of resistance, such as pressing against a table or wall. Because they place joints under greater strain, they should only be done after you've been properly instructed by your therapist.

For exercise to be worthwhile, you have to do it regularly. Here are a few general guidelines to help you get in shape—without getting out of whack:

- Start with three days a week, and build up to three times a day, ten minutes each time. That should be enough to catapult you out of the couch-potato crowd. You don't have to start off doing ten minutes a shot: Build to ten minutes, and that may be a good goal for you.
- If you've been out of action for a while, start with simple movements and do them more slowly than you think you can, until you're sure of what you're capable of doing. You don't have to

go to the gym or the local track: Walk around the house a few times. Do two minutes in the morning, two at lunch, and two in the evening, then add a minute or two every week; before you know it you'll be up to ten minutes at every session.

- Don't push any joint you're exercising to the point that it becomes painful. Adopt a slow, steady rhythm that gives your muscles a chance to relax between repetitions, and don't overdo it. You'll know you've got a successful exercise program if you can do something for at least ten minutes while maintaining a conversation. If your muscles are aching two hours or more after you've finished exercising, or they're worse the next day, you've done too much. Slow down, do fewer repetitions, or find another form of activity that doesn't cause you any pain.

- Try to breathe steadily, inhaling through your nose and exhaling through your mouth, letting your stomach rise and fall with each complete breath. If you feel suddenly faint or dizzy or sick to your stomach, if you experience tightness or pain in your chest or severe shortness of breath, stop immediately. If the symptoms continue, contact your doctor.

- There may be times when especially painful joints force you to modify your regimen, or put it on hold for a few days. Check with your doctor about "working" through flares, when a joint or joints are acutely painful or inflamed (hot, swollen and tender). Because of the up-and-down nature of arthritis, there'll be days when the exercise you accomplished with ease yesterday is impossible today. Cut back on what you'd normally do and build back up gradually as your strength or flexibility returns. And don't be too hard on yourself if you *do* miss a day or two; just make sure you get back to your routine as soon as the flare subsides. Muscles lose their "tone" in a few days to a week, and it's easier to lose strength and flexibility than it is to restore it.

- Try keeping an exercise diary. Some people find it encouraging and a useful way of measuring their progress. Keep in mind that walking and other activities of daily living (sometimes referred to as ADLs) are important for your overall health, but they can't replace therapeutic exercises designed to increase or maintain a joint's strength and range of motion.

- Choose a specific time for your daily exercises, and stick to it. It takes a long while for something to become a habit, but any activity's easier to maintain once it has. Choose a time of day when you're not tired or generally experience the least pain and stiffness, or when your medication has the greatest effect. Try different times until you discover what works best. Most people find it tougher to exercise right after meals, for example; give yourself an hour or two after eating before you get to it.

- If you're doing fairly active exercises, make sure you "warm up" before you start with a little stretching to loosen and relax your muscles, and, at the end of the session, repeat the procedure to "cool down," the way sprinters work out the muscle strain after a race with a slow jog. You can ease the pain and stiffness in a joint with massage or hot and cold applications before exercising—but not *too* hot: Use only mild heat that's soothing on the skin, for about twenty minutes, or a cold pack in a towel for ten or fifteen minutes. You can also alternate hot- and cold-water applications. That's called a contrast bath: Soak your hands or other joint in warm water for three minutes, then plunge them into cold water for a minute, repeating the procedure three times. Some people prefer to take a real bath or stand under the shower for a few minutes, either before or after exercising, or both.

- Any kind of exercise you're going to do that involves being on your feet will be easier and more comfortable if you're wearing good shoes and insoles; they'll also help protect your joints. If your feet are already sensitive, think about having proper inserts made that will cushion and support them.

Should you engage in weight-bearing exercise and activity? It used to be that doctors advised against it if patients had OA in a joint, but we now know that even weight-bearing activity and walking—if it doesn't cause severe increased pain—can be an effective and safe way to exercise. "In our first research study," Marion Minor says, "we only accepted people who had weight-bearing arthritis, that is, arthritis in their hips or knees or feet. Those people walked and did aquatic exercise in the pool and didn't have any trouble. They didn't walk too fast or work too hard, and they did appropriate warm-up exercises to get ready to be more active. We also found that people who did moving exercises actually decreased joint swelling and pain.

"But choose activities that don't cause increased pain; if walking causes increased pain, then choose aquatics or a bicycle or something else that gets you ready to walk. Stairs are not a particularly good form of exercise for people with arthritis in their hips and knees. It puts a lot of stress on them, so keep stairs to a minimum and try to do other things for your cardiovascular health."

Range-of-Motion Exercises

Range-of-motion (ROM) exercises are the key to maintaining maximum range of motion and flexibility (not strength) in arthritic joints. They involve gentle movements that exercise each joint as fully as possible. Many ROM exercises can be done before you get out of bed in the morning, and some may alleviate the morning stiffness associated with certain forms of arthritis.

- Hands are most easily exercised on a tabletop, with your forearms and hands face down. Keeping your palms flat on the table, lift each finger and thumb (of both hands) one after another as high as you can without causing pain. Once all your fingers are up, raise your whole hand, bending it gently back, with your forearm still resting on the table.
- Exercise your wrists simply by slackening the tension in your fingers and bending your hand back and forth in all the normal range of motion, several times. Then relax.
- With your hands flat on the table and your fingers together, slowly slide your first finger toward your thumb and hold. Repeat the motion with your second finger, then the third and fourth, until all your fingers are together. Repeat three times.
- Hold your hand straight up, with the fingers extended. Now slowly bend the fingers down to your palm without bending the large knuckles. Open and repeat three times. For the thumb, hold your hand open, with the fingers straight. Reach your thumb across your palm and try to touch the base of your little finger. Hold, relax, and repeat.

- You can do your elbows lying down, with your arms lying close to your body. Keeping your upper arms flat on the bed (or floor), raise your forearms so that they're perpendicular to your body. Now rotate them slowly, so that you're looking alternately at your palms and the back of your hands. Repeat several times.

- Still lying on your back, with your arms flat at your sides, move them out, as though you're making "an angel" in the snow, then return them to their original position and repeat. This exercises one plane of motion for your shoulders. For another plane, stay flat, with your arms at your sides. Now raise one arm at a time through an arc directly in front of you until it's flat on the bed or floor over your head (as if, while standing, you tried to touch the ceiling). Return it to the original position, then repeat with the other arm.

- You can exercise your neck standing or sitting. Turn your head slowly so that you're looking over your right shoulder, then turn it back to face forward. Stop. Then turn it to look over your left shoulder. Repeat. Now try tilting your head to the side, so that it comes as close as you can bring it to your shoulder without pain. Repeat on the other side, and repeat both motions twice more. To work the back of the neck, tuck your chin down onto your chest and hold, keeping your neck straight (you should be able to feel the muscles on the back of the neck pulling slightly).

- For your back, stand with your hands on your hips and your feet shoulder-width apart. Swivel your head and shoulders to the right and hold. Return to face forward. Swivel to the left and hold. Repeat.

- You can exercise the muscles of the lower back in a vertical direction by lying on your back and trying to press your back into the floor. Hold and repeat.

- Sit up for the hips. Stretch your legs out in front of you, then roll them in, so the toes of one foot are pointing to the toes of the other foot. Then roll your legs in the opposite direction, so your toes are pointing away from each other.

- Also for the hips, lie flat on your back with your legs about six inches apart. Slide one leg out to the side as far as you can, keeping the toes pointed up. Slide it back, and repeat with the other leg.

- A variation that exercises both the hip and the knee is done from the same position, toes pointing up. Instead of sliding the leg out to the side, hold the knee straight and rotate your leg, so that your toes are pointing out. Hold and repeat with the other leg.
- You can work your knees while you're sitting in a chair. Make sure the chair is high enough so that you can swing your legs. With your thigh on the seat of the chair, raise one leg from the knee and hold it out straight in front of you, bending your knee back as far as possible (without pain, of course).
- Another knee exercise can be done while lying on your back with your legs extended. Bring one knee up to your chest and hold, then lower it slowly to the floor. Repeat four times, then follow the same pattern with the other leg.
- The "towel grab" is one of the best ROM exercises for the arch of the foot and the toes. Standing up or sitting, with a towel under your foot, try to pull the towel toward you, in bunches, with your toes. (You can get the same effect by trying to pick up marbles with your toes.)
- Sitting on the floor with your legs extended in front of you, rotate each foot in turn, describing circles in the air, first in one direction, then the other.

These are just a few of the many exercises that can be done to increase the joints' range of motion. For more exercises and proper instruction in performing them, consult a physiotherapist or occupational therapist. There are also modified strengthening exercises you can learn to do that will strengthen muscles around the joints, conferring greater stability as the muscles become stronger. Again, consult a therapist to ensure you're doing them without placing undue stress on arthritic joints.

Dance, Dance, Dance...

Just as the glories of dance conceal its aptitude for injury, so too does injury mask a less predictable potential: its use as therapy. Dance therapy exists in a host of incarnations; it's been used with AIDS patients as a form of physical conditioning; with the poor, the disabled, and the hearing-impaired to ease social and psychological problems; in kinesiology, to develop strength and flexibility; with people who have suffered neurological damage to re-establish proper motor function; and as a way of promoting mind-body centering.

Dance is the kind of activity that inspires unbounded enthusiasm in its devotees, and just because people have arthritis doesn't mean they should give it up, says Sydney Lineker, director of program development with The Arthritis Society's Consultation and Therapy Service: "I don't think there are too many kinds of dance they *shouldn't* do, really."

A light dance program can improve circulation, increase strength, and improve overall range of motion. Lineker does warn people to avoid abrupt, jerky or twisting movements on ill-supported or swollen joints, "but I don't think dancing generally puts a lot of impact on the joints, because it's fluid. And the socialization can't be underestimated. I think that's what keeps people involved and doing this as a type of exercise."

Lineker keeps limitations to a minimum. The chances are, if someone has arthritis, particularly RA, they're hurting before they step onto a dance floor. She advises these people to watch for "an unusual increase in pain or a sense the joint is swelling or feeling numb. You really have to listen to your body, and if something becomes painful that wasn't painful when you started, you'd want to stop.

"We're realizing that the benefits of being active and doing some kind of aerobic activity probably outweigh the risks of staying home and doing nothing—even if you have arthritis." A speaker at a recent physiotherapy seminar told Lineker and her colleagues that people need to hear, "'Do you have a prescription to sit at home and do nothing? Because we're advising you wrongly if we're making you feel that incapacitated.'"

Lineker's only caution is that you be sensible and don't do anything that will make you feel worse. If you're not sure dancing is appropriate, talk to a doctor or a physiotherapist. But basically, she says, "Get out there and live your life."

11

Widgets and Wizards

Occupational Therapy and Assistive Devices

In every matter that relates to invention, to use,
or beauty or form, we are borrowers.

—*Wendell Phillips*

Occupational therapists (OTs) with training and experience in rheumatology have a special role in the care and treatment of people with arthritis. They treat clients referred to them by a physician or other health professional by assessing joint function and evaluating all aspects of a person's activity—work, leisure, and self-care—so as to design ways to help them minimize or avoid disability.

Because of their arthritis, people may lose their ability to perform the everyday tasks they once did with ease. An OT can teach them ways to get around their disabilities, sometimes with assistive devices, sometimes with splints specially designed for resting or for working, sometimes simply by modifying their activities to reduce stress and strain on sensitive joints, or with advice on how to avoid fatigue.

A full assessment provides a clear picture of the client's issues, says Ilene Cohen, an OT with The Arthritis Society's Consultation and Therapy Service (CTS) in Toronto: "If they can barely move and can't get up and down from the couch or the toilet, that's where I start. I'll get them the assistive devices they need to help them function in their most critical activities. We do a total joint count and a functional inquiry in terms of range of motion, stress pain, and whether they've got effusions—swelling in the joints. We also do a history to find out how long they've had the disease, what kind of medical treatment and therapy they've had—so you really get a feel for where a person's at medically and what they've been through."

Education is a major part of the job—on two levels. In B.C., for example, OTs work as part of the outpatient day program team, the children's program, and the fibromyalgia program at the Vancouver, Victoria, Cranbrook, and Penticton clinics, teaching components of the osteo- and rheumatoid arthritis hand classes, as well as the hip and knee education classes. They also play a teaching role in the division's affiliate program, in which practising health professionals are trained in arthritis management at the Vancouver clinic. In that program, OTs, PTs, nurses, and social workers are given a general grounding in arthritis and are then split into groups for further training in their specialty, with special instruction in making and fitting splints and insoles.

A similar program operates in Ontario, both for practising health professionals (by mid-1995, more than a hundred OTs from across the country had been trained in arthritis management since 1977) and students in university health programs. Trainees are taught how occupational therapy functions as a discipline within the rheumatology program. "The treatment of rheumatology is multidisciplinary," Cohen says. "It affects everything. Physios have to know about OTs so they can make appropriate referrals, because OTs can have such a major impact on patients with arthritis. Within the last three or four years, we've started taking trainees out into the community with us to do assessments, to give them the other aspect of therapy and the reality of what these people go through and what their issues are in the community."

In practical terms, OT tasks can be divided into two categories: joint protection, including the use of splints and other protective devices, and energy conservation, which means adapting activities and learning principles to apply to any situation. Some of it is simple mechanics. Fatten the handle on a utensil, and you increase the surface area of the grip, which confers a noticeable mechanical advantage. Add a long handle to any kind of tool or utensil, and you ease the load by increasing leverage, thus reducing strain. Another simple trick: Let larger joints do the work instead of smaller ones. In other words, don't carry a purse or briefcase in a hand weakened by arthritic fingers if you can carry it over your shoulder with a strap.

"Part of OT training is task-analysis, breaking things down into their component parts and trying to problem-solve for those things," says Hazel Wood, regional director of the CTS in Toronto. "You might have an assistive device out of a catalogue, but it doesn't quite work for somebody with arthritis, because it may have been designed for somebody with another condition. So you've got to modify it, and another therapist might not think to do that or might not have the time."

If a client is having trouble with stairs, for instance, an OT would look at balance, perception, cognition, everything specific to the arthritis. Then they'd take it a step further: "Down the road, what's the prognosis? Do we expect the client's condition to worsen? If so, then we've got to build that into whatever assistive devices we recommend. OTs are trained to do that across the board, but the more you work with a certain clientele, the more you practise different things and come up with different ideas."

A major component of occupational therapy through The Arthritis Society, at least in Ontario and B.C., is the Outreach Program. In B.C., for example, where the program is most developed, OTs take turns driving to regional health clinics throughout the province twice a year, four weeks at a time. Once a year they also fly into remote areas for a week of assessments and treatment. The service is expensive (donor dollars make it possible), but in the long run it makes more sense to have an OT fly in to a remote area than to ask twenty-five or thirty patients to fly to Vancouver. Travelling can be an ordeal for people with arthritis, and the treatment may not be as effective as it is in their own community.

Visiting clients right in their own homes or workplaces allows OTs to assess the client's environment for problem areas and suggest modifications to make tasks easier. "We don't do renovations, but we do make recommendations," Cohen says. They can range from simple modifications—a raised toilet seat, half-steps on stairs, easy-access cupboards and counters in the kitchen—to major overhauls.

One major assessment, for a man with severe RA, was paid for by his insurance company. At $10,000, it's hardly a typical case, but it illustrates the effect such modifications can have. Before they were done, the man was totally dependent on his wife for every aspect of daily life; he couldn't even get out of bed by himself. Cohen recommended a long list of devices and renovations, from simple devices to major items, including a special wheelchair. She also suggested renovations to make the bathroom and various doorways wheelchair-accessible.

As a result, the man became basically independent. The initial expense was steep, but in terms of long-term health costs, it may well prove to be a bargain. The man's wife is freed to work if she wishes, and the man won't need attendant care for his daily needs. Nor will he need to be institutionalized, and the changes mean he'll be able to continue to work at home.

Not everyone's got ten grand for alterations, of course, but then all most people need is a little ingenuity.

Mother of Invention

When Jan Watkins was first diagnosed with RA, she went through the usual emotional sequence—fear, denial, anger, and so on—then got on with her life. It wasn't easy, and it didn't happen overnight. 1995 was the first year, she admits, that she managed to get off the roller coaster of depression: "I seem to have lost my downs, more or less, not because I've learned to control them but because I've learned to avoid them. I'm very realistic. People say, 'Oh, it's your attitude.' Well, attitudes change. What you've got to prove to someone is that they *can* do it."

Watkins has done it by ingeniously adapting every aspect of her house and lifestyle to the demands of her disease, while maintaining a steadfast refusal to be overcome by it: "My whole life now is how to meet the challenge of staying in my own home, which I want to do until I die. I've had endless people tell me I can't do this, and that makes it even more of a challenge. I've even got an advocate [her husband, from whom she's been divorced for twenty-five years], and if they tell me I've got to move out I tell them, 'Phone my advocate.'

"I take a very tough stand. You have to be tough to survive alone with a disease like this. Otherwise you get people who want to help, and they don't know that you're helping yourself. The tide is changing, to try to get people to stay in their own homes. I've got a life now that I've adapted to. I've made my house suit me like a glove, and there's no reason why I should fall or have an accident if I'm careful. If I *do* fall or have an accident, it's curtains: I couldn't live in this house on my own."

Watkins "probably wouldn't fit too many of the criteria" one would assume necessary for someone to manage alone with a chronic illness, says Hazel Wood. "Yet she's doing it. She sort of expands the definition. It's in society's interest to try to keep people at home. It tends to be cheaper, even if in the short run it doesn't look like it. You might say, 'Well, look, Jan needs all these different adaptations and so forth, and that costs money,' but if you break her spirit and she starts to lose her willingness to live, then what are the costs? You end up having social work come in and all kinds of other resources.

"I think we have to go with what people want, and they have to tell us how much safety and bother they're willing to compromise to stay at home. But then they also have a responsibility to put something back into the system. If people can afford it, personally I think there needs to be some sharing."

By just about any standard, Watkins is doing her share. Most pertinently, she goes to a great deal of effort to make her discoveries about adapting to arthritis known to as many people as possible, and her discoveries—in aids and adaptations to her environment—are no small matter. In large part, they're the main reason she's been able to pursue her ruling passion: the small forest of trees she's planted on her Southern Ontario property over the past decade or so, for which she was awarded a 1995 Niagara Escarpment Achievement Award.

For the first five-and-a-half years after she arrived from Cockney London over thirty years ago, Watkins planted whatever she could lay her hands on. It was a busy time: "That's when I did all the changes on my house, the plumbing, carpentry, fought with developers, taught full time, and planted like crazy. I never saw the inside of the house. I had no furniture and didn't want any. I was hardly ever in."

The pastoral whirl came crashing to an end in the early 1980s. Suddenly she couldn't turn taps, grip a doorknob. There'd been no warning, no redness or swelling, but she was diagnosed with fairly advanced RA. "I couldn't teach anymore, so I had to rent for five-and-a-half years." She returned in 1987, when her disease went into remission. "That's me then," she says, proffering a photo of a previous life: "You wouldn't recognize me, would you? I don't think I look fifty-three." The observation is apt, untinged by regret. "Now I look like ninety-three."

Watkins' assessment is confirmed by her shrunken frame, twisted hands, and feet left two sizes smaller by operations to remove eroded bone. She rises from her chair with painful slowness, her wrists are in splints, her hips and shoulders are terribly weak, and, in early 1996, both knees were replaced. Treatment with gold and prednisone was an agony of side effects—worse than the disease: "As luck would have it," she says, "I haven't been able to take these drugs, these immunosuppressives, so the disease has ripped through me. But at the same time, I've been able to maintain more mental balance because of it.

"Disability's got so many options if you're a person who thinks a little," she says. "Sometimes I look back and think, how did I think of all these things in three years? Necessity is the mother of invention, that's all. I've learned to adapt physically and now I'd like to try to help others. I'd like others to know it's not impossible."

There's no point wondering why arthritis has happened to you, she says: It's just the law of averages. "So, stop asking, 'Why me?' What you should be asking is, 'How can I solve this problem?'" For Watkins, it's an obvious question. A former high school math teacher with a degree in chemistry, Watkins worked for several years as a research assistant in the chemistry department at McMaster University in Hamilton, Ontario. Although her RA eventually cut the job short, it was good training in problem-solving, and she's put it to good use.

She still has the use of one finger and thumb on each hand, but she's slowly losing her grip—literally. She refuses to let it defeat her: "I've been so successful in the last couple of years that I say, 'It won't phase me. I'll think of something else.'"

A disabled person, Watkins believes, has to learn to do things for him- or herself. A healthy person can do everything ten times faster, but it doesn't matter—there's no rush. It's more important to learn to do things for yourself. If you come to depend on other people every time you drop something on the floor, you lose your independence and any positive self-image you may have had. So, she says, "why not devise a little method where you can pick it up yourself?"

Watkins uses a variety of reachers made from bamboo canes, with one-inch hooks or rings screwed into the ends: "I can pick up anything that's under, over, above with this," she says. "The purposes are a hundred fold, but you won't think of them until you can't do something." With a little careful manoeuvring, she can undo the Velcro fastenings and take off her shoes, and, she points out, demonstrating the technique, "when I'm standing behind my wheelchair, I can even take my brake off."

Watkins' house is a showplace of devices, many of her own creation or adaptation. Most favour function over form—a window handle, for example, has a ready-made extension: a vacuum cleaner crevice tool—but she argues that it's more important to be scientific than artistic. A portable half-step for climbing stairs is a box of empty Ensure cans tied and hauled with a string, improbably named "Dog." A friend made a comelier model out of wood for her, but it wasn't as light, and thus not nearly as useful. While OTs might balk at the "dog," Watkins defends the vertical strength of the empty cans, held in place by the box, lifted in stages with the knotted cord. It's not a thing of beauty, but it works.

In a closet, hangers are hooked on hangers to bring clothes down to a level her shoulders can handle; a board is levered into the open drawer of a dresser, providing table space next to the bed. In the kitchen there are endless devices: A vise attached to the end of a table grips an X-Acto knife in a cardboard sheath, a fixed blade for opening mail or intractable packaging. A butter knife hangs by a string from the handle of the fridge door. "Can you open your fridge with no hands?" Watkins asks, showing how: She wedges the blade between the rubber seal and the body of the fridge and simply leans on it to open the door.

"The general public doesn't understand what a lever does," Watkins observes, "and arthritics have to understand the lever if they're going to help themselves. Most of my devices have a little lever in them somewhere."

The patio door opener is another good example. "This was one of the first things I did, because I couldn't open this door," she says, pointing to a long wooden handle leaning across the door. The handle is tied by a string to the frame, to which it's held by a bolt at the bottom. Leaning against it causes the handle to press against a second bolt, set out from the frame of the door—the fulcrum of her lever—which in turn forces the door open. It's ingeniously effective.

Ilene Cohen believes most of Watkins' devices are "terrific; she has some excellent ideas." Cohen has the professional's concern, however, that some of Watkins' ideas might go astray in others' hands. She hesitates to endorse "the dog," for example, with its body of empty cans. While it might work for Watkins, she says, who's as light as a bird and very careful, it might be dangerous for someone heavier or less cautious. Still, Cohen says, "people can learn a lot from her; it's the principles that are important, not necessarily the individual devices."

Watkins has been compiling her inventions for the last couple of years in a pamphlet. "Practically everything in there," she says, "nobody else helped me with—*could* help me with—yet there are things I could not do without. Many I discovered; others I had to sit down and think about. What bothers me is, how many people are losing their homes because they can't do what I'm doing?"

Watkins has been working on that larger problem. One of her solutions is RAIV—Rheumatoid Arthritis InVentors—a not-for-profit forum designed to bring people with RA together to share ideas and solutions to problems with physical access. Watkins is eager to share her own inventions; her list, complete with photos and instructions, is available to anyone who asks (see Recommended Resources).

She's not trying "to get to the moon," she says, just stir up a few ideas. She'd like to see other people taking up the challenge of RA: "You've got to have something to stir your mind. If you can meet that challenge physically, if you can say, 'Yesterday I couldn't do that; today I can,' then you've achieved something in life you couldn't have done without the disease."

Watkins' latest enthusiasm is reserved for the Internet, which is "wonderful" (she can be reached at jwatkins@wchat.on.ca). Put aside your doubts and fears, she says; it's not as difficult as some people fear. A friend got her up and running in a matter of hours, and that afternoon her son in Vancouver received her first message via electronic mail.

She uses pencils gripped between the first and second fingers of each hand to peck out her messages. Her wrist splints help, and she's devised a style that allows her to type for up to an hour-and-a-half at a time, but it's still painful: "If you do the wrong things, it can be agony. You've got to work out solutions all the time.

"I don't like the word 'courage,'" she says, "and I hate to see the word 'brave.' I'm not courageous or brave—I'm just being very human. You don't know until you get a disease like this how strong the will to survive is. I've been through tough times before, so this is just one more awkward situation. You've got to know when you're beaten and give up. But never expect you're beaten and give up before you've proven it. If I have anything to say, that's the most important thing."

Finding Help

How's this for ironic? You can get professional training in everything from bricklaying to brain surgery, but the business of living—the trickiest, most important occupation of all—is pure amateur hour, extended indefinitely. Most of us bumble through without making too much of a hash of it, learning from example, advice and experience, but at the best of times it can be a pretty solitary affair. And when a disabling illness imposes itself on us, we may feel we've stumbled onto a lonely path indeed. Like an explorer thrust into suddenly rocky terrain, we may feel we're going where no one has gone before.

The fact is, there are few unexplored regions on the map of human experience, and those who have lived with disabilities have left plenty of markers. You just have to know where, and how, to find them.

Ilene Cohen illustrates the problem with the story of a woman she consulted who'd been taking sponge baths for years because her arthritis made it too difficult for her to get in and out of the bathtub. She was being seen by a rheumatologist, Cohen says, "so how come she slipped through the cracks? I think because she just didn't say the right stuff to the doctor to twig him that she was having problems managing."

If the woman *had* said something, the doctor could have referred her to an OT. She may not have realized there were solutions available, Cohen speculates, "so she didn't think there was anything she could do about it and just kind of puttered along." When Cohen *was* finally sent in, she immediately gave the woman a bathseat: "After years and years, she could take a shower. And it was so simple."

There's help to be had in the form of innumerable aids and devices that can increase your independence and make life easier—*if* you ask for it. Ask your doctor or nurse; ask your OT, physiotherapist, or social worker; ask any health professional you deal with. "There are so many alternatives to help people function better," Cohen says, and the number of ingenious devices available to help you cope with weak, stiff joints is almost unlimited. No matter what the nature of your disability, no matter what task you need help performing, it seems someone has been there and thought the problem through.

That said, we have to add a caveat: Just because you have arthritis doesn't mean that every piece of equipment made for people with arthritis is going to work for you. No one's joint function is exactly the same as anyone else's, and a tool or device designed for someone with mild OA may not be ideal for someone with severe RA—for that matter, it may not be equally suitable for two people with mild OA. Make sure the device you're thinking of buying works for you before you put down your money, Cohen advises. Otherwise you're liable to end up with a closetful of doorstops and paperweights.

If possible, have an OT visit you in your home to do an assessment of your needs and joint function before you go shopping for new devices: "People learn new ways of doing things by seeing OTs and explaining what hurts and *when*," Cohen says. "We can alter their methods or try new equipment that doesn't hurt so much."

OTs can also explain what's available; some may even have equipment to sell. The great advantage is that the OT can demonstrate how an item works. For example, Cohen says, "when someone walks into a medical-supply store for a raised toilet seat. The salesperson says, 'Well, how high do you need it?' And they don't know. That's the real advantage of home therapy: You can set them up with what they need, with what works. There are a lot of things people need that we don't supply, but we advise what to do and where to get them."

If you don't have access to an OT, keep in mind that you can try most assistive devices right in the store. Some suppliers will even let you take devices home for a trial run. "Usually these companies are pretty good," Cohen says. "Things like toilet seats they won't lend, but some places will let you rent."

By all means, consult the professionals—from the suppliers of aids and devices to the members of your health-care team—but don't be afraid to improvise. Many of the best solutions to disability impediments are engineered by individuals like Jan Watkins. Not everyone can be an inventor, but most people can contribute an idea or two, even if it's only in finding new ways to use existing tools and utensils.

How? Learn to be flexible. Discover ways to alter your lifestyle to meet the demands of the disease, and exercise as much ingenuity as you can muster to deal with the minutiae of daily life. From the time you wake in the morning ("How do I lift my stiff, aching body out of bed?") to the time you go back to bed at night ("I can't reach my toes—how am

I going to get my shoes and socks off?"), you may need a whole new bag of tricks to ease your burden—and your mind.

Ask your doctor for a referral to an OT for an assessment of your home or workplace, or take the initiative for yourself. Most large urban centres have design centres with model kitchens, bathrooms, and offices filled with cleverly engineered devices. If there's one near you, check it out; you may find something you can use, or you may be inspired by their ideas to create a few aids of your own.

There are lots of ways to adapt your environment. Start by making your activity centres, be it kitchen or workplace, as convenient as possible. Organize materials so you can reach them with a minimum of twisting and stretching, preferably from a seated position.

Beyond the lightweight and ergonomically designed housewares available—knives, scissors and clamps, touch-activated lamps, over-size buttons on the phone, and grab bars and nonslip mats for the bathroom—are all sorts of economical tricks. You don't have to buy expensive cutlery—build up the handle of your paring knife with tape; replace round doorknobs and taps with lever-type handles, or build them up with rubber grips or elastics.

Clothing is infinitely adaptable. Try Velcro fasteners in place of buttons, and equip zippers with pull rings for easier use. Loose clothing is easier to get in and out of. Slip-on shoes are preferable to shoes with laces, and shoehorns are available with extra-long handles, so you don't have to bend over. In winter, a long coat offers more protection for sensitive joints from the frigid air, and if it has large pockets, you may be able to dispense with a handbag or shoulder bag. For women, front-closing bras and wrap-around skirts are much easier to put on. Clothing in easy-to-care-for fabrics needs little or no ironing or hand washing.

Even your car can be adapted for ease of use: You can have a swivel seat installed, which makes getting in and out a snap; there are special "one-handed" seatbelts available; and you can avoid some twisting and turning by mounting a multipart rearview mirror. For stiffened hands and fingers, get a built-up handle for your ignition key and a padded cover for the steering wheel.

Arthritis imposes a lot of barriers on everyday life, but don't let it stop you. Staying as active as you can—mentally and physically—is a healthy way of dealing with the disease.

The Kindest Cut of All
Surgery

To do a great right, do a little wrong...
—William Shakespeare, The Merchant of Venice

Surgery isn't something any of us likes to contemplate, but it *is* something that some people with arthritis will have to consider. So, consider this: If you have advanced arthritis; if your life has become an endless round of medications for pain; if your ability to perform the simplest activities of daily life is steadily diminishing, surgery just might turn your life around.

Barry Baker, executive director of the Canadian Orthopaedic Foundation, recalls "a little old lady from Gander, Newfoundland," who participated in her community's annual Hip, Hip, Hooray walkathon (to raise money for orthopedic services and research) after having had joint replacement surgery. "Oh," she said, in an accent that was equal parts Celtic ancestry and blessed relief, "I left all me pain in the O.R. [operating room]."

For many people with arthritis, orthopedic surgery is an answer to prayer: an end to pain, and a renewed contract with life. The word "orthopedic" comes from the Greek words *orthos*, meaning straight, and *pais*, for child, a formulation designed to emphasize the childhood origin of many musculoskeletal problems. Orthopedic surgery is the surgical prevention and correction of those deformities; orthopedic surgeons are medical doctors trained in its practice.

The first thing to understand about orthopedic surgery is that it isn't an admission of defeat, says Dr. David E. Hastings, head of orthopedic surgery at Toronto's Wellesley Hospital, nor a last resort when all else fails. One patient's arthritis might best be managed with conservative measures, such as medication and physiotherapy, while another—someone with OA in one hip, say—might be better served, in terms of pain relief and functional improvement, with an artificial hip. As Hastings puts it, the idea of conservative *versus* surgical treatment is obsolete: "In many cases, surgery is the conservative approach and the denial of surgery is radical."

At the same time, most arthritis *can* be managed with conservative (that is, nonsurgical) measures alone—medication, rest, exercise, physiotherapy, perhaps assistive devices and modified activity planning. Almost inevitably that will be the first approach. By far, the majority of people with arthritis never require surgery.

The choice depends on what stage patients' arthritis is at when they're first assessed, says Toronto rheumatologist Dr. Arthur Bookman: "If they come in early enough, we'll set out a program for them to prevent progression of the disease through exercise, medication, weight reduction, and sometimes bracing. They'll usually not be interested in surgery until it's absolutely necessary, but then they may start coming back a great deal, and they may then be appropriate for surgery. If we feel the gains are worth it, we'll tell the patient."

Keep in mind that some people—especially those who aren't medically fit or who suffer from heart disease—are not suitable candidates for surgery. If surgery will entail a significant risk to life, beyond the normal risks of any surgery (such as infection), it will be ruled out. The success of any procedure also depends to a great extent on the patient's attitude and willingness to comply with post-operative physiotherapy or other rehabilitation programs. "We try to select our patients that way," Bookman says. "If I have an eighty-five-year-old lady who's bright, spry and well motivated, I might send her to have her knee fixed, but someone who sits in a chair all day and doesn't know how to do any exercises I'd keep away from surgery."

There's usually no rush. There are exceptions requiring immediate surgery—cases of infection, tendon rupture, or where bone displacement is placing undue pressure on a nerve—but, for the most part, arthritis simply isn't an acute condition, which is a good thing, given that it takes more than five months, on average, to get from your GP's or rheumatologist's office to the O.R. As long as you're not in any real distress and you don't have to wait *too* long, cooling your heels can actually be a good thing. It gives you ample time to prepare, physically, mentally, and materially; it also gives you a chance to monitor your condition, which may go into remission or stabilize at a tolerable level. However, if someone is becoming totally disabled, if a hip bone is rapidly disintegrating, say, most surgeons can bump a patient onto their urgent list, which will usually get the person into surgery within a few weeks.

Is Surgery the Right Choice?

Opting for surgery is a decision each patient has to make conjointly with his or her physician and/or rheumatologist and surgeon. Perhaps nowhere else in the management of arthritis is the team approach more important. The average GP sees more people with OA (which affects one in ten Canadians) than a rheumatologist (whose specialized understanding is essential in treating RA, which affects one in a hundred), but both are limited to the "conservative" management of musculoskeletal problems—that is, everything short of surgery.

While a GP will sometimes send a patient with OA to a rheumatologist for treatment, if either feels a patient requires surgery, says Bookman, usually that physician will go as far as making a diagnosis and determining what the main problem is, "then we'll refer the patient on to the surgeon we think most appropriate for the type of problem we're dealing with. The final decision as to whether the patient's actually going to be operated on is the surgeon's."

Rheumatologists and orthopedic surgeons may also exchange diagnostic expertise. A surgeon will occasionally send him a patient, Bookman says, "regarding a diagnosis or looking for conservative avenues of management, since surgery doesn't seem appropriate." On the other hand, if a rheumatologist feels there's some kind of internal problem with a knee, he or she may ask an orthopedic surgeon to do a second assessment, sometimes with an arthroscopic procedure.

"Each patient is an individual," says orthopedic surgeon Dr. Paul H. Marks at Toronto's Arthritic and Orthopedic Hospital. "Each situation, even with seemingly similar injuries, may be different in each patient, and the surgeon needs to be cognizant of that. He or she needs to spend time discussing the various options with the patient. What are the pros and cons of initially pursuing a conservative treatment? What are the risks and benefits of surgery?"

Marks stresses the importance of patient education. He'll often ask patients to come in for a discussion to educate them about all the risks and benefits. Then he'll ask them to go home and think it all over, write down any questions they may have, then come back again to talk them over. That way, he says, "they're fully educated. If the surgery is two hours, and the commitment for rehabilitation is six months—and both are equally important—the patient needs to be prepared for that. So, I spend quite a bit of time making sure all the cards are on the table and we're all talking the same language beforehand and there are no surprises. Then patients are motivated and they'll go whole-hog into their rehabilitation, which hopefully will improve their outcome."

What can you reasonably expect from surgery? The most important thing is reduced, often *no* pain in the affected joint, as well as improved function, mobility, and flexibility. No surgery—be it the repair of a torn ligament or a total joint replacement—can equal the capabilities of a normal, healthy joint, but it can free you from pain and restore a good deal of your functional ability.

Both OA and RA can sometimes be helped through surgical intervention. Because the disease process in certain types of either inflammatory or degenerative arthritis can result in, or in some cases be caused by, damage to the soft tissues surrounding a joint—including muscles, ligaments (which attach bones to bones), and tendons (which attach muscles to bones)—treatment may also include surgery in these areas, either as a preventative or corrective strategy.

Possible procedures include: a synovectomy, the full or partial removal of a diseased joint lining; resection, the removal of all or part of a diseased or damaged bone; osteotomy, in which part of the bone in a joint is cut away, allowing the joint to be realigned; arthrodesis, or fusion, of the bone ends in a joint; and arthroplasty, a full or partial replacement of the joint with artificial components, as in total hip or knee joint replacements. Other procedures are designed to repair damaged ligaments, ruptured tendons, and torn menisci, the cartilaginous pads that cushion knee joints. Some procedures require full, open surgery on a joint or the tissues around it; some can be dealt with arthroscopically, a relatively noninvasive technique in which tiny instruments are inserted inside a joint through small incisions.

Orthopedic surgery is less common in other types of arthritis. Beyond minor procedures, says Hastings, "there's not much place for surgery in gout" (though sometimes the pain and distress of a badly affected toe may be relieved by surgery). People with lupus sometimes suffer a complication called avascular necrosis in their hips (often as a result of prolonged treatment with prednisone), which causes joint degeneration. Most patients are good candidates for total joint replacements. Lupus patients are also prone to "lupus hand deformity," a problem that can often be improved through surgery.

In severe cases of ankylosing spondylitis (AS), hip and shoulder replacements may be employed, and major surgery is sometimes required to correct curvature of the spine caused by the disease. Unfortunately, in AS, the ligaments and tendons surrounding the vertebrae and connecting the spine to the ribs may harden and tighten, forming bony outgrowths that can overgrow and "freeze" a replacement joint, making surgery extremely difficult. In such cases, the patient will have to make the decision for or against surgery with his or her surgeon.

A Sporting Chance

Vancouver Canucks star forward Pavel Bure is one. Toronto Argonauts quarterback Doug Flutie is another. So is former Kansas City Royals outfielder Bo Jackson. They're just a few of the zillion-dollar athletes who've sustained injuries in the line of duty that prompted top-flight medical attention.

Sure, sports injuries to pampered athletes attract more attention than the local grocer's bum knee, but what's that to do with you? Plenty. Just as AIDS research got a huge infusion of interest and funding after Rock Hudson was stricken with the disease, injuries to star athletes can lead to new treatments for arthritis-related problems. As team doctor to the Toronto Argonauts football squad in the 1960s, for example, Dr. Robert Jackson revolutionized sports medicine with arthroscopic surgery, and, before long, the grocer's bum knee was benefiting, too.

At Toronto's Arthritic and Orthopaedic Hospital, Dr. John C. Cameron sees a lot of meniscal tears—one of the commonest injuries in sports (menisci are shock-absorbing pads that sit atop the femoral cartilage in each knee). Before arthroscopy, if a meniscus tore near the back of the knee, surgeons couldn't gauge the extent of the damage, so they'd remove the entire meniscus. "The problem is," Cameron says, "when you take the meniscus out, the surface area of contact between the femur and tibia gets smaller, so the load goes way up. Basic mechanics. The articular cartilage over the end of the bone can't tolerate that increased load, so it starts thinning, developing craters and holes and eventually disappears." The result? Arthritis.

With arthroscopy, surgeons can do partial menisectomies, which show promise of much better results. Compared to full, open knee surgery, Cameron says—which leaves a ten-inch scar across the front of the knee—arthroscopy leaves a little puncture hole. "We had a guy today who hasn't been able to straighten his knee for a month," Cameron says. "He's a carpenter, so he's been off work all that time. He should be back at work next Monday." With open surgery, he'd have been killing time for another month.

Dr. Marks is orthopedic consultant to the National Women's Basketball Team and the Canadian Freestyle Ski Team, and head orthopedic surgeon to the NBA's Toronto Raptors. About half of his practice is knee problems, the other half "shoulders and a smattering of other things you'd see in weekend warrior athletes, like elbows and ankles and back pain as it relates to sports injury."

A common sports injury is a full or partial tear of the anterior cruciate ligament in the knee. "If you follow those patients for ten or fifteen years," Marks says, "a significant percentage of them would go on to degenerative change in their knee with regard to the articular cartilage." Marks and colleagues are studying the synovial fluid in these patients' joints to try to determine which elements—proteins, for example—protect cartilage and which destroy it.

One interesting finding in their preliminary data comes from specimens they've taken from the "normal" knee in a patient with one bad knee. They've found that the proteins they're studying in the "bad" knee are abnormal even in the "good" knee. If true, that would suggest something new: a systemic component to OA.

The point is that, if you can identify patients at risk—"and these are very active young people who have injured themselves," Marks points out—"there may be a future for gene therapy or increasing the protective proteins in the knee to prevent degenerative change.

"We're not always dealing with high-level, elite athletes," Marks says. "Sometimes they're just recreational athletes or average people who want to keep active, but [injuries] affect their lives just as much as they may a professional athlete. In medicine, it's always better to try to prevent a problem than to try to fix it afterward. We can reconstruct a knee ligament, but to prevent the injury in the first place is a better strategy. No matter how good our reconstructions are, the gold standard is still the normal joint. No surgical procedure can reproduce that. I'm a surgeon and I like to operate, but my job is also to help people avoid operations if I can."

That's where the future lies, Marks says, "in preventative strategies, becoming minimally invasive with the things we do, trying to understand the biology of these systems and how we may be able to alter those things and prevent future wear and tear in joints. We're just on the eve of understanding some of these questions. There's a lot of work to be done, but the next ten or twenty years are going to be very exciting in medicine."

Arthroscopy: The Needle with an Eye

It took time and technological refinements for what people once called "the needle with an eye" to catch on in a big way. With one flexible tube equipped with a miniature camera and a light source, a doctor could identify a problem. With a second incision, and a second tube equipped with a surgical tool, he or she could effect a repair. "The market really came about with the ability to operate with the 'scope," Jackson says, "and the concept that if you can see pathology, if you can see something's wrong, you should be able to devise some way through another puncture wound to deal with it. So, operative arthroscopy and the treatment of torn cartilages and ligaments, the treatment of arthritis and so on—that all evolved with the development of the instrumentation."

With further miniaturization, arthroscopy may eventually be used in every joint in the body. Needle arthroscopes, which are even narrower in diameter than ordinary arthroscopes, are already being used, but their capabilities are limited and surgeons' enthusiasm still muted.

Needle arthroscopy is "being toyed with" in a number of centres, says rheumatologist Dr. Arthur Bookman at The Toronto Hospital, Western Division, "but it's a limited tool. The advantage is that the patient doesn't need a general anesthetic, and with the right equipment and setting it can be done in an office or an out-patient facility. It's mainly used for diagnosis and sometimes to flush things out, but they can't do much more than that. And the vision [that the needle 'scope provides] isn't as good, so it's not being used widely in Canada."

"Flushing things out of a joint" (it's called an arthroscopic lavage) is a helpful procedure in some cases. OA of the knee might be initiated by trauma, such as a torn ligament, or a congenital defect, such as bow legs, but the result is the same: Stress is applied unequally across the surface of the joint, causing wear, much as a loose or misaligned tire on a car wears. Over the course of time, minute fragments of cartilage are worn away and absorbed by the lining of the joint, which becomes inflamed and sore.

To relieve the source of the inflammation, Jackson and his colleagues sometimes do an arthroscopic lavage, flushing out the joint with a saline or lactate solution to rid it of the accumulated debris—some of which is microscopic in size—as well as all the enzymes produced by the body "to try to digest these little fragments." With an arthroscope, a surgeon can also mechanically smooth off any loose bits that are about to be shed into the joints, "so these people feel better immediately if you get them in the early stages of this," Jackson says.

The misalignment or instability that initially caused the problem hasn't been addressed, so flushing out a joint won't halt the disease process, but it can certainly delay it, and there's been no evidence of any harmful effects. The procedure can also be repeated, if necessary.

Patients are urged to take it easy for two or three days after the procedure—no shopping sprees or exercise—but after about a week or so they can do anything normally. "I don't ask them to stay in bed, and you don't splint their knees, and they keep walking and doing normal things," Jackson says.

In the meantime, the technology continues to inch forward. Newer, smaller cameras—weighing no more than an ounce or two—have been developed using fibre-optic applications. The next step will be even smaller, digital imaging devices that will make current lenses obsolete.

There are other new applications in development, including attempts with laser arthroscopes to "re-bond" injured tissues, rather than simply remove them.

It may even be that, because of its diagnostic capabilities and its potential to effect minimally invasive repairs of early arthritic damage, arthroscopy will confer preventative advantages: "Because we see things earlier," Jackson says, "before they become irreversibly damaged—if there's a small tear or chip in joint tissue, we can fix it with minimal intervention, so you don't run into problems of wound healing and complications of major surgery. So, we may see in the next few years a significant decrease in the amount of degenerative arthritis of the knee."

Surgery Sites

Back and Neck

As many as 80 per cent of all Canadians—even the rich and famous—will suffer from a back problem at some time in their lives, but surgery, which might be seen as a definitive means of "fixing" mechanical shortcomings of the back, is seldom an alternative, says Ottawa physiotherapist Rob Karas: "When surgery is used for the right reasons it's very effective, but that's a very low percentage."

Ottawa orthopedic surgeon Dr. Donald Chow agrees. He recommends back surgery for only a minority of patients. "I look at a spinal surgeon being able to do three things," he says: "If nerves are compressed, we can decompress them. If there's abnormal motion—called instability—in the spine's joints, we can stabilize the spine by fusing these joints. And if an unstable spine moves into an abnormal position or alignment, we can realign it."

Except in such cases, Chow says, the best strategy is physical fitness, monitored and maintained independently by the patient. He offers the same advice to recovering surgical patients, who are no less in need of taking charge of their own health: "It's important that patients realize that a lot of their care is really up to them. We could do beautiful surgery on a bulging disc, but if you don't get yourself into shape, or you continue to lift improperly or sit too long at your desk, you may wind up with more back problems than if I were to send you out gardening without any surgery."

While the majority of neck and back problems have relatively straightforward causes and solutions, some complex, serious conditions can occur. Osteoporosis, chronic thinning of the bones, can weaken the vertebrae, predisposing them to fracture under stress. In rheumatoid arthritis (RA), the vertebrae of the neck can become unstable and shift out of alignment, putting pressure on the nerves in the spinal column. In such cases, arthrodesis (fusion) may be the only solution.

Other arthritic disorders related to the spinal column may be even more subtle. Some, such as osteomyelitis, can result from a bacterial infection; in RA, the body's immune cells attack healthy joints, including those of the back. Ankylosing spondylitis is a form of arthritis affecting the lower part of the spine that can fuse its various parts. If identified early enough, anti-inflammatory medication and strengthening exercises may prevent permanent deformity, but in extreme cases leading to kyphosis (excessive curvature of the spine), a vertebral osteotomy — removing a wedge of bone from one or more vertebrae—may be helpful, though it involves a risk of paraplegia.

Lumbar spinal stenosis is narrowing of the spinal canal as a result of osteoarthritis. It begins with pain in the legs and buttocks that's relieved by bending forward at the waist (the so-called "simian stance" some people assume to avoid pain). The condition, which can result from overuse, injury or aging, causes joint cartilage and intervertebral discs to deteriorate, so nerves in the spinal canal become compressed, causing pain in the lower back and legs. In extreme cases, a laminectomy may be done to remove bone and soft tissues encroaching on the spinal canal. Because of the possibility of damage to the spinal nerves, though, this is one case where surgery *is* almost always a last resort.

Shoulders and Elbows

"The shoulder joint's a little different from most of the joints in the body," says Toronto orthopedic surgeon Dr. Paul H. Marks. "Unlike the hip, which is a ball and socket and really quite stable, the shoulder joint is more like a golf ball on a tee. It's very shallow and has quite a universal range of motion, more than most any other joint in the body."

Because of its structure, the shoulder depends on the surrounding soft tissues to maintain its stability, including the rotator cuff and biceps tendons, and the capsular ligament, which completely encircles the synovial capsule and the joint within it. Inside the joint capsule, various ligaments act as static stabilizers, holding the shoulder in place, while small fluid-filled sacs called bursa reduce the friction between tissues and bone.

Because the shoulder isn't a weight-bearing joint (though it sustains a good deal of force from lifting and repetitive activity), it usually isn't subject to the same kinds of wear-and-tear degeneration that leads to OA in the hips and knees, nor is it as frequently affected by RA as some other joints. However, repetitive motions can wear and irritate some of the soft tissues that enclose the joint (such as the rotator cuff tendon, which can be affected by overhead motion, as in tennis players and baseball pitchers), causing synovitis (inflammation of the synovium), tendonitis (inflammation of the tendon), or bursitis (inflammation of the bursa), and a number of surgical approaches have been developed to deal with them. Inflamed synovial tissue (the joint lining) can be removed (a synovectomy), either through open surgery or, less invasively, using an arthroscope; eroded cartilage can be excised and the joint surfaces "debrided"—smoothed and cleaned out; even the bone surfaces can be shaved down (an achromioplasty) to make more room for a compressed tendon.

Before a surgeon operates, of course, he or she is likely to try a range of conservative strategies, including aggressive, active physiotherapy, anti-inflammatory medications, modifying activities, or employing various devices that might help the patient. Usually only after conservative treatments have failed do they consider surgery.

There are a number of different factors that come into play in terms of "overhead" athletes who injure themselves. Usually the problem isn't as serious as a fracture or a dislocation of the joint—a major trauma or a macrotrauma; it's more often what doctors call a microtrauma, or repetitive microtrauma. Although microtraumas may not be serious in themselves, over time they tend to accumulate, and their cumulative effect is to cause injury to the various structures of the joint. "It's sort of like taking a paper clip," Marks says. "You get so many bends out of it and then it just breaks."

The rotator cuff, for example, is a sheath of muscles and tendons that cover the scapula, or wing bone (the shoulder blade), where it meets the clavicle, or collar bone. Because the shoulder's not a deep ball-and-socket joint like the hip, it's dependent on the soft tissues that surround it, as well as various ligaments within the joint capsule, to maintain its stability. Performing any repetitive activity that puts undue strain on those tissues or takes it above what Marks calls "a certain threshold of repair," may cause microtraumas. The tissues may become inflamed, as in tendonitis, or become worn where the rotator cuff tendon passes under the roof of bone called the achromium, which forms a point in the shoulder where it connects with the collarbone. With each repetitive motion, the tendon gets caught under that roof of bone. Over time, if it isn't given a chance to recover, it can cause injury.

Sometimes tissues become stretched as a result of repetitive microtrauma. As the shoulder loosens over time, it may develop subluxation, in which the bone ends no longer meet properly in the joint (as opposed to dislocation, in which the joint pops right out and a doctor has to put it back in). Because the joint doesn't have the static ligaments or structures to hold it in place anymore, the other structures—such as the rotator cuff and biceps tendons—try to take over that function, and they have to work overtime to keep the ball on the golf tee, Marks says, "and they sometimes develop tendonitis or wear and tear.

"It's a complex system. We're just starting to understand the mechanics of all of this. Certainly degenerative change or osteoarthritis in the shoulder is less common than we might see in some of the other joints, for example, the knee."

One of the most common examples surgeons see of arthritis in the shoulder is in patients who've dislocated a shoulder and then had surgery to strengthen and tighten the surrounding tissues to keep the humeral head from popping out again. Sometimes, though, surgeons are *too* efficient: Studies now show that over-tightening shoulder muscles can accelerate arthritic change in the shoulder. The patients' shoulders don't dislocate anymore, but ten or fifteen years down the road some of them develop degenerative change, or OA. Thus, doctors are far more cautious than they once were in surgeries to repair shoulder instability.

Rotator cuff tears are sometimes seen in patients in their thirties, after falls and other accidents, but they're more often associated with patients in their fifties and beyond. Again, there may have been an earlier accident that's eventually led to pain in a shoulder. Over time, the normal shoulder mechanics are out of whack, and there may be some degenerative change as a result.

The predominant criterion for operating is pain, and surgery can usually do "a pretty good job of settling down those symptoms," Marks says, but there are no guarantees that surgery will improve function. Even if they can reconnect a tendon and get it to heal, the muscle quality may have atrophied so much that the patient never regains full muscle strength, which is what often happens with baseball pitchers: The surgeon may be able to control or reduce the symptoms for a while, but if the pitcher gets back up on the mound and starts hurling, the injury will almost certainly recur.

If the articular cartilage in a shoulder joint is completely worn out, the patient may be a candidate for a total joint replacement, as a result of OA in someone in his sixties or seventies, perhaps, or earlier in someone with RA. While total shoulder joint replacements still aren't as common as hip or knee replacements, they're now considered a good option, and they're improving in their sophistication and mechanics.

A complete prosthesis consists of a humeral component—a ball on a stem composed of various metal alloys that's inserted in the humerus, or long bone of the upper arm—and a plastic socket that replaces the glenoid cavity of the scapula. When the socket is replaced, most often the plastic insert is cemented in place, though sometimes it's only necessary to replace the humeral component. If the synovial capsule is inflamed, it may be removed during the surgery, but it generally will at least partially regenerate. Whether or not it becomes inflamed again depends to a great extent on whether or not the inciting factor can be arrested. The inflammation may be part of a cycle of irritation, pain, and swelling that has to be broken with physiotherapy, anti-inflammatory medications, or cortisone injections.

Replacing an elbow with an artificial implant is more problematic than a shoulder. The elbow is a ginglymoid, or hinge joint, an articulation between the upper ends of the two bones of the forearm (the radius on the thumb side, the ulna on the pinkie side) and the lower end of the humerus of the upper arm. The functional demands on the prosthesis are extreme. Not only does it have to provide a wide range of motion and rotation, it has to provide a good deal of leverage, too, and because the hands are used so much there's always a risk of the prosthesis loosening.

Elbow surgery's also complicated by the proximity of the nerves that pass over and under the joint to the hand. A misstep in the O.R. could leave the patient with a good deal of stiffness of the joint after surgery, or even nerve damage. Surgeons have to be extremely careful during any elbow operation that they don't injure or leave one of the three main nerves in the arm (ulnar, median, and radial) inappropriately aligned with the bones of the joint. The ulnar nerve may be the biggest problem. It passes from the upper arm over the elbow and down the ulnar side of the forearm, carrying sensation to the pinkie and ring finger. Any abnormal pressure exerted on the ulnar nerve can cause pain and pins and needles (think of knocking your "funny bone") or weakness and clumsiness in the fingers, sometimes resulting in permanent damage.

Occasionally abnormal pressure on the nerve can be relieved through an operation called ulnar nerve transposition. During a forty-five-minute procedure, the nerve is transferred from its normal position at the back of the elbow joint so that it runs across the front of the elbow. Physiotherapy will be required after surgery to strengthen the muscles around the elbow, but the patient can usually resume normal activities after about six weeks.

Tennis elbow (properly known as lateral epicondylitis) is a repetitive strain injury that affects not only tennis players, but anyone— labourers, carpenters, even dentists—who overdoes any activity that places undue strain on the muscles and other soft tissues of the elbow, causing them to become swollen and inflamed. Usually only conservative treatment is required, including rest, physiotherapy, and sometimes inflammatory medications, but if there's severe tendonitis, a minor arthroscopic procedure may be employed to relieve the condition. In even more serious conditions, a tendon transfer may be required, in which the affected tendon is detached from its normal point of attachment to a bone and reattached in a different place. This allows a different muscle to take over the work of a muscle that isn't working properly, but it usually takes several months before the patient learns to use the new muscle properly.

Despite the technically demanding nature of most shoulder and elbow surgery, patients are generally satisfied with the results. Surgeons now have nearly thirty years of experience to draw on, and refinements are constantly improving techniques and equipment.

Hands and Fingers

Given that your hands account for a quarter of all the bones and joints in the body, it's not surprising that a lot can go wrong, and it's not just joints and bones, of course: each joint is secured by ligaments and encased in a synovial capsule. In addition to the small intrinsic muscles within the hand itself are long muscles that flex and extend the fingers; they originate in the forearm, and are attached to the fingers by tendons that pass through sheaths and pulleys across the palm or the back of the hand.

Rheumatoid arthritis (RA) is the most common cause of problems in the hands, though other forms of arthritis, including osteoarthritis (OA) and lupus, also attack joints in the hand and wrist—in a number of different ways. One of the most common changes is joint subluxation, in which bones shift out of alignment, not quite meeting, not fully dislocated. A problem that's often seen in rheumatoid hands is ulnar

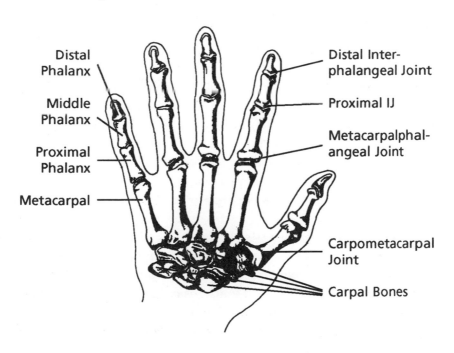

Distal Phalanx

Middle Phalanx

Proximal Phalanx

Metacarpal

Distal Inter-phalangeal Joint

Proximal IJ

Metacarpalphal-angeal Joint

Carpometacarpal Joint

Carpal Bones

drift, a deformation at the MCP joints that causes the fingers to turn out toward the little finger. Despite the name, there's little that's graceful about swan neck deformity, in which a PIP joint bends backward while the DIP joint flexes. In another problem with an elegant name—boutonnière deformity—the PIP joints remain fixed in a bent position, with the DIP joint straight or bent backwards. More prosaic, dorsal tenosynovitis refers to swelling of the long tendons on the back of the hand.

Depending on the deformity, there are a number of surgical procedures possible, including a synovectomy, which is the removal of an inflamed synovial capsule in a finger or wrist joint. In an osteotomy, the surgeon excises a wedge from a bone to realign it with the bone it meets in a joint. Arthrodesis is a slightly more radical procedure, in that it fuses the bone ends of a joint together, eliminating any further movement in the articulation, but also pain. Arthroplasty is a full or partial joint replacement with an artificial implant.

OA and RA generally affect different joints in the hand. In RA, the MCP and PIP joints—the two largest finger joints—are involved. In OA, the MCP joints are usually unscathed; it's the DIP, or small, joints—the fingertips—that bear the brunt of the attack, and only occasionally the PIP joints are affected, too.

For all the surgical advances of recent years, hand surgery in RA still has a long way to go. "We can relieve pain and we can relieve deformity," says Dr. David E. Hastings, head of orthopedic surgery at Toronto's Wellesley Hospital, "but the amount of function we improve is not high." The problem is especially acute in RA, because it's a progressive disease: "Very often, you operate on one set of joints, like the MCP—the big knuckles—and then the patient gets active RA in the smaller knuckles. You may have got everything lined up fine, but their hand doesn't work any better because the next line of joints down, or maybe the wrist, is acting up."

The only total replacements Hastings does in the hand are silastic implants—made of silicone—for the MCP joints. The silastic implant works like an internal splint, holding the fingers more or less in alignment until the soft tissues heal. It functions more as a spacer than as an artificial joint. "Artificial joints in other areas of the hand in RA have been singularly unsuccessful," he admits, partly because the quality of bone in people with RA is too poor: "If you put in a hard metal hinge, the bone just collapses around it. They just don't work."

Hastings rarely operates on osteoarthritic deformities in the PIP joints at the ends of fingers. "Those run a course," he says. "They hurt for two years or so, then tend to stiffen up and almost fuse themselves. You're left with knobbly looking ends to your fingers, but functionally they're not bad. And the pain goes."

In lupus patients, there's a hand deformity that can be quite severe. It resembles rheumatoid deformity, Hastings says, "where it looks like there's ulnar drift and the hand is sort of closed up." In lupus, though, articular cartilage isn't destroyed. Instead, the tendons and ligaments shorten. To correct it, Hastings developed an operation in which he excises about a centimetre of bone from each of the metacarpals: "That allows the tendons and ligaments to stretch out, and the hands look virtually normal, with nothing plastic in them. Functionally it's quite important, and the patient ends up with very good-looking hands."

Hips

Three days before Christmas 1994, singer/dancer Liza Minnelli checked out of a Los Angeles hospital, eager to be with friends and family for the holidays. If she could have danced with joy—a step or two from *Cabaret*, perhaps—she would have, but Minnelli made her exit on crutches, five days after having had one badly deteriorated hip replaced with an artificial implant. "I feel so much better I can't tell you," she told reporters. "I suffered with degenerative arthritis for ten years and never told anyone. I was ashamed of it. I don't know why."

It was pain that finally convinced Minnelli, forty-eight, to have her traitorous hip replaced. No doubt the absence of pain after her operation made her wonder why she'd waited so long, but then she'd hardly be alone in that: Lots of people put off hip surgery until they can barely walk, until they wake up at night when they roll over in bed. Yet for most of the thousands of people who have the procedure done every year, a new hip is a new beginning.

From one perspective at least, it's not a bad idea to put it off as long as you can. It doesn't make sense to leave it until you're *in extremis*, but, because artificial hips are only expected to last ten or fifteen years (perhaps longer with current implants), your doctor will try to prolong the life of your existing hip for as long as possible with conservative measures, such as medications and physiotherapy.

That, says Dr. Maurice A. Bent, chief of orthopedic surgery at North York General Hospital in Ontario, "lessens the chance that they're going to require a revision"—that is, a second operation to replace a deteriorated implant. "If you have to have it done when you're fifty, you can virtually be guaranteed that you're going to have to have it revised at least once in your lifetime."

A hip *can* be done more than once, but it's never as good the second time, and it's worse the third time. The bone stock isn't nearly as good, plus the risks of infection and other complications are much higher every time you go through the same scar and tissue.

Believe it or not, artificial hips have been in use for over a hundred years (nineteenth-century surgeons used prostheses made of ivory and glass), but the procedure wasn't a big success until the 1960s, when British surgeon Sir John Charnley developed a prosthesis with a polyethylene socket that was cemented with methylmethacrylate, a dental glue. The glue is specially formulated to help implants, be they artificial hips or dental inlays, keep their grip in a moist environment.

Hip implants have been greatly refined since Charnley's time, but his basic design is still used today: a molded polyethylene cup implanted in the worn-out hip socket, or acetabulum, and a stainless-steel ball—which fits into the cup—attached to a stem that's inserted into the length of the femur, or thigh bone.

Implant components can be cemented, uncemented, or a combination, a choice determined by the patient's age and physical condition. Neither glue nor cement, implant adhesive works like the grout in bathroom tile, Bent says. "It's a space-occupying material with minor adhesive capability. Its real function is to fill the space between prosthesis and bone." The liquid cement flows into minute cavities and cracks in the bone surface, creating a finely bonded, rigid enclosure for the stem of the prosthesis.

Uncemented models have a porous surface that allows bone to actually grow into the implant over time. It's usually chosen for a younger patient, who presumably will need at least one revision, because it's easier to remove than cemented models. The down side is that it takes longer for the bond to become secure and the patient to regain full function, but a younger patient's bone generally grows more quickly into the prosthesis. Elderly people have softer, more osteoporotic bones and, while they will get some ingrowth, it may be more fibrous soft tissue that doesn't calcify as effectively. In addition, Bent says, "the basic bone structure on which we're laying the prosthesis isn't as strong, so there's a greater risk it may crack or be a problem. Most people over the age of sixty-five would have a cemented prosthesis, at least a cemented femoral stem, and many people under sixty-five would have an uncemented prosthesis."

Again, it depends on the patient's physical condition: "You could have a sixty-five-year-old who's quite osteoporotic, has had a very sedentary life and never exercised, and the bone may be of very poor quality. Conversely you might put an uncemented prosthesis in a seventy-year-old who's jogged all his life and has excellent bone quality." (The Queen Mother walked out of hospital, using a pair of canes, after having had a hip replaced in late 1995—at age ninety-five.)

Patients are usually urged to get up on crutches the day after surgery, which takes about three hours. For the first four weeks, they only put "featherweight" pressure on the new hip, gradually progressing to canes, then one cane, after a few months. "Usually I'd encourage them to use a cane for at least three months after the surgeries," Bent says.

What can you expect of your new hip? Relief from pain, first of all, then gradually improving functional ability. High-impact sports are out, but occasional doubles tennis might be OK, and swimming, bicycling, even golf, shouldn't be a problem. Get your surgeon's approval before you leap back into the fray, but you should be able to expect "pretty normal living," Bent says, "except you have to remember you have an artificial hip that's not part of you. It's fixed in place by bonds that can be broken down by repetitive, excess movements."

There'll be a long period of adjustment—up to a year in most cases—with several months of regular physiotherapy to get muscles and soft tissue back in shape, but most people can expect dramatic and long-lasting results. "We now have what we think is a better stem design and better cement technology, and many of these new hips may last more than fifteen years," Bent says. "But how much more—twenty? twenty-five years?—we just don't know."

Knees

The knee has been called the "prince" of joints. Perhaps, as Dr. Allan E. Gross suggests in his 1989 book, *Surgery, A Complete Guide for Patients and Their Families,* that's because it's "pampered with tape and braces and revered by those who love to flaunt their knee incisions like duelling scars."

On the other hand, it might be because the knee is complicated, easily hurt, and difficult to replace. Unlike the simple but well-protected ball-and-socket of the hip, the knee is exposed, a masterful hinge joint able to bend (flexion), straighten (extension), and capable of about ten degrees of rotation inward and outward.

The knee consists of three bones: the lower end of the thigh bone (the femur), the upper end of the shin (the tibia) and the knee cap (patella); one surface of each is protected with cartilage where they meet. There's also a pair of cartilaginous half-moons in each knee atop the cartilage of the femoral heads that act as shock absorbers. The joint cavity is enclosed in a synovial capsule filled with viscous lubricant.

On either side, the capsule is reinforced by strong connective tissue—the medial (inner) and lateral (outer) collateral ligaments. The posterior and anterior cruciate ligaments strengthen the joint from its interior. Stabilizing the knee over all these other tissues are two major muscle groups, the quadriceps in front and the hamstrings behind.

A chronic injury in one or more ligaments—a partial or complete tear, for example—can lead to instability in the knee, which may cause a misalignment of the bones in the joint and, eventually, osteoarthritis. These can often be repaired, but research suggests that even after ligament reconstruction some patients are still at risk of developing degenerative change.

Cartilage (and sometimes the menisci) that's eroded in the knee by arthritis leaves the bone ends exposed. They may become "eburnated," polished and smooth from rubbing together. Because the bone ends have a rich nerve supply, that rubbing eventually becomes very painful and the knee extremely stiff. Any kind of weight-bearing—standing, walking, climbing stairs—becomes almost unendurable. Surgery may be the best answer.

There's a variety of approaches, depending on how advanced the degeneration is. (Most are also applicable to the hip, as well as other joints.) Fusion, for example, fixes the joint in place, bone to bone. While the joint will no longer bend, fusion does relieve the pain.

For RA patients, occasionally a synovectomy—removal of the inflamed lining of the joint, which is often done arthroscopically—can in some cases slow down the progress of the disease into adjoining tissues and postpone more radical surgery. Removing the lining eliminates the major source of inflammation, "and hopefully the cartilage can be preserved," says Gross. The operation is generally only successful for very early disease in a relatively healthy joint: "Once the cartilage is destroyed, a synovectomy doesn't help." The synovium will regenerate after surgery, but it may redevelop with the disease process intact, and although the operation can be repeated, Gross says, "it probably won't be that rewarding."

Another procedure sometimes helpful in the early stages of arthritis is an osteotomy—cutting and realigning the bones so that some of the patient's weight (in hips and knees) is shifted onto good cartilage. (The procedure is occasionally performed in lupus patients with minimal disease involvement.) A metal brace holds the bone in position until it heals, usually in eight to twelve weeks, with optimum improvement about a year after surgery. If it's done early enough, an osteotomy may delay or even eliminate the need for total joint replacement.

Total knee replacement is still a relatively young procedure, trailing hips by a decade or so, but the technique has definitely caught up: Total knee surgery now achieves results as good as total hip surgery. Where total knees are sometimes less successful is in RA patients who have multi-joint involvement, says Dr. Hastings: "If you hear of somebody who's very unhappy with total knees, it makes you wonder if she's got bad hips. If you have that combination—bad hips, knees and feet— you've got to really look at your priorities." In other words, if several joints need replacing, it may be best to begin with the largest joints (hips) before proceeding to the knees and ankles.

Surgeons prefer to postpone knee surgery as long as possible with conservative strategies, unless the patient is in severe distress. As with any total joint replacement, the less often a revision is necessary the better. Any surgical procedure involves a risk of infection, though that's becoming increasingly rare, and in hip and knee surgery blood clots can form in the legs, which can break off and travel to the lung, causing a pulmonary embolism. Normally blood thinners are administered to prevent the problem.

A total knee joint procedure is an exercise in cabinetry. A ten-inch incision is made in the front of the knee, carefully skirting the tendons and muscles that hold the patella in place. Once the joint is exposed, the end of the femur is shaved, using guides and cutting blocks, to fit the femoral component. (It may or may not have a stem, depending on the quality of the patient's bone.) The tibia is similarly prepared to receive the tibial component, which has a stem cemented or press-fitted into the shaft of the bone; a plastic plate is added on once the metal component is fitted in place of the original cartilage. The back of the patella is shaved to receive another plastic plate that's moulded to fit the groove in the femoral component. If the synovial tissue is inflamed, it's usually removed.

The procedure takes about two hours, with components snugly fitted and bones correctly aligned: Perfect alignment reduces the possibility of uneven wear and maximizes the "life" of the new joint. Tubes are left in the wound for a day or so after surgery to drain excess blood, and the knee is wrapped and cooled with ice-packs or small refrigeration units to reduce blood loss. Patients remain in hospital for a week to ten days, undergoing intense physiotherapy and perhaps pool exercise. Physio will continue on an out-patient basis for four to six weeks to help the patient regain maximum range of motion; the patient is also tutored in exercises to be done at home for several months afterward.

Because the knee is so much more complex than the hip, rehabilitation and recovery require a greater effort on the patient's part, and there are greater limits on the activities he or she will be able to do, but swimming, golf, even a little slow dancing shouldn't be a problem.

Feet

RA is also a common source of foot deformity, says Dr. Bent, "and we do various procedures for it, depending on the problem, including arthroplasties and fusions."

A common procedure is excisional arthroplasty of the metatarsal heads—the ends of the long bones in the foot (that is, replacing one or both of the bone ends of inflamed joints with a prosthetic implant): "RA patients often have deformity in the metatarsal-phalangeal joint due to excess pressure, and an excisional arthroplasty may help a great deal. If they get metatarsalgia [pain over the metatarsal bones] from pressure under a metatarsal head, we usually do an osteotomy of the metatarsal and just let it come up and get out of the way a little bit, so they don't get the pressure on the plantar surface [sole] of their foot."

OA is very uncommon in the foot, Bent says. "It's usually in the metatarsal phalangeal joint of the big toe—hallex rigidus—which just means osteoarthritic change in that joint." It can occur at any age, sometimes from an injury like stubbing your toe. Usually the bony overgrowth will be removed, which should relieve the pain. "It's a simple or early procedure, often very successful," Bent says. "If that fails, we might take away all this roughened bone and fuse the joint so it doesn't move, or do an incisional arthroplasty, which removes a bit of the proximal phalanx and creates a false joint."

OA in the ankle is almost always secondary to trauma, an injury or a congenital deformity, such as polio or something that's caused unusual wear. It's not like the hip or knee joints, which tend to erode just from wear and tear.

Severe arthritis in the ankle that doesn't respond to conservative treatment usually means a fusion procedure (prosthetic implants are only rarely used because complications and early failure rates are high). The ankle is a mortise where the two leg bones (the tibia and fibula) meet the large bone at the top of the foot (talus), just above the heel bone (calcaneus). If the joint gets into trouble, Bent says, "you have to take the articular surface [the cartilage] off the top of the talus and the end of the tibia until you have raw bone surfaces. Then you hold those together and fix them, usually with screws, so that they grow together."

With the ankle fused, patients can no longer move their ankle, so they walk with more of a flat-footed gait, but they still have enough motion in the forefoot to compensate—and no more pain. There's a fairly long recovery time with any major ankle or foot fusion procedure, because of course the ankle and foot bear the body's entire weight (thus, surgeons encourage overweight patients to shed a few pounds before surgery, if possible). The patient will in most cases be on crutches for several weeks, until the bones have had a chance to grow together, but people generally function very well after such operations.

Gout is almost always managed conservatively by a rheumatologist with medications, but it can produce degenerative, osteoarthritic change. If it does (most often in the big toe), the toe may have to be fused or corrected with another surgical procedure, such as an incision arthroplasty, "but that's very uncommon," Bent says. "You don't see many patients who have gone on to have gouty arthritis." Most attacks of gout on the big toe are treated with medication for the acute episode, after which the patient will be prescribed another medicinal agent to lower and maintain a proper level of uric acid.

There are any number of other problems people with arthritis are prone to in their feet—clawtoes, hammertoes, Morton's neuroma, to name but a few—some of which can be treated with medications and/or orthotics, such as pads and lifts for the shoe. If surgery's the best option, though, try not to be overly anxious about it: Most surgical techniques for the foot provide excellent results. You may never go back to rock climbing or jumping out of planes, but you should be able to get around on your retooled feet just fine.

New Knees for Old

"I was in such bad shape I thought I was going to die," Carol Beswick says in her soft Caribbean accent. "There were times I prayed to die, because it was so, so painful. I didn't really think of taking my life, I just prayed that one day I'd sleep and not wake up." What kept Beswick, forty-one, going was her daughter, Camille, who turned sixteen in early 1996: "When I'd think that way, I'd say, no, I want to see my daughter grow up. I want to know she's going to be able to take care of herself."

Beswick was a twenty-five-year-old college student and new single mom when her arthritis began, with swelling and pain in her right elbow. A couple of months later, the joints of two fingers on her left hand started to swell up. By the time she finished school and landed a job as a data entry operator with Canada Customs, an ankle was also affected. Then she had her first really bad flare: "Practically all my joints were involved. I woke up one morning and I couldn't get out of bed."

A rheumatologist had some fluid from her elbow tested and diagnosed her with rheumatoid arthritis. He gave her cortisone injections in her elbow for the pain, but he didn't really explain what she was facing. "In the early stages they just say this is what you have, RA," Beswick recalls, "and I want you to take some of this, a coated Aspirin, and I want you to come to the clinic once or twice a week. They would inject my joints with cortisone, maybe once a month, different joints at different times. This continued for a while, and the pain just kept progressing, and I would be taking off from work all the time."

In early 1983, a new rheumatologist, closer to where she worked in Scarborough, Ontario, had her hospitalized. For three weeks, she was prodded and poked, tested and injected. In her condition, they finally concluded, Beswick shouldn't even be working—a daunting prospect for a single mom with a toddler to take care of. Fortunately, Beswick's sister Heather had come up from Jamaica and stayed to help out, and the initial treatments, a combination of gold injections, water therapy, splints for her hands, more Aspirin, and lots of rest—seemed to be helping.

Over the next several years, Beswick was up and down, mostly down, with flares and remissions, but the RA was taking over. The pain was becoming consistently bad, she was still on regular gold injections and taking lots of Aspirin, she suffered periods of deep depression, and her mobility was slowly eroding. She could handle a few light chores, but she relied on Heather for help with Camille. She couldn't even comb her own hair, because her shoulders were so bad.

From 1990 to 1992, her condition worsened. Nothing seemed to help, and she landed in hospital again. This time she saw a physiotherapist who asked if she'd been in touch with The Arthritis Society. "You've been sick for thirteen years, and nobody told you about them?" the physio asked. "Well, no," Beswick replied. "And he said, 'I'm going to sign you up right now,' and I thank God. I didn't know they had social workers you could sit and talk to, and physiotherapists and occupational therapists. That was what I needed, to really understand what was happening with my arthritis, to be educated about it."

That same year, Beswick was referred to an orthopedic surgeon for her knees. He took x-rays and gave her the news in no uncertain terms: "He said, 'You have to make up your mind. You have no cartilage left in your knees. You're too young, but you can have surgery done now or wait till later—and be in a wheelchair and go through all the pain.'

"By then," Beswick says, "my arthritis was so bad I couldn't comb my hair, I couldn't wash myself, I couldn't feed myself, let alone walk. Just to take one step was agonizing..." She decided to go ahead with total joint replacements, both knees, four months apart.

"After the first operation it was very painful, but after I started going on it I felt better. I didn't have all that pain I'd experienced before. I was able to put my foot down and walk with a walker, then a cane." The second operation, though, wasn't as good. Beswick's right knee doesn't bend as much as it should, making it difficult for her to sit comfortably, for example, in the back of a car: "My patella doesn't move at all in the right knee, but it doesn't pain."

Beswick still has arthritis "all over," and since the operation her right ankle has been very painful. She walks with a limp, but she *can* walk, and the pain in the knee, while it isn't totally gone, is bearable. "Before I had to think when I got up," she explains. "Now I can just get up. OK, there's going to be a little discomfort, but not like before, when I felt I wanted to faint because the pain was so bad."

Without a doubt, the results would have been better if the operations had been performed earlier, something Beswick's going to have to consider as she contemplates the continuing deterioration of her other joints. Her right hip is "acting up a little bit," and the other hip may eventually be affected, too, either by the progression of the disease, or because of the uneven wear her hips are subjected to because of her mismatched knees.

"I don't even want to think about having my hips replaced right now," she says, "but it's a possibility. My hands are still the same, my elbows, my shoulders—it's affected my shoulders real bad—and my elbows have gotten worse."

Overall, though, Beswick is better than she was. The knee surgery has given her a measure of independence she didn't have before, and The Arthritis Society occupational therapists have helped set her up with labour-saving devices to make her domestic tasks easier, and given her instruction in how to perform those tasks with the least possible stress on her aching joints. "I have to make ways of doing things," she says, "but I feel much better that I'm doing things for myself, because before my sister and my daughter used to be doing everything."

She's even doing occasional volunteer work for The Arthritis Society, attending meetings to talk about her arthritis, and she's agreed to take part in a program at the Sunnybrook Health Science Centre in

Toronto, teaching medical students about the *real* world of arthritis. Given her condition, "you can't help but think about the future," Beswick says, "but I try not to. I say, whenever I reach the river, then I'll cross over the bridge, but now I don't want to think about it. I just want to thank God for what I have and try to make it better, if I can."

After Surgery

Major surgery on a joint may take two or three hours. Getting full range of motion, strength, and flexibility back in that joint often takes months. That's where post-operative components such as physiotherapy and the advice of an occupational therapist come in. They're among the most important determinants in the success of your surgery.

As an outpatient physiotherapist (PT) with The Vancouver Arthritis Centre, for example, Bruce Clark sees people who have had a wide variety of surgical procedures. Usually the patient has been in hospital for a week to ten days, receiving daily in-patient physiotherapy. Then a PT such as Clark will take over, seeing the patient for forty-five minutes three times a week for the first two or three weeks, then twice a week for a month. During a typical session, he might apply ice to reduce pain and swelling, and prescribe specific exercises for the patient to do at home between treatments to restore range of motion and muscle strength.

Education is a key part of the job. If a surgeon suggests a patient lose weight before surgery, Clark says, a physio would explain why: "Anyone can tell an overweight person to lose weight—they hear it all the time. It's important to explain to the person the stress they're placing on the joint because of the extra weight, and how this could affect the long-term result."

Since the early 1970s, hard-pressed surgeons have been sending individual patients to The Arthritis Society's B.C. and Yukon Division for education sessions on surgery. By the mid-1980s, total joint replacements were being done with such frequency that The Society started monthly education classes for groups of people considering hip and knee surgery. Among other things, the ninety-minute classes cover the anatomy of the joint, the disease process, conservative treatment principles, indications for surgery, surgical procedures, risks and benefits, post-operative strategies, and long-term results, with question-and-answer periods included. People who require information beyond the scope of the classes are dealt with on a one-to-one basis.

Some Vancouver surgeons send all their patients to the education classes before they make a decision regarding surgery. This, says Clark, "is truly informed consent. A patient who understands what's going on is more comfortable with the entire procedure. They understand the process, the rationale, the timing of events, and so on." Patients thus become willing participants in the process rather than feeling like pawns in an overwhelming experience.

"There's a lot of work required by the patient in the rehab process," Clark says, "and an individual who understands this and agrees to it is then part of the team. As a physiotherapist, I don't want my clients to do exercises for *me*. That will last two weeks. I teach them all the benefits and get them to understand how exercise helps. That way they'll do it for themselves, for the rest of their lives."

Rosaleen Crooks is a physiotherapist at Toronto's Wellesley Hospital, which has a pre-admission program for people who are about to undergo hip or knee joint replacement surgery. Again, the aim is patient education: "We show them a video to explain what will happen and the type of procedure they're going to have, and we give them a short booklet that discusses what they need to bring into the hospital with them. It gives them some basic exercises to go through before they come in, but it's primarily designed to organize their discharge planning, and to facilitate their discharge before they come in."

How much exercising an individual can do to prepare for surgery depends to some extent on the nature of the disease. Someone with severe RA, for example, may have too much pain in the joints to endure any real degree of exercise, though they can be instructed in simple manoeuvres, such as getting in and out of a bathtub or techniques that help with dressing and walking with crutches.

Those are some of the things the Wellesley program videos address. Seeing such manoeuvres, Crooks says, "helps patients realize that they too will be able to do this after their surgery. It's all very well for somebody like me who's never been through a joint arthroplasty to tell them that they're going to be able to do this or that, but after actually seeing it on film and then discussing it with the therapist, they're much better prepared, and they realize that they will be able to function after their surgery."

From evaluation studies, Crooks' department has confimed that pre-operative instruction helps to decrease patients' anxiety and increase their knowledge retention. And, whether they're going straight home or to a rehab setting after surgery, they're ready: They've been given help planning and organizing whatever home therapy or other services they may require after surgery. It's not just preparing for post-operative exercise and physiotherapy; it's also all the minutiae of daily living. Will they need meals prepared? Do they have someone to take care of the dog, water the plants, pay the bills? Planning ahead can take some of the anxiety out of surgery and better prepare the patient for the post-operative work, and a better prepared patient is more likely to be a compliant patient. That is, says Crooks, "they've given themselves empowerment. If they don't have any knowledge of what they should and shouldn't do or be prepared for, obviously it's more difficult."

One of the tangential benefits of this approach is that patients are discharged from hospital "more expediently," Crooks says. "Length of stay has significantly decreased in the last few years. Where patients used to stay in hospital for fourteen days after total joint arthroplasties, it's decreased to from five to eight days." That means huge savings in health-care costs, but it doesn't mean patients are simply left to their own devices. Depending on their condition, they may require a stay at a rehab facility or they may go home—that's a decision, says Crooks, "that they can come to with their doctor and therapist as to what they feel they can cope with and what they're able to do."

Where physiotherapy has the biggest role to play, of course, is post-operatively. In the past, patients were instructed to take it easy, stay in bed, sometimes for weeks, to give tissues a chance to heal. Not anymore. It's now known that taking that approach simply increases recovery time. Muscles and other soft tissues grow weak from inactivity, and the recovery curve actually gets steeper with every day they're not used. So, physio usually begins within twenty-four hours after surgery, depending on the patient's recovery and how well the operation went (that is, whether or not there were any complications, such as infection, that might preclude immediate activity).

Generally a PT will be at your bedside the day after your operation, encouraging and helping you to stand and walk a few steps with a walker if you've had hip or knee surgery. Whatever joint has been operated on, you'll be taught to gradually progress from minimal movements to more advanced activity, all of it designed to restore your full range of motion as quickly as possible. How fast and how well you regain range of motion depends to a large extent on your willingness to work at it, because exercise promotes healing.

Over the next days and weeks, it's also a good idea to get some advice in the use of assistive devices by an occupational therapist (in some centres, a PT may perform that function as well). If you've had surgery on one of the weight-bearing joints, you'll need to ease back onto your feet with a steady progression of walkers, crutches, and canes, and you'll have to learn to "featherstep," and how much weight, with each successive day, you can put on your new joint.

You'll also need some advice about movements and positions to avoid, especially in the first weeks and months. If you've had a hip replaced, for instance, you'll learn to rest your weary bones in armchairs, which are much easier to get in and out of, and avoid chairs in which the level of the seat is below your knee level (you might as well put that low-slung sports car away for a while).

Upper-extremity surgery has its own set of adaptations. Since there's no weight-bearing involved, the learning curve isn't as fraught with anxiety about falling, but you'll still need to learn how much motion in a shoulder, say, is appropriate on a progressive basis. Just learning to dress is a whole new ball game. Welcome to the world of reachers, long-handled shoehorns, and dressing sticks, just a few of the ingenious devices that can help you get in and out of shoes and socks, or get back into your pants and slip into a shirt or blouse.

People who've had hand, finger, or wrist surgery will be given another regimen entirely, scheduled around a progressive series of dressings and bandages, though physiotherapy will most likely begin well before the last of them is removed. You may also be fitted for various kinds of splints, depending on the nature of your operation, that are to be worn at various times (sleeping, say, or working) to provide support and proper alignment for the affected joint or joints.

Again, whatever physio- and occupational therapies it's suggested you do, *do* them—with as much enthusiasm as you can muster. You'll heal faster and regain the fullest possible range of motion, flexibility, and functional ability sooner and better.

The Future of Surgery

Surgery has come a long way in the past generation, with a constant influx of innovations, both here and abroad. As today's discoveries make current practice safer and more efficient, ongoing research holds near-miraculous possibilities for the not-too-distant future.

For example, Swedish researchers at Sahlgrenska University Hospital in Göteberg have taken samples of healthy articular cartilage from the knees of patients with cartilage defects and used it to grow new cartilage in tissue culture. Once they had enough material, they went back into the patients' knees, excised the damaged cartilage, and inserted the test-tube cells, called chondrocytes, in the joint. Although the procedure is still considered experimental, the Swedish researchers viewed the initial results as extremely promising.

That kind of experimentation, though, is just the tip of the iceberg. Remember the *Star Wars* films? In one, the young hero, Luke Skywalker, has a hand lopped off in a laser-sword fight by the nefarious Darth Vader. A few scenes later, a new hand, as good as new, has been grafted back onto young Luke's arm—an undeniable benefit of living in "a galaxy far, far away."

Sci-fi nonsense? Maybe not. As Robert Langer and Joseph P. Vacanti reported in the September 1995 issue of *Scientific American*, engineering replacement tissue isn't just movie fantasy. Langer is a distinguished professor of chemical and biomedical engineering at the Massachusetts Institute of Technology; Vacanti, his collaborator for nearly twenty years, is an associate professor of surgery at Harvard Medical School and director of the Laboratory for Transplantation and Tissue Engineering at Children's Hospital in Boston. Most of the knowledge and technology to rebuild bones, specific tissues, and even organs, they say, is already in place.

Such marvels are based on the manipulation of ultra-pure, biodegradable plastics or polymers, descendants of the kind of degradable sutures developed for surgery two decades ago. Using computer-aided design and manufacturing techniques, organ and tissue engineers will shape the plastic into the form of the elements—muscle, blood vessels, bone, skin, and so on—to be "regrown." The plastic will provide a kind of scaffolding, which will be "seeded" with cells of the relevant tissue. As the cells grow and divide, the plastic degrades, until only living tissue remains. The new, permanent tissue will then be implanted in the patient.

It may not be as far-fetched as it sounds. Langer and Vacanti's team has already engineered artificial heart valves in lambs from cells taken from the animals' own heart vessels, and for several years human skin has been grown using polymer bases, then grafted onto burn victims. Eventually, Langer and Vacanti believe, whole organs will be designed, manufactured, and surgically implanted in patients.

They believe that, given the right conditions, the body's own cells will manage the intricacies of organ reconstruction, leaving surgeons to handle the plumbing—connecting the new organ with patients' nerves, blood vessels, and lymph channels.

Similarly, they wrote, "engineered structural tissue will replace the plastic and metal prostheses used today to repair damage to bones and joints. These living implants will merge seamlessly with the surrounding tissue, eliminating problems such as infection and loosening at the joint that plague contemporary prostheses."

The ultimate will be the production of complex body parts such as hands and arms: "The structure of these parts can already be duplicated in polymer scaffolding, and most of the relevant tissue types—muscle, bone, cartilage, tendon, ligaments, and skin—grow readily in culture. A mechanical bioreactor system could be designed to provide nutrients, exchange gases, remove waste, and modulate temperature while the tissues mature."

The only problem left to overcome is finding a way to induce nervous tissue to regenerate—an obstacle Langer and Vacanti are confident will soon be overcome. As Luke Skywalker might say, may the Force be with them.

To Look, and Look Again
Immunology and Research

*False facts are highly injurious to the progress of science,
for they often endure long; but false views, if supported by
some evidence, do little harm, for everyone takes a salutary
pleasure in proving their falseness.*
     —*Charles Darwin*, The Descent of Man

Advances made in the care and treatment of people with arthritis in only the last generation are little short of miraculous, and even greater advances lie before us. Where only a few years ago there were no disease-modifying agents for rheumatoid arthritis, now there are at least five. Where once a woman with lupus who became pregnant was advised to have an abortion—for her own safety—now both mother and child can almost always be saved. Where complications from many forms of arthritis were once often fatal, now they can be treated, and the patient can expect to lead a full life. Where surgery and medications and overall care were once basic and largely ineffective, refinements have been made in all areas that have immeasurably improved the lives of people with arthritis.

The source of all this beneficence? Research. Innumerable scientists, working alone or in collaboration in clinics and laboratories, have painstakingly, incrementally, increased our understanding of arthritis. In doing so, they've created more successful surgical techniques, developed new treatment approaches, and devised safer and more effective medications.

Blood Secrets
Magnified 25,000 times through an electron microscope, macrophages

are Stephen King's worst nightmare. Misshapen, spiky blobs of lurching goo, they descend on hapless victims like The Thing That Ate Manhattan, enveloping and devouring them with gustatory efficiency. In a horror film, macrophages would be the monsters.

Macrophages constitute just one battalion in the remarkable army our bodies marshall in our defence against a teeming host of bacterial and viral invaders that constantly threaten to overcome us. We call this unseen army the immune system. Against most ordinary foes, such as cold viruses and minor bacterial infections, the immune system is a good protector. Pitted against more insidious foes, like cancer and AIDS, it's often overwhelmed. And, in some conditions—known as autoimmune diseases—the immune system turns traitor and attacks our own healthy cells, which is what happens in such forms of arthritis as lupus and rheumatoid arthritis (RA), amongst others.

Blood is the battlefield where the immune system plies its trade. Pulsing through the average adult's circulatory system (a complex network of veins, arteries, and capillaries) are about five-and-a-half quarts of the red tide the ancient Sumerians called "the vital force of life." Our understanding of the blood's intricate role in our affairs (among other things, it transports nutrients and hormonal messengers, hauls waste, clots wounds, and fights viral and bacterial infections) only really began with the invention of the microscope in the late sixteenth century. By modern standards, it was a crude instrument, but it was sufficient for Anton van Leeuwenhoek, a Dutch amateur scientist with a gift for observation, to identify red blood cells in 1674. Others had seen the "flattened disks" before, but van Leeuwenhoek was the first to describe them fully as "red globules 25,000 times smaller than a fine grain of sand."

Known to scientists as **erythrocytes** (from the Greek *erythros*, meaning red), these tiny cells constitute about 45 per cent of the blood. Their job is to haul oxygen from the lungs to each of the body's 60 trillion cells via an iron-containing protein called hemoglobin, which binds to oxygen molecules released by the lungs (a process called oxygenation) to form a loose, unstable compound called oxyhemoglobin. Whenever one of these oxygenated red cells encounters another of the body's cells that's "gasping for air," it releases its oxygen in exchange for the depleted cell's carbon dioxide, which it then carries back to the lungs to be exhaled.

Red cells, though, don't have any direct involvement with the immune system; that's the province of white blood cells (**leukocytes**, from the Greek *leukos*, meaning white), six hundred times fewer than their red kin. There are five types: eosinophils, basophils, neutrofils, monocytes, and lymphocytes. **Eosinophils** and **basophils** are key players in inflammatory and allergic reactions, while **neutrophils** and **monocytes** are constantly engaged in phagocytosis (its root means "to eat")—an apt description of how these cells dine on foreign invaders, dead cells, and the daily accumulation of other biological debris. Billions of these **phagocytes** ("cell eaters") are produced in the bone marrow every day, from whence they travel through the circulatory system, the body's tissues and organs, engulfing and breaking down captured materials.

Neutrophils are relatively short-lived. Not so monocytes: triggered by chemicals exuded by bacteria or dying cells (chemotaxis), monocytes puff up like fat men at a feast, ballooning to ten times their former size to become those lurching **macrophages**—literally "big eaters." They live for years, and in the face of an otherwise unmanageable foe, they can fuse together to form giant cells or swell their numbers by reproducing.

Lymphocytes—comprising some 25 per cent of all white blood cells—are the front-line soldiers in the immune system. Unlike other white blood cells that "crawl" through the bloodstream, most lymphocytes (which are derived from parent cells in bone marrow called stem cells) take up residence in body tissues, especially lymphatic tissue. They take their name from lymph, a clear fluid that flows in a secondary circulatory system, moving nutrients and oxygen in the blood beyond the capillary system into all the body's cells.)

From here, things get complicated, but a deeper understanding of the immune system will help as you take a more active role in your treatment.

Immunity

First, a few more introductions: An **antigen** is any substance—usually a bacterium or a virus—that "turns on" the immune response.

This response (it's often referred to as "the immune cascade") consists of two main components: **humoral immunity** and **cell-mediated immunity**. To understand the difference, we have to go back to lymphocytes, of which there are two basic types, **B cells**, which mature in bone marrow, and **T cells**, which undergo further differentiation in the thymus, a small gland directly beneath the breastbone. B cells are the agents of humoral immunity; T cells are the agents of cell-mediated immunity.

Both systems can be activated by the presence of antigens. In humoral immunity, B cells produce one of the body's most potent weapons against invaders—protein **antibodies** composed of gamma globulins, also known as immunoglobulins. Antibodies are target-specific; that is, each type binds to and destroys only one specific antigen. For example, an antibody that attacks enterococci bacteria will ignore a flu virus, and vice versa. In fact, the 10 trillion B cells we each cart about in our blood are capable of fabricating more than 100 million distinct antibodies at any one time, each composed of four tiny protein chains. They form Y-shaped sites (two to an antibody) expressed on the cell membrane as receptor molecules. When a receptor recognizes its antigen—the enemy it was specifically created in the bone marrow to attack—the antibody binds to the antigen, causing the B cell to proliferate in a "clonal-selection process" that produces a variety of deadly progeny, both more B cells and freewheeling antibodies. These proteins don't destroy foreign organisms themselves; they merely "mark" the invader chemically for destruction by other elements of the immune system.

One of the most potent of these is **complement**, a brigade of enzymes that fracture in response to the chemical signals that are emitted when an antibody binds to its antigen. The fragments thus created also bind to the antigen in a precise sequence; once the last one is in place, the enzymes act like chemical dynamite and literally blow the antigen apart. In addition to attracting complement, antibody-antigen groupings—called immune complexes—draw any nearby macrophages, which require little prompting to dig into a big meal. Immune complexes can also bind with other antigens or proteins or even other antibodies (a process called agglutination), serving larger dishes to patrolling macrophages and neutrophils.

Cell-mediated immunity can be roused into action by B cell activity, which divide and differentiate into plasma cells that secrete antibody proteins—soluble forms of their receptors that bind to antigens, either neutralizing them or precipitating their destruction by scavenging cells, such as macrophages. (The response of phagocytes to foreign invaders is a non-specific immunity—they'll eat any material they encounter.)

Macrophages and B cells activate T cells in a similar fashion: They break the antigen they've engulfed into tiny fragments (called **antigenic peptides**), which are joined to molecules called **major histocompatibility complex** (**MHC**; *histo*=tissue, *compatibility*=acceptance, and *complex*=a group of closely linked genes) and transported to the surface of the cell, where they're placed on display, so to speak. T cells have receptor molecules on their surfaces that are capable of recognizing portions of different antigenic peptide-MHC combinations. When they do, they leap into action, producing **lymphokines**, chemical messengers that stir up other elements of the immune system, including more B cells and macrophages.

T lymphocytes are if anything even more important to the immune response than B cells. Even if all the body's B lymphocytes were healthy and active, without T cells an effective immune response would be impossible. Unlike B cells; there are three types of T cells, whose only apparent difference is function: The first, known as **CD-8**—**killer**, or **"cytotoxic"**—cells bind directly to the antigen, inflicting a fatal wound upon it. Exactly *how* it knocks off its victims isn't clear, but the process is probably closer to the enzyme action of complement than the devour-and-destroy technique favoured by macrophages.

The second type, **CD-4**, or **helper cells**, are activated by an antigen to stimulate the production of vast numbers of lymphokines that in turn accelerate the production of other elements, such as B cells and other T cells=specific to the triggering antigen, thus promoting inflammation.

T helper cells may be the big guns in the immune system, since even one helper cell can activate hundreds of B cells and macrophages by releasing its lymphokines (which include various **interleukins, interferon-gamma, tumor necrosis factor,** or **TNF, colony stimulating factor, lymphotoxin,** and **T-cell replacement factor**). One type of lymphokine activates B cells and macrophages; another behaves as a "migration inhibition factor" that orders lymphocytes to remain on the job. Others kill adjacent infected cells or broaden the immune response of lymphocytes to include different target antigens. By contrast, **suppressor T cells**, as their name suggests, have the opposite effect—damping down B and T cells.

A select number of both B and T cells remain in the blood long after the invader has been destroyed to serve as **"memory"** cells: lymphocytes that will quickly mount an attack (in four to five days) on any subsequent invasion by the same antigen. These memory cells are the basis of the "bestowed" immunity that results from an infection or vaccination.

Autoimmunity

All this activity characterizes the immune system when it's working properly. In so-called **autoimmune disorders**, various players in the immune defence fail to make the crucial distinction between self and nonself—a breakdown German immunologist Paul Erlich (1854-1915) labelled *horror autotoxicus* to describe the then-unthinkable condition—and actually turn their formidable resources against the body. There are a wide variety of autoimmune disorders, affecting some 5 per cent of all Western adults, including multiple sclerosis, Graves' disease, insulin-dependent diabetes mellitus, and a range of arthritis-related conditions that include rheumatoid and psoriatic arthritis, scleroderma, Sjögren's syndrome, and lupus.

The immune system can turn against the body in a number of ways. For example, if too much interleukin 2 (IL-2) is secreted—for as yet unknown reasons—the T suppressor cells will fail to curtail the immune response after the antigen is destroyed, leaving healthy tissue under continued attack from its own defence forces. Because an infection often precedes the onset of an autoimmune disease, scientists have long suspected that autoimmunity could be triggered by a virus or bacteria in people with a predisposition to a certain disease.

Normally, a pathogen invades the body, and the immune system gears up to fight it off. But for some reason, in an autoimmune disorder the immune system doesn't stop, turning on its own body's cells, perhaps due to "molecular mimicry." Some viruses and bacteria are evidently able to fool the body into granting them free access because they contain stretches of amino acids (the building blocks of proteins) that look like cells in the body. After responding to the invading virus or bacteria, the immune system is then primed to attack the corresponding body component.

Research studies have shown links to molecular mimicry and immune response in rheumatic fever and RA. However, not everyone infected with a microbe mimic will develop the corresponding disease, evidently because not everyone has exactly the same type of HLA (human lymphocyte antigen, a set of MHC genes on the surface of all human cells that identifies them to the immune system as "self." HLA molecules determine which fragments of a captured antigen are displayed on the surface of a macrophage to stimulate T cells to react.) One individual's HLA structure may bind an antigen that mimics body cells so that it can be "displayed" for destruction by the immune system, whereas another may bind an antigenic fragment that's unique to the pathogen: It doesn't mimic "self." In both instances, the immune system is mobilized and the pathogen attacked, but in the latter case the immune cascade knows when to stop—when the pathogen has been eradicated. Nine out of ten people with ankylosing spondylitis (AS), for example, have the genetic marker HLA-B27, compared to about one in twelve people in the normal population, but some people who don't have that marker still develop the disease, and some people who *do* have it *don't* develop AS.

In other words, when it comes to HLA and immune response, everybody's different. It's known, for example, that people who carry the HLA molecule designated DR4 are about six times more likely to develop RA than people who don't, but not everyone who has HLA-DR4 *does* develop RA. Even identical twins don't always react the same way. And in lupus, which has been associated with certain HLA types, only about one out of four twins of people with the disease also develop lupus. When they do, their B cells produce an abnormal amount of antibodies that swamp the suppressor function and attack the body's own tissues. Why is a hotly debated question.

Research in Action

Despite the gaps in understanding, much has been learned in recent years as a result of the pressing need to understand how the immune system works and how it sometimes fails to ward off disease. This has led to the creation of new labs and countless new research teams. While many are engaged in work that has no direct bearing on arthritis, any advance made in one area almost inevitably leads to gains in others.

Research has already made a big difference to lupus patients; whereas once a diagnosis of the disease was accompanied by a grim prognosis, now the majority of people with lupus live long and basically normal lives—thanks to more complete understanding of the condition and the development of safe and effective medications. Similarly, gout, which used to sentence victims to chronic pain and disability, can now be effectively controlled with diet and appropriate medications. A growing number of people with RA have been spared the irreversible damage that used to result from the traditional "go low, go slow" approach—a treatment strategy that only changed after research revealed that earlier and more aggressive treatment was the way to go. And, not many years ago, many scleroderma patients succumbed to kidney failure; researchers developed medications that have saved thousands of lives.

But what *is* research—what's its essence? One answer is provided by Dr. Kenneth Pritzker, chief of pathology and head of the Connective Tissue Research Group at Toronto's Mount Sinai Hospital: "Some years ago, I went to a former professor and chairman of pathology in Toronto and said, 'Listen, I want to look at this particular problem, but I'm concerned that other people have looked at the same problem, and I'll be asking the same questions.' And he said, 'Well, why do you think it's called *re*-search? You're looking *again.*'

"Actually," says Pritzker, "there's a lot of truth to that, because you're looking again and again and again. Research is a systematic and repetitive investigation to try to ascertain new knowledge by exploring questions that are answerable or potentially answerable in some depth over time. And that's all there is to it."

Defining it, of course, doesn't tell half the story. Research has made major inroads in treatment and understanding of virtually every form of arthritis over the last generation, and physicians and scientists predict even greater advances in the years to come. Technologies that weren't even conceivable fifteen or twenty years ago are permitting rapid and exquisitely complex investigations into areas that were once beyond the limits of research, and the rapidly expanding search for answers in genetics and immunology demonstrates real promise of even further advances.

Much of the best arthritis research being done today can be attributed to the efforts of The Arthritis Society (TAS), the largest sponsor of peer-reviewed arthritis research in Canada. From its beginning in the late 1940s, TAS worked at encouraging a multidisciplinary approach to the problems of arthritis. As Dr. Ed Keystone, director of the rheumatic disease unit at Toronto's Wellesley Hospital, recalled in a 1984 issue of *Arthritis News*, "Our first recruits were clinicians, experienced physicians who were equally at home—and adept—in the classroom, at the patient's bedside, and in the laboratory. These early clinician pioneers blazed the trail...by initiating the first multidisciplinary and collaborative efforts. It was because they were teachers and researchers *and* patient-care physicians—with their fingers in a lot of pies—that we were able to nudge and stimulate the interest of other physicians, scientists, and researchers in other disciplines in our cause.

"Almost before we knew it," said Keystone, "we were finding these early specialists sharing information with their colleagues, trading knowledge and experiences and, consequently, stimulating each other to even greater heights and potentially more productive avenues of investigation."

The starting point was attracting some of the bright young M.D.s to rheumatology with fellowships, then funding them for an extra year or two to learn the intricacies of basic science research. In the early days of Society-funded research, these young doctors represented something entirely new: the first hybrids in arthritis research. Bridging the gap that previously existed between the lab and patient care, they were able to make enormous contributions. Suddenly the study of arthritis was no longer divided into separate camps, one dealing solely with the causes of disease, the other with its consequences. The battle began to be fought on a combined front, equally benefiting research efforts—and patients. By the mid-1970s, Canadian arthritis care was considered the best in the world and the standard against which the practice of rheumatology elsewhere was measured.

With that in mind, it's worth looking at some of the research currently funded by TAS. According to its executive summary, TAS committed $5.3 million (most of it coming from donors) to research being done across the country in 1995–96, including twenty-seven new projects, each of which "is unique in the world and does not duplicate work being done anywhere else." In any given year, the summary states, "between fifty and a hundred researchers receive funding to pursue ideas which, according to the experts in their fields, are the most promising in terms of improving our current treatments of arthritis and, ultimately, eliminating arthritic diseases entirely."

- In Montreal, Dr. John Esdaile, who holds a number of senior positions in research and rheumatology at McGill University and Montreal General Hospital, is leading a team of specialists that's trying to answer why some people with lupus *don't* suffer heart attacks and strokes, despite the fact that people with lupus are five times more likely to have a heart attack and twenty times more likely to suffer a stroke than "normal" people. Their aim is to identify the causes, risk factors, and markers, or clinical clues, for heart attacks and strokes in the patients taking part in the study, with a view to learning how to prevent them.
- In a joint study in clinics and laboratories in Canada, England, the U.S., and Italy, researchers have been working on a long-standing problem: What causes rheumatoid arthritis? Their finding—that a common intestinal bacterium known as *E. coli* (*Escherichia coli*) could be one of the triggers that sets off the disease—is more clue than conclusion, one of the collaborators noted: "It's really only a start toward solving the puzzle," said Dr. Ed Keystone, director of the rheumatic disease unit at Toronto's Wellesley Hospital. "In fact, it raises more questions than it answers, but it puts us on the right track in terms of research."
- Dr. Mary Bell at the Sunnybrook Health Sciences Centre in

Toronto is studying the efficacy of a six-week course of home physiotherapy for the treatment of RA, assessing any improvement in patients' symptoms and comparing them to a similar group that's not receiving the treatment. The study could play an important part in determining how widely funded such services will be in our increasingly cost-conscious future.

- At Laval University in Quebec, Dr. Pierre Borgeat, a professor in the department of physiology, is studying the use of methotrexate in the treatment of RA. Specifically Borgeat is trying to determine methotrexate's effect on adenosine, a natural substance released by blood cells that's implicated in inflammation. His results could lead to the development of new and even more effective medications for the treatment of inflammatory conditions.

- In osteoarthritis research, Dr. Wayne Marshall at The University of Toronto and The Toronto Hospital, Western Division, is investigating nerve changes in the joints of people with OA to find out whether the loss of these nerves can cause the joint to "wear out." His findings could signal changes in the way treatment is designed to preserve or heal the nerves.

- Dr. Glen Thomson at the University of Manitoba in Winnipeg is studying the connections between food poisoning and reactive arthritis, with a view to identifying high-risk patients and developing specific therapies.

- At the University of Western Ontario, Drs. Mark Speechley and Manfred Harth are attempting to measure the prevalence and impact of fibromyalgia on health-care services in a mid-size Canadian city (London, Ontario).

- In Quebec, Dr. Artur deBrum-Fernandes at the University of Sherbrooke is studying bone metabolism in the hope of developing new treatment and prevention strategies for osteoporosis, in which bones become weakened and break easily.

- In Toronto, Dr. Robert Inman is trying to determine how the HLA-B27 gene interacts with bacterial infections to produce reactive arthritis, such as Reiter's syndrome.

- At McGill University, Drs. John Mort and Peter Roughley are using biochemical methods to track the pathway of cartilage destruction in different types of arthritis. By identifying the various enzymes involved in cartilage degradation, physicians may in future be able to inhibit them more effectively.

New Frontiers

There's a good deal more arthritis research going on, of course—some of it TAS-funded, some not. Researchers are studying the nervous system, for example, looking for ways to affect the way the brain functions, through both psychotherapies and medications, to see whether chemical messengers in the brain can affect the immune system—and the course of some forms of arthritis. Other researchers are focusing on viruses, which may act as "triggers" in some kinds of arthritis.

In September 1995, researchers reported that they were set to begin clinical trials into a new treatment approach for RA called photodynamic therapy. The technique, which is employed against some cancers and psoriasis, uses ultraviolet light to activate a previously injected drug that's absorbed by cells lining an inflamed joint. Once activated, the medication kicks off a chemical reaction that destroys the harmful cells. "If we're correct," says Keystone, "it's conceivable that someone could stand in a big light box and, with one treatment, be relieved in all affected parts of the body."

One of the most promising fields of study has produced another new treatment approach for people with RA and other rheumatic diseases called "biologics"—compounds made from naturally occurring human or animal proteins that target the excessive concentration of white blood cells in inflamed joints.

"Some biologics are incredibly powerful," Keystone says. "After a single injection, an RA patient may go into remission for months, even a year. Studies show that some patients do very well after a single infusion of these agents and need no other therapy."

Biologics are still highly experimental, but, in current clinical trials, they're showing enormous promise, and they appear to be relatively safe, with few reported side effects. Current immunosuppressive medications take a scattergun approach, suppressing not only the bad, anti-self response, but also the protective immune response, leaving the patient open to a host of infections. By contrast, biologics are designed to work like guided missiles, or "smart bombs," targeting a specific cell that's creating a problem, while leaving the rest of the immune system intact. Keystone predicts that 20 to 25 per cent of RA patients may soon be treated with biologic agents, probably in combination with currently available medications.

Biologic therapies are one of the fruits of the growing convergence in immunology, molecular biology, and genetic engineering. Molecular biology's task is decoding and analyzing the most minute particles of human life, including the DNA (deoxyribonucleic acid) that determines every aspect of our makeup, from eye colour, height, and skin tone to predispositions for the development of certain chronic illnesses.

Genetic engineering is the manipulation of the information encoded in genes for any number of purposes: Insulin can be produced in bacterial "factories," for example, using monoclonal antibodies made by splicing human insulin genes into bacteria genes and letting them reproduce. Genetic engineering is also employed in cheese-making, growth hormones used to stimulate milk production in cows, and the production of micro-organisms that feast on garbage and oil spills.

Researchers are also turning to genetic engineering to treat auto-immune forms of arthritis, such as RA and lupus. Investigators at the Kennedy Institute for Rheumatology in London, England, for example, have produced a monoclonal antibody that binds to and eliminates tumor necrosis factor (a chemical messenger released by T cells). A single dose of the antibody suppresses the immune system for up to ten weeks without weakening the body's overall immune response to infection, and RA patients receiving the antibody report increased joint mobility and reduced stiffness. Similar results have been achieved elsewhere by researchers using monoclonal antibodies targeted at other elements implicated in the disease.

Easily the most controversial direction in current genetic research, though, is gene therapy—to many people, two words that are synonymous with "playing God." Gene therapy involves the replacement of faulty genes with healthy, or "corrective" genes in a patient's cells to cure or alleviate the symptoms of disease. But that's just the beginning of gene therapy's potential.

There are at least four categories of human gene therapy, only two of which are feasible with current technology, but the other two are only a short leap away, and it's those imminent possibilities that have some people worried. Dr. W. French Anderson, director of the Gene Therapy Laboratories and professor of biochemistry and pediatrics at the University of Southern California School of Medicine, argues against using either of what he calls enhancement genetic engineering or eugenic genetic engineering, in which genes would be introduced into a person's cells to "enhance" a simple characteristic, such as height, or "improve" a more complex characteristic, such as intelligence.

Somatic and germ line gene therapy, however—in which normal genes are introduced into someone to correct a condition arising from a genetic defect, or are introduced into the reproductive cells of a parent so their children would be free of the disease—Anderson applauds. In fact, he led a team that performed the first gene therapy on a human subject: In 1990, he and his colleagues removed white blood cells from the immune system of a four-year-old girl, who suffered from severe combined immunodeficiency (SCID). The child had inherited a faulty gene from her parents that normally produces the enzyme adenosine deaminase, which is essential to a properly functioning immune system. Without it, she was defenceless against infection.

The white blood cells Anderson and company removed were infused with corrective genes and then returned to the girl's circulation. Four more infusions were administered over the next four months, and her condition improved. With follow-up treatments, Anderson's patient was transformed from a sickly, housebound little girl into a healthy, vibrant nine-year-old who loves to do everything "normal" children do.

Gene therapy, Anderson believes, will constitute a "fourth revolution" in medicine over the next century (after public health measures, such as sanitation systems, which greatly reduced the spread of disease in populations; surgery with anesthesia; and the introduction of vaccines and antibiotics). Anderson foresees a time when the vast majority of disorders will be eased or even cured by the delivery of "selected genes into a patient's cells."

In fact, there are some four thousand diseases known to be caused by a congenital defect in a single gene, including cystic fibrosis,

Huntington's disease, and SCID, and a good many other conditions—including certain forms of arthritis—are the result, in whole or in part, of some dysfunction of one or more genes in the body's defences. With the completion of the Human Genome Project (the $1 billion effort to decipher what scientist and writer Robert Shapiro has called "The Human Blueprint"), the function of each of our estimated 100,000 genes will eventually be revealed. The information derived from that long international study, Anderson writes, "should make it possible to identify the genes that malfunction in various diseases."

Used wisely, gene therapy holds the promise of real solutions to disease. Just as it changed the life of one four-year-old girl, gene therapy could—in time—change the lives of countless people with arthritis, which is what all research is aiming toward. The question is, are we willing to pay what it will cost to achieve the goals of research? Increasingly the answer to that question appears to be a resounding *no*.

The Slippery Slope of Research Funding

Business and industry have long recognized the key role of research in keeping a company healthy—and what happens when R&D dollars drop. In 1993, Northern Telecom Ltd.—the fifth largest telephone equipment company in the world in 1992 and one of this country's corporate giants—stunned the investment community by posting a staggering $1-billion (U.S.) second-quarter loss. At the same time, NorTel revealed plans to lay off 5200 people, including some 2000 Canadians—almost nine per cent of its worldwide work force.

The company, said *The Globe and Mail*, "is reeling from years of poor management, under which it alienated some of its chief customers and failed to meet the R&D spending vital to retaining its product edge." The company's relentless focus on short-term profits had seriously undermined its long-term competitive position, one result of the former CEO's "fundamental absence of long-term vision."

On the same page of that day's *Globe* was a story in which then Prime Minister Kim Campbell "reaffirmed her support for Canada's health-care system and social safety net," but said "both need to be overhauled significantly." Campbell's statement to reporters appeared to be an invitation to provincial governments "to concentrate limited resources ever more on 'medically necessary' services."

The two stories were chilling in their implications for medical research. One, the cautionary tale of NorTel's setback, was a vivid illustration of what happens in a competitive environment when a company lets its research and development slide. The other story was a reminder that funding resources are becoming scarce, and retrenchment is the order of the day. For arthritis researchers, the implications were grim. Already in crisis, the future of arthritis research was threatened by funding shortfalls that could set it back years.

A dismally consistent pattern was outlined in a paper written by Dr. André Beaulieu, former chairman of The Arthritis Society's Medical Planning Committee and currently director of the Rheumatic Disease Unit (RDU) at Laval University in Quebec. The paper, "Helping the Arthritis Sufferer in the 1990s: The Essential Role of Excellence in Research," tracked the money allocated by The Society to arthritis research from 1981 to 1991. Over the ten-year period, Beaulieu found, there was an almost constant growth in absolute dollars, an increase of 103 per cent, or 7.7 per cent annually, with the rate slowing to 4 per cent annually in the last four years of the study.

While those figures sound at least moderately encouraging, the reality is otherwise. Since 1991, funding has been slowly drying up: In 1991–92, The Society allotted $8 million to research; for 1995–96, the figure had eroded to $5.3 million. Because of rising administrative costs and the real need to devote more money to clinical and patient programs, there have been fewer and fewer dollars available for research. Part of that shortfall, clearly, is a result of governments' wrestling with overall health-care costs—trying to concentrate "limited resources ever more on 'medically necessary' services."

"It's all very well for governments to say they're going to cut health-care costs," says Bonnie Thorn, vice-president, medical and scientific programs at The Arthritis Society, "but somebody has to pick up the slack, and the pressure falls on organizations like ours, which are mission-oriented. People are saying, 'Well, if I'm not getting the kind of care and services I used to get from the government, I should be able to get them from you.' Consequently there's a bigger demand on our fundraising dollars, to put them into client services, so there's even less money for research, because that's the only place it can come from."

Putting an even greater strain on research funds is the fact that inflation in research has very little to do with inflation as measured by the Consumer Price Index. Put simply, the cost of doing lab work has risen exponentially. A relatively unsophisticated everyday-use centrifuge in 1981, for example, cost $4,252. The same machine in 1991 cost $9,637—127 per cent more. A cell incubator, another common device, sold for $5,119 in 1981, a price that ballooned to $12,301 in 1991—or 140 per cent inflation.

Another crucially important factor contributing to the inflationary trend is the ever-increasing complexity of research required to make progress. As scientists learn more about the workings of bodily systems (such as the immune system and our genetic heritage), the problems they encounter become more complicated, and of course far more expensive. These costs are calculated under what scientists call "sophistication inflation."

Beaulieu noted that a scientist working with proteins in 1981 "could remain competitive with relatively simple pieces of equipment, such as easy-to-prepare chromatography columns, a non-computer-assisted UV monitor and fraction collector. The total cost of a state-of-the-art chromatography system was in the range of $6,000. Ten years later, the same protein scientist couldn't perform adequately without equipment collectively referred to as HPLC [high-pressure liquid chromatography] or FPLC [fast-protein liquid chromatography], the cost of which [was] $60,000."

In that same ten-year period, molecular biology and genetic engineering came up with sophisticated reagents, such as monoclonal antibodies and cytokines, that have become basic needs, the sine qua non of quality research. All have been affected by the sophistication inflation factor. A 1991 investigator, Beaulieu noted, would easily spend "15 to 20 per cent of a research grant buying sophisticated material that did not even exist" in 1981.

The Future of Arthritis Research

The crisis in arthritis research funding is very real, says Denis Morrice, president and CEO of The Arthritis Society. "The plain fact is, arthritis doesn't appear to be an urgent health priority in Canada—for the government or the general public. Yet it's clearly one of the most expensive burdens on the health-care system."

The numbers support Morrice's contention: According to the independent data research company IMS, in 1992, Canadian physicians wrote just under 28.7 million prescriptions for arthritis medications, a whopping 13.7 per cent of all prescriptions written in Canada that year. Yet arthritis research remains dramatically underfunded, and, says Morrice, "for arthritis, research *is* the answer."

Unlike such conditions as heart disease, arthritis can't be prevented. "There isn't any lifestyle change that's going to prevent rheumatoid arthritis or scleroderma or lupus or many other forms of arthritis," says Morrice. "By all means, stop smoking, go swimming every day, jog, and so on. But it won't prevent arthritis. The only thing that will prevent arthritis is research. Let's find the cause and the cure."

That's not getting any easier, despite advances made in the understanding of the disease in recent years. A lot of very good scientific research—with clinical implications—is being cut back, and it relates purely to dollars, says Edmonton rheumatologist Dr. Paul Davis: "The amount of money available for supporting researchers has gone down. We're seeing people with highly rated research, by peer review, being approved—but not funded. And we're seeing good researchers with excellent academic records of productivity losing funding, not because they're poor researchers, but because, in a highly competitive market, the smaller pie must be shared with fewer people."

What many people fail to realize, Davis says, is that the short- and long-term implications of the funding deficit are much the same. Even when you're established as a researcher, he says, "loss of support for one year may be manageable if you get lucky with some slush funds, but after just one year, you can't get back into the system, because in that one year your productivity will have gone down. And, from there, you're losing researchers, and because you can never build back from where you were, you end up being far behind the rest of the field. You can't stop a lab for twelve or eighteen months. A lab has to be vibrant and productive. Stop it for a year and you've probably stopped it forever."

The fact is, says Calgary orthopedic surgeon Dr. Cy B. Frank, the current crisis in research funding "is going to make it difficult for new people to come into this area. Young people are not going to consider research in a field if they see senior people shutting down their labs, people who have previously been successful. It won't take long for word to spread that this is not a good thing to do, and that's going to have a catastrophic effect on our ability to recruit other people into this area. It will also mean the permanent loss of bright people who have been making contributions in the past."

The Human Perspective

Before we see the end of the current crisis in research funding, both government and society will have to recognize just how big a problem arthritis represents. And under current accounting methods, that's not about to happen. "People don't die from arthritis," says Dr. Elizabeth Badley, director of the Arthritis Community Research and Evaluation Unit in Toronto, "they live with it."

What people have to understand, she says, is that arthritis "is largely an invisible disease. People who have it are often limited in what they *can* do because it hurts *to* do things. They're more likely to stay at home, so you don't see them out in the street as much. And how do people who may look perfectly healthy convey to family and friends that they're in pain or can't do something?"

One of Badley's colleagues measures grip strength in people with arthritis. Whenever another family member is there, "she'll give them the meter and say, 'This is what your relative can squeeze. You squeeze that amount,' and they'll discover they just have to flick their fingers. This average person has hardly registered the grip, but that was the *maximum* grip somebody with rheumatoid arthritis could do. And their family didn't realize. They suddenly think, 'No wonder they can't open jars...'"

Because of that lack of recognition, Badley says, "arthritis hasn't got the immediacy of heart disease and cancer and AIDS. You can't really compare it with those conditions." Unfortunately, when you're competing for research dollars, comparisons are unavoidable. And as long as the basis for comparison is mortality rates, arthritis will trail such ailments as heart disease, cancer, and AIDS. To put arthritis in perspective, to measure the enormous impact it has not only on individuals but on society as a whole, you have to find another frame of reference.

One way to take account of arthritis is in terms of disability years, and "arthritis is by far the single largest cause of disability, way above everything else," Badley observes. "Because arthritis is so very, very common, even if only one in ten Canadians with osteoarthritis has a serious disability, it's still the most common reason for disability in the population. By the year 2020, it's estimated there'll be almost a million Canadians with disabling arthritis."

Another view looks at quality of life and "healthy years of life lost." The idea is that if someone dies before the average age for a full lifespan, they've lost years of life—as many as seventy years if they die in childhood. Most people with arthritis, though, will probably live a full lifespan; what's lost is the *quality* of those years. With that in mind, researchers ask people to evaluate their arthritis through quality-of-life surveys. They then attach a value to every year that that person spends sick; the more sick they are, the higher the value, and the more it counts toward healthy years of life lost. Very serious arthritis might count for three quarters of a year, moderate arthritis half a year, and so on.

By that measure, someone who develops serious arthritis at fifty and lives to age seventy-five would score "higher" than someone who suddenly dies of a heart attack at sixty. On a mortality scale, the person with severe arthritis would be well behind "fatal" conditions; extrapolating "healthy years of life lost" across society as a whole, though, the impact of arthritis suddenly becomes obvious.

Department of Future Medicine

The effect of curtailing research is what might be called "the NorTel Factor." The NorTel Factor is what happens when long-term results are sacrificed for short-term gains and expediency. The recession of the early 1990s cut into everyone's budget, but, like NorTel, a dwindling investment in arthritis research now will mean years of retrenchment, with inestimable consequences for its future.

When arthritis research funding from all sources, government and private sector, is counted relative to GDP, Canada is "near the bottom of the pole," according to Keystone. "We're below the U.S., Japan, Germany, France, England, and Sweden." In the overall picture, arthritis research funding fares even more poorly compared to other health conditions, despite the fact that arthritis is the leading cause of disability in Canada, indeed in almost every industrialized country.

"People know that arthritis cripples," says Morrice, "but they don't realize how many are disabled. And if they knew just how much it costs in health-care dollars to treat arthritis, they'd be justifiably out-raged that arthritis isn't a national priority, like AIDS or cancer or heart disease."

For The Arthritis Society, forced to stretch shrinking resources across an ever-increasing number of costly services, it's a critical dilem-ma. Keystone doesn't blame people for wanting more money injected into patient care—better canes, crutches, orthopedic care, new therapies: "You have to understand where they're coming from. There is no cure, so they say, 'at least make me feel better.' I agree. But my concern is that, if we continue to keep addressing that immediacy, it's like putting money into building a better iron lung at the cost of funding a vaccine."

The bitter irony of that choice, according to Beaulieu, is that "the inability of arthritis scientists in Canada to profit from real growth in the funding of their research programs will unavoidably have major consequences on patient care in the medium to long term."

It goes back to the RDU (rheumatic disease unit) network. In that, says Keystone, "we created a unique setting—putting academic rheumatologists in every medical school across the country. The reason we set up RDUs in the first place was to ensure the highest quality care for arthritis patients, vis-à-vis somebody with a heart problem or what-ever, so there'd be real expertise in terms of physicians, nurses, OTs, and other medical professionals specially trained to look after the arthritic patient."

All rheumatologists in Canada are trained at universities with RDUs, whose mission is "to provide exemplary care and teaching while maintaining an active research role." More often than not, the financial support of The Arthritis Society, which provides about 70 per cent of all funding for arthritis research in Canada (though empty coffers have meant that only half of applications judged meritorious in 1995–96 actu-ally received funding), "has provided RDUs with the critical mass in clinical manpower required to deliver the excellence in patient care and teaching expected in university hospitals," according to Beaulieu. In turn, The Society's financial support, allied with the organizational structure of the RDUs, has been sufficient to attract "the attention of deans and department heads, who in most cases provided the necessary additional assistance that would not have existed without the initial support of The Arthritis Society."

As a result, rheumatology has acquired an increased visibility in the university setting, while RDUs have developed into a particularly fertile environment for the training not only of rheumatologists but also of allied health professionals, such as nurses, physio- and occupational therapists.

The impact and high profile that RDUs have acquired, though, can't and won't be maintained without strong research programs: "Deans and department heads monitor performance of their staff by giving high priority to research achievements," Beaulieu pointed out. "University support is more than likely to be withdrawn if faced with weak research accomplishments within RDUs." Thus, diminished funding of arthritis research will not only lead to "diminished efforts in finding a cause and cure for arthritis, but also to a decreased capacity to compete within universities for long-term rheumatology manpower support and training positions. In the long run, this will result in less protected arthritis patient-care facilities as other sub-specialty programs take the lead. The consequences of funding less research can only lead to…a significant decrease in the quantity and quality of patient care."

That would be a serious setback, given the inroads research has made in recent years, says Keystone—cause and cure aside: "We've cut the number of our hospital beds down in recent years, not just because the government said it wasn't going to fund us, but because of the higher quality of patient care. Has it saved the health-care system money? Enormously: fewer beds, less surgery, less disability, and less economic impact in terms of disability in the workforce."

So, what needs to be done? Revenues, obviously, need to be increased. One major source of funding, for example—the government-sponsored Medical Research Council—needs desperately to be addressed. From its $235-million 1993 budget, only about two per cent went to arthritis research, even though arthritis was (and is) the leading cause of disability in Canada.

Research, says Keystone, "is no more than the Department of Future Medicine. Basic research is our medicine for the future; we have to provide more full-time investigators. We have many clinician-scientists, which is excellent, but the highest quality, the best bang for your buck, are the full-time investigators—the 90-per-centers. This is the most expensive field, but it's the area we really have to target."

1 4

A Meanness to an End
Arthritis and the Future of Health Care

"The time has come," the Walrus said, "to talk of many things..."
—*Lewis Carroll,* Through the Looking-Glass and
What Alice Saw There

Canada, it would appear, has developed a chronic illness, a cond-ition, according to its doctors in Ottawa, Calgary, and Toronto, not unlike arthritis.

In certain of its extremities, there appear to be symptoms of Raynaud's phenomenon, experienced as a distinct coldness and loss of function from reduced blood flow. A consistent stiffness characterizes the country's morning newspapers that eases little as each day pro-gresses, and a severe and prolonged inflammation is apparent in at least one of the country's members, for which some specialists have sug-gested radical surgery (to date, the patient has demurred but may yet accede to its physicians' recommendation).

Certainly there's heat and tenderness throughout the body, increasing loss of energy and function and a great deal of pain. Psychological symptoms as a result of the prevailing condition abound: bouts of depression, periods of confusion, and loss of interest in and dissatisfaction with many of the work, leisure, and intellectual activities previously enjoyed.

The diagnosis would seem to be unmistakable. Like more common forms of arthritis, however, the cause of Canada's malaise isn't clear, though some specialists have formed theories. The most popular (in fact, almost the only) is The Deficit, a chronic condition the body nor-mally keeps in check but that has, for reasons only partially understood, proliferated. The treatment regimen prescribed by specialists is extreme, to say the least, involving drastic restrictions in diet and work activities (collectively described as "tightening the belt") and increased reliance on medical management procedures currently employed in the American health-care system. The patient's prognosis is uncertain.

Canada's condition is indeed serious, if not critical, but the diagnosis of its ills and the measures being taken to promote its recovery are very likely going to achieve a result most Canadians (I sincerely hope and believe) would never consciously select. For people with arthritis—*real* people with *real* arthritis—their friends, families, and caregivers, that result is most vigorously to be inveighed against. This end to which we seem to be ineluctably devolving has already begun, with the un-ravelling of key threads in the fabric of our society.

The Devolution of Care

Foremost among society's unravelling threads is our health-care system, which is undergoing substantial reform. It, along with our other social programs, is one of the central wefts in our national makeup. The generous philosophy out of which it was woven is often hailed as one of the defining characteristics of this country and of our identity as Canadians. Now the reforms being wrought upon it by a self-interested autocracy, with its "neo-conservative" agenda, threaten to tear it to pieces, undermining everything generations of Canadians have sought to achieve.

We'll return to the dire turn this trend implies for health care—and what it could mean for people with arthritis—but it's worth uncovering the roots of current policy to see more clearly where it's headed.

In his 1995 book *Whose Country Is This Anyway?*, columnist and former political organizer Dalton Camp laments current politicians' "abandonment of the poor." They have "bought the case for a capitalism beyond accountability—which agrees to sell, barter, or trade any principle or progam for the public good in the interest of more satisfactory tax rates, less tedious regulation, and private-sector dominance over the public interest," and prefer to "betray their people rather than disappoint the bondsmen and the bankers and the conglomerate press."

The end of all their manipulations will be to turn Canada into a country our forebears wouldn't recognize, a nation indistinguishable from the American enterprise.

This is not American-bashing; it's simply a recognition that our two countries are very different entities. We may have difficulty defining ourselves as Canadians, but the society we've created is very much our own, uniquely shaped by the skew of language embedded in our laws, constitution, history, and traditions. In the current climate of "reform," however, it's getting harder and harder to tell us apart. Their right hands firmly on the tiller, our captains of industry, elected office, and the media are steering the national agendas of both ships of state on the same course, each equally determined to roust the bogeymen of '90s public policy: debt and taxes.

As Camp wrote in *Whose Country Is This Anyway?*, under the direction of such masters, we're finding it easier "to consider forgoing the accepted standards of social services, to accept the argument that the Americans have known better all along about these matters, and that while the bankruptcy of social policy is inevitable, society's needs can safely be left to charity."

The current shallows of American political philosophy hardly represent a new passage; the only question is how we got sucked in. The theme goes something like this: If the wealthy are doing well, then the country will do well, and some of the profits of the wealthy—underwritten by tax breaks for corporations and the rich to encourage them to "stimulate" production—will inevitably "trickle down" to the impecunious, in the forms of more jobs, a livelier economy, etc. This argument has been swallowed whole by Canadian policy-makers.

The fact that such policies don't seem to work only means that governments take responsibility for acting more firmly. Obviously if the economy isn't positively humming after an infusion of such generous incentives, it's because we're living too high off the hog (as *The Wall Street Journal* scolded us in 1995). The result is a federal deficit that's soared completely out of control. The solution to the problem? Massive cuts in social spending. Never mind that those most keenly affected are those least able to afford it; as well-heeled government leaders sympathetically inform us, "we're all going to have to tighten our belts."

You'd think this would be a tough sell, particularly in a country such as ours, but, as Linda McQuaig notes in her 1995 book, *Shooting the Hippo (Death by Deficit and Other Canadian Myths)*, spurious arguments about the "dependency" of the socially disadvantaged "have helped weaken the public's support for [social rights]." Constantly reiterated mantras about "the debt wall" and the imminent collapse of our economy have convinced an apparently willing populace that our overly generous social welfare system has to be cut down to size, including — according to endless media reports — our bloated health-care system.

Deficit Mania and the Wealth Gap

How did we reach this point? We've been overwhelmed by the spread of deficit mania, what Michelle Weinroth, writing in the October 1995 *Canadian Forum*, calls "supranationalism," which "has made corporate profit its emblem of glory and global competitiveness its new morality."

"Global competitiveness" is the catchphrase CEOs cite as they announce this year's company profits, almost in the same sentence that they announce this year's layoffs. The result is a growing disparity between the haves and have-nots, and, as Michael Rachlis and Carol Kushner point out in *Strong Medicine: How to Save Canada's Health Care System,* "a mountain of evidence from epidemiology, sociology and immunology supports the conclusion that widening the gap between rich and poor increases illness....It doesn't look like a coincidence that populations with the best health — like the Japanese and the Swedes — have the narrowest gap between rich and poor. By contrast, countries with the greatest amounts of income inequality — like the United States — demonstrate the worst health indicators. In fact, the United States, despite its enormous wealth, has the greatest proportion of people in poverty of any wealthy nation and also displays some of the worst health outcomes in the industrialized world."

The reason the wealth gap is growing here is because recent fiscal policy in Canada has been structured by the Bank of Canada's ongoing battle to eliminate inflation — despite mounds of evidence that demonstrate the folly of its ways. Unfortunately, the complexities of high finance are beyond the grasp of most of us (for a shrewd dissection of current fiscal policies, pick up a copy of *Shooting the Hippo*); we've simply had to trust that our financial and political gurus know what they're doing. Well, it's plain to see that they may know what they're doing, but it isn't necessarily in the best interest of all the people.

Members of the elite are, by definition, well heeled. From their perspective, if current fiscal policies result in a steady level of high unemployment, so much the better: Job cutbacks aren't a threat to them. And, as McQuaig notes in *Shooting the Hippo*, maintaining a high level of unemployment means they can pay lower wages to workers competing for scarce jobs. "The deficit, on the other hand, represents a potential for higher taxes, which scares the elite, partly because there is always the danger that the public will demand that the tax system be made more progressive. Furthermore, the solutions proposed for deficit reduction— cutting back government spending—are exactly what the elite wants anyway. It is quite willing to pay for its own services privately—from private medical insurance to private schools—if it can be spared having to contribute to the cost of providing these services for everyone else."

The success of "deficitism," writes Michelle Weinroth, "resides in its capacity to enact a national *drama*, an all-consuming tragedy that disarms and robs popular consciousness of critical thought. Such an ideology relies on exaggerating the political reality and on animating feelings of horror before a proclaimed catastrophe...by destabilizing the otherwise balanced judgement of public opinion."

In the meantime, the first wave of cuts to provincial transfer payments has induced the provinces to chop social programs—including health care. Every province has closed or merged hospitals and cut beds; services have been reduced, eliminated, or removed from coverage; health-care premiums have been increased and user and prescription fees have been implemented or are under consideration. Such actions, writes Maude Barlow, national chairperson of the Council of Canadians, in the November 1995 issue of *The Canadian Forum*, "contradict [Liberals'] soothing words about protecting the basic principles of Medicare. Indeed, its actions are facilitating the entry of U.S.-style health care."

In fact, U.S. companies already have their feet in the door, intent on prying open the Canadian health-care sector—what they see as "one of the largest unopened oysters" in health care today.

Private or Public?

For-profit clinics first surfaced in Canada, to much hue and cry, in Alberta. After months of spirited sabre-rattling, the Alberta government eventually agreed to change its policy with regard to the clinics, which were in contravention of the Canada Health Act, because they were charging patients "facility fees" (in addition to the medical portion of bills, which were paid by the public system). The clinics were basically operating as a "second tier" of service, which critics have long argued undermine the principles of universal and equal-access health care by allowing those who can afford to pay extra to "jump the queue."

The fact remains that a two-tier system already exists to some extent, with clinics from coast to coast offering everything from abortions to orthopedic surgery to clients prepared to pay for faster service. A glaring example hit the front page of *The Globe and Mail* in January 1996, when it was reported that a woman had "jumped to the top of the waiting list" by paying to have an MRI (magnetic resonance imaging) procedure done at Toronto's St. Michael's Hospital, rather than wait her turn (in about six months) under the Ontario Health Insurance Plan, or go to Buffalo, New York, to have it done.

U.S. health management or maintenance organizations (HMOs) have also begun pilot programs called Comprehensive Health Organizations (CHOs) in Canada that provide and purchase services for their members, Barlow writes, "on a non-profit, publicly funded basis, with the goal of providing consumer-driven, community-based health care." This sounds like a good way to reduce health-care spending, until you realize that CHOs were the way American HMOs began in the early 1970s, before funding cutbacks forced the shift to for-profit HMOs. And the way even *non*-profit CHOs operate—with both CHO and patient shopping around for services to get "the best bang for their buck"— undermines the principle of universal, accessible, and comprehensive health care. "In a climate of funding cuts," says Barlow, "it is not difficult to envisage a shift to for-profit CHOs....This would open the door to U.S. companies, who could not be discriminated against under NAFTA. It is not a huge leap to the entry of the HMO megacorporations from south of the border."

Canadian power-brokers have already aligned themselves with the same American exponents of managed care who trashed our health-care system in the protracted debate over U.S. reforms, raising every imaginable scare tactic and exaggeration to convince their fellow citizens that our version of Medicare was definitely *not* the way to go. Now those same interest groups are starting to work on Canadian hearts and minds, trying to undermine our confidence in our system by stirring the deficit-mania pot and creating confusion among the public—employing what's known as "the chaos theory of market restructuring," says Joyce Nelson, writing in an issue of *The Canadian Forum:* Private interests first create the perception that a given market— in this case, the Canadian health-care system—is rife with chaos, then they step in with their own "solutions."

Colleen Fuller of the Health Sciences Association of British Columbia stresses that American health insurers' ability to break into the Canadian market is "totally dependent on the serious erosion of the Canada Health Act," which, notes Nelson, "specifically excludes private, for-profit administration of health insurance." But, as government cutbacks steadily erode medical services that were previously covered by public health-insurance schemes, those who require such services could be thrown, say Rachlis and Kushner, "into the arms of the private insurance industry." And that means that before long, we'll be enjoying the tender mercies of managed care. So, let's take a look at the American model—after all, that's basically the version our power-brokers will end up buying, perhaps not at first, but eventually, inevitably, as private companies turn health care into a competitive market.

Managed Care

What *is* managed care? Suzanne Gordon and Judith Shindul-Rothschild, writing in the May 16, 1994, issue of *The Nation,* describe it as "a byzantine system in which insurers and employers herd patients and families into health maintenance organizations or networks of approved physicians and other providers and hospitals, all competing to provide the cheapest services..."

It sounds like a good way to ensure low-cost efficiency, but there are problems, beginning with the way managed care companies keep their costs down. Health maintenance organizations which are paid to provide health coverage for companies' employees, "don't have to cover all illnesses or all people," notes Nelson, "but can pick and choose those likely to need the least medical care as a cost-saving measure."

The horror stories coming out of the States about managed care are legion. Frances D. Boylston of Montreal, writing to the editor of *The Globe and Mail* in July 1995, told the story of her thirty-five-year-old cousin in Atlanta, Georgia, who had to turn down a lucrative bank job because he'd suffered a heart attack three months earlier: "The insurance company of the prospective employer said that he could be insured only after a year and only on the proviso that he does not miss even one day of work due to illness."

Boylston's sister "was reduced to asking friends for their antibiotic medications for her severe bronchial infection because she had 'used up her benefits' for that kind of illness, and had to wait 183 days before seeing a physician for 'a related illness.'" Another of Boylston's cousins has a twelve-year-old daughter with multiple physical handicaps. This woman "is indentured to her job," Boylston wrote: "If she were to switch companies, no insurance company would cover the child's needs."

Gordon and Shindul-Rothschild cite the case of a nineteen-year-old girl with "a very rare and difficult to treat mental illness—obsessive-compulsive disorder (OCD)" who was suicidal. She was refused treatment at the only psychiatric facility in the state with an OCD inpatient clinic because *her* insurer doesn't have a contract with that facility: "'There are nights when I stay up cradling Robin in my arms because she can't stop crying,' the anguished mother recounted. 'She says she can't stand to go on living this way. What's so terrible is that there's help for her and [the insurer] won't let her get it. No one can cure her, but they can help *her* to live with OCD.'"

Isolated cases? Not at all. Managed care companies are in business to make money—some of them to the tune of 20 per cent annual profits. They accomplish this end in a number of ways. First, most simply won't insure certain people (that is, people with health problems, such as Boylston's cousin's daughter—or someone with disabling arthritis), or they charge prohibitive fees.

Next, they restrict which health-care providers, clinics, and hospitals clients can use (as in the case of the woman with OCD); those on the company list are generally chosen "by the criteria of cost and their willingness to follow a managed care plan's guidelines on which services are appropriate and when," say Gordon and Shindul-Rothschild. And, because care companies shop around to find the least costly services from doctors, clinics, and hospitals, patients may be forced to change physicians with dismaying regularity, dissolving whatever relationship of trust and understanding they may have built up and creating real discontinuities of care. For those with a chronic condition like arthritis, that relationship may be crucial to their standard of disease management.

Then there's what Gordon and Shindul-Rothschild call the bureaucratic mismanagement of "invisible diagnosticians"—what care companies call "utilization reviewers," nurses and physicians who may have no specialty training in the field they're evaluating, and who never examine patients but nonetheless decide the course of their treatment: Your attending physician prescribes a medication, for example, but then has to call the reviewer to see if the company plan will pay for it. For an arthritis patient whose doctor is trying to find a safe and effective NSAID, the quest may be severely limited by the care company's list of "acceptable" medications.

The final irony of managed care, write Gordon and Shindul-Rothschild, "is that it raises rather than lowers health care costs, as studies by numerous government agencies and health care researchers have shown." University of British Columbia economist Robert Evans told *Maclean's* in July 1995 that "most of the advocates of privatization are saying that we have got to get more money into the system. But that is essentially saying, 'Abandon the target of cost control, and let's keep this system expanding.' If you want to try to manage your system more tightly so as to live within your constrained means, then you have to stay with a single payer."

It only makes sense: If you have dozens of competing companies all carrying their own administrative and infrastructure costs in addition to squeezing a profit out of the system—on top of the costs of marketing and advertising—there's no way it could be cheaper. "Study after study—as well as the experience of governments in Europe and Canada—has documented that a single-payer financial reimbursement mechanism is the only way to save money and increase access while maintaining quality and continuity of care," say Gordon and Shindul-Rothschild. "As patients are learning every day, managed care does little but manage the care right out of the system."

Everyone has a stake in universal programs, argue Rachlis and Kushner. Current funding levels are more than enough to provide all Canadians with high-quality health care, they say—in fact, if we managed the system better, we could actually *add* services. But, if political leaders are determined to privatize, cut back on benefits, and implement user fees, "Medicare in Canada will soon be a fond memory. What we'll end up with instead is a two-tiered system where ability to pay rather than need determines who gets care. Overall costs for health care will rise, not fall, as private insurance steps in to fill the void left by retreating government programs. The wealthy and the healthy will do fine. Poor people—and especially those who are sick—will not."

Health-Care Options

So, where does that leave people with arthritis? On the outside, if current trends prevail. Managed care looms before us like some hideous spectre, unimaginable, but entirely possible. The principles and the reality of equal and accessible universal health care won't disappear all at once; it will be more like arthritis—a quiet, unseen erosion. Clearly, given that governments are determined to control (that is, cut back) spending on health care, the first thing that has to be done is become more cost-conscious in the way services are delivered. If, as Rachlis and Kushner suggest, there's already enough money to make the system work, what kind of changes need to be made—and what role can people with arthritis play in making sure the *right* things happen?

There's been a slew of treatment regimens proposed for health care in recent years, but one of the most sensible and concise hit the newsstands in July 1995, when *Maclean's* published its ten-point "Prescription for Medicare." Of their ten proposals, only three were strictly government-controlled measures, beginning with the recommendation that government remain the principal payer, as Robert Evans has suggested. Number two on the list was "Change the way doctors are paid" (from the current fee-for-service structure), and number eight recommended controlling drug costs more effectively.

Interestingly enough, of the remaining seven recommendations, all are already being applied, in one way or another (with only slight modifications, such as the substitution of the word "arthritic" for "elderly" in number seven), by arthritis-care providers. That would suggest at least *some* care providers are on the right track, if *Maclean's* is any gauge. Number three, for example, is "Improve the efficiency of hospitals." Number four is "Change who does what in health care"; number five is "Ensure that all groups work together"; number six is "Make sure that medical procedures actually work"; number seven is "Keep elderly people at home as long as possible"; number nine is "Set up more community health centres"; and number ten is "Allow patients greater say in their care."

To see just how those recommendations mirror some of the most innovative strategies in current practice, let's take a quick look at just two programs, bearing in mind that many of the *Maclean's* proposals echo other treatment strategies right across the country. Many of these same strategies, if they were implemented in the care of other conditions, could have a profound effect on the cost and effectiveness of our total health care.

Alternative Approaches to Arthritis Care

Inevitably, as administrators scramble to find more cost-effective and therapeutically effective ways to deliver services to a growing number of people with arthritis—some of them inspired by clinicians' recognition that the status quo in patient service is outmoded—they're going to turn to models of care like The Arthritis Program (TAP) at York County Hospital in Newmarket, just north of Toronto. It's one of a small number of programs offered around the country that are taking a fresh approach to health services, combining patient education and customized patient treatment as the key to arthritis management.

TAP began in 1982 by completely overhauling its approach to the way patient education and treatment are delivered, placing patients at the centre of their own care. Instead of the traditional one patient, one health-care provider—doctor, physiotherapist (PT), occupational therapist (OT), etc.—TAP took the view that it would be more efficient to assemble a team of health professionals specializing in arthritis and have patients with similar diagnoses see them collectively. That way, the team could take ten to twenty people at the same time, leading them through classroom sessions to a better understanding of their disease, medications, disease management, coping strategies, and exercise techniques, among other things.

"We were giving generally the same information to everyone with RA or OA who came through, and the waiting list was growing," says OT Lisa Stevenato. "We felt we could provide a better forum to give the info to more people, and those who needed ongoing treatment could be screened for that treatment during the process." TAP offers an effective way to provide the information, "with people in groups with others who have similar problems that support them. It also gives them an opportunity to hear other people's questions that they might not think of or didn't have a chance to ask their doctor."

TAP isn't just a classroom program or a teacher-pupil situation, says the team's social worker, Patrick Clifford. It's the embodiment of a philosophy about disease management that involves a number of integrated activities, professionals, and processes. It begins with patient education. Patients' understanding of the disease and its treatment—something physicians rarely have time to provide in a one-on-one setting—are essential, but it has to be disease-specific. Group approaches offered elsewhere still often lump people with different forms of arthritis together, whether they have RA or osteoarthritis or fibromyalgia, despite the limitations that imposes on the amount of relevant information that can be conveyed. TAP's first program focused exclusively on inflammatory arthritis; whether patients had RA, lupus, scleroderma, psoriatic arthritis, or another form of inflammatory arthritis, most of the information being presented met their needs. And, when the Ministry of Health provided additional funding (for a total of just under $300,000) in the early 1990s, they expanded TAP to provide programs for people diagnosed with fibromyalgia, OA, and juvenile arthritis.

The program requires a firm commitment on the patients' part, including time, to begin with—the inflammatory program, especially: It's three weeks long, Monday to Friday, 9 a.m. to noon (TAP tried full-day sessions, but by mid-afternoon their students were flagging). Early research into the program's approach showed that with a minimum of 75 per cent attendance, outcomes improved dramatically. Entrance is by referral from an outside health professional—the patient's family physician, for example, or from within the hospital itself.

Patients referred to The Arthritis Program are slotted into the first available group, based on their diagnoses; with new sessions beginning at the start of every month, they usually don't have long to wait. Anyone else coming into the hospital with a suspected rheumatic complaint is referred to the rheumatology department, where they're seen and assessed and an appropriate recommendation made, which may include referral to TAP. (In fact, all program participants are given a complete assessment, including a medical history, before starting the program, which provides a baseline from which any progress the patient makes can be measured.)

If someone comes in with an acute problem, he or she can be moved to the head of the line. "People don't have to sit on a waiting list while their active inflammatory process, or their active OA or FMS, progresses to the stage where they can't function," says Nadine Bellman, one of the team PTs. "They book right into the next available education program. We try to accommodate them as quickly as we can."

The inflammatory program is divided into three parts: education, group treatment, and custom treatment. The program consists of about twenty-four hours of education and treatment from the team (each member gives at least one of the instructional lectures), starting with daily, 110-minute lectures. Over the three-week period, they cover a wide range of subjects, including the disease process, medications, physio- and occupational therapy, treatments that are within patients' control to administer, and how to conduct day-to-day self-assessments, as well as psychosocial aspects of the disease, such as social supports, emotional issues, and relationships with family, friends, and co-workers. The sessions are open, spirited affairs, with participants encouraged to raise questions arising from personal experience.

Each class includes individual treatment—about six hours in all—including splints if patients need them, insoles, and other assistive devices. Participants are also allotted individual time with a PT, an OT, and Marie Chambers, the rheumatological pharmacist, to go over issues that may be causing problems or to answer questions that weren't answered in the classes. Patrick Clifford is available for consultation if they have psychosocial problems to discuss—a lingering depression, for example, or outside support service requirements. In addition, everyone has about four-and-a-half hours of pool therapy, half an hour three times a week, and they see the rheumatologist with the team in "rounds" once a week.

Team rounds are another TAP innovation. Each week of the inflammatory program, every patient has a meeting with the entire treatment team to discuss his or her case. Each team member provides an updated assessment of the patient's progress in terms of any goals that were set at the beginning of the course, changes in symptoms, response to medications, etc. Patients are encouraged to take part by providing information, but also by asking questions or making observations. If they've experienced an unusual side effect from recently prescribed medication, for example, or they've been having trouble with an exercise regimen, they can raise the issue. Having the entire team on hand sometimes provides a view of problems that may not be apparent to individual members. It also allows each member to reinforce and provide added perspective on the messages the others are sending, which may help ease a patient's anxiety about treatment decisions they've been asked to consider.

The process is different for people with FMS, says Chambers. While the team approach, rounds, and the opportunity for individual consultations within the actual program are much the same as in the inflammatory program, people with FMS take part in "what we call a fibro blitz, generally before we see them," Chambers says. "It's a morning of education, basically to make sure these people know what FMS is. We want them to realize that, if they don't fit the picture of FMS, they need to go back to the physician that referred them."

Participants are assessed and evaluated and given a range of practical strategies in self-management of their condition. At the end of the class, if they'd like to take a more comprehensive session, they can sign up for the full program, which consists of eight classes spread over eight weeks and is divided into three sections: education, integration of information, and pre-aerobic exercises. During that period, participants also consult individually with team members, as required.

The OA group goes to night school, from six to eight one night a week, three weeks in a row. (The brevity of the course reflects the fact that there are fewer complications involved with and fewer treatment strategies available for OA.) "In week 1, one of the rheumatologists does the medical perspective," Chambers explains, "then I do medications. Week 2, the PT and OT do exercises and function. Then in week 3 they're split off, according to whether they have back or neck or knee involvement, and they're instructed in specific exercises. We've learned that people have a building-block need to learning, and that if the information is presented out of order, then the learning potential is decreased."

Usually people attending the classes already know what kind of arthritis they have, and they may have some basic knowledge about it.

"What we're working to teach them is how they're going to better manage their arthritis," says Chambers. "Some people are newly diagnosed, a lot aren't. We have a real mix. It's whenever they happen to trip upon us, sometimes even fifteen years into the diagnosis."

One of the basic tenets of all sessions is that they achieve some measurable outcome, that they'll affect the course of each patient's disease or improve his or her functional measurements. Because of the mix— young and old, new to arthritis, and old hands—the TAP team has designed the overall program so that it meets a wide variety of needs and abilities. Although TAP is an out-patient program, they know they've reduced hospital visits and the average length of stay in their patient group when those people *do* need to be admitted to control their arthritis or deal with complications. "We make sure people are fully involved in their care," says rheumatologist and TAP medical coordinator Dr. Carter Thorne. "We empower people." It's not enough for people to simply accept that they have RA or OA or FMS: "They have to have the ability to influence the course of their disease."

In other words, they're taught how to help themselves to the full extent of their capabilities, and how to recognize when they should seek appropriate aid. In that way, they not only become better arthritis self-managers, they learn to use support services more appropriately and cost-effectively.

"Our position is that the principles of the program should be used in other places, and that access to programs of this type should be the norm," Thorne says. In 1991, TAP helped set up a clinic in Kenora, in northern Ontario, based on the TAP principles, but using Arthritis Society assistance and other local resources. To date, outcomes in Kenora are achieving results similar to those in Newmarket.

A Variation on the Theme

At Sunnybrook Health Science Centre in Toronto, rheumatologist Dr. Mary Bell heads the Rheumatology Medical Day Treatment Program (RMDTP), which developed as a result of bed closures at the hospital in 1992. Until then, Sunnybrook had been treating people with inflammatory arthritis primarily on an in-patient basis, with twelve rheumatology beds; the average length of stay was twelve to fourteen days.

The bed closures meant they wouldn't be able to service as many people with inflammatory polyarthritis in an in-hospital setting, Bell says, so they looked at the idea of managing them in an ambulatory setting: "We studied our in-patient population, looked at what their needs were for hospitalization, where all the investigations and treatments took place while in hospital and what happened upon discharge. We tried to develop a program that simulated the in-hospital stay, so patients could sleep in their own beds and eat in their own homes, but come in and achieve the same goals they would have as in-patients."

The result was the RMDTP, which immediately realized tremendous cost savings, because patients weren't in hospital overnight, requiring care from nursing staff and other health professionals. The program was designed to be nine half-days in length, to approximate the amount of care and instruction patients would have received as in-patients over twelve to fourteen days (with two or four of those days on weekends, when there'd be no active treatment in the way of physical or occupational therapy, professional nutritional input, etc.) The same rheumatologists, pharmacists, OTs, PTs, social workers, etc., who had treated in-patients were involved in the new program.

In the first six months, they found they were able to service the needs of all their RA patients very effectively, with very few people admitted to hospital for RA (the five remaining in-patient beds were saved for people who were acutely ill and required intensive investigation and management). This allowed them to expand the program to people with other arthritic conditions.

To ensure continuity of care after patients leave the program, RMDTP maintains community links with The Arthritis Society's Consultation and Therapy Service. "People come into the ambulatory program and get a full, multidisciplinary assessment and management," Bell says. "Upon discharge, they're linked directly with community resources as required, and a follow-up plan is created so that they aren't lost in the system with respect to ongoing care. Family physicians, as the gatekeepers to care, are always informed of assessments and recommendations, what's been done and what hasn't been done that requires their assistance in the community."

The inflammatory program begins with a multidisciplinary assessment day, where the patient is assessed by Bell, an OT, a PT, and a nurse, to get a baseline on the patient, establish perceived needs, and discover where the team might be able to help. "Then we work with the client to discuss the findings of the assessment and what the coordinated goals would be and what might be achievable within the nine half-days," Bell says. "They bring a record from their GP. As the physician involved in the team, I do a screening assessment, a medical history, and a physical. If there's anything that's required for safety's sake, we obtain those recommendations prior to starting into the program, but rarely is that necessary. They're all screened before entering."

Much like York County's arthritis program, every day at RMDTP has a slightly different spin. After the initial assessment day, each half-day begins with a forty-five-minute hydrotherapy program in a heated pool, followed by a fifteen-minute break with a cold drink, because people feel a little tired and a little dehydrated. They move into an interactive, wide-ranging educational session, with the discussion directed by a different member of the treatment team (Bell, a rheumatological pharmacist, an OT, a PT, and a social worker) each day: the importance of exercise to well-being, medications, coping and self-management skills, weight control and nutrition, alternative medicine, the importance of doctor-patient communication, and so on.

Education sessions are followed by group and individual exercises. If someone requires occupational therapy—splinting, for example—there are periods of time for that, too. "You get a lot in in the nine half-days," Bell says, and, where there are issues that aren't addressed in that time, they're dealt with on an out-patient basis, though that's rarely necessary. "All the members of the team are available for individual consultation when required," Bell says. When patients have emotional or psychological needs, for example, they might have an individual consultation with the social worker. If someone's lost his or her job, a social worker can also help explore community agencies that can provide assistance, such as drug cards from welfare or initiating changes in their environment, "where people really need to change from a house to an apartment. Where individual consultation isn't required, it's not utilized, and that's really to save health-care dollars."

Physical improvement and knowledge gains are measured with self-administered questionnaires. "Clientele have demonstrated improvement in self-efficacy, a reduction in anxiety, and an increase in knowledge around arthritis as a result of the program," Bell says, "so it's proven its effectiveness over time."

Bell doesn't see their program "as being the only intervention. Most of these people are encouraged to look at the Arthritis Self-Management Program for ongoing education, to look at connections with The Arthritis Society's Consultation and Therapy Service staff, and to get into dialogue with their physicians about their care. We really advocate their full participation."

To date, the program has proven extremely effective in treatment, developing patient self-efficacy, and dollars. (Sunnybrook has done a cost-effectiveness study they hope to publish in 1996 or 1997.) With the money they've saved from the inflammatory program, they've been able to set up a separate program for osteoarthritis patients. They've avoided duplicating services that are available elsewhere in their area, such as pediatric arthritis. Similarly, they don't deal with lupus, fibromyalgia, or scleroderma patients, all of whom have excellent resources available to them in the Toronto area, though they may expand the program to include people with ankylosing spondylitis.

People have really begun to endorse this kind of ambulatory care, Bell says, "and the feedback from patients is that they like it better, because they don't lose contact with their own families. They don't feel like patients. They feel like people who are consumers of care, and that helps their self-esteem and helps them maintain their lives. That's been a very strong message that's come from our program.

"We've tried to have the best of both worlds," Bell says. "That is, by assessing each individual for his or her needs, and co-creating goals for management, and having the opportunity to get individual attention for specific needs, we can maximize the impact of group intervention to cover general needs, and use individual intervention for individual needs. It's efficient to do that, because it saves dollars."

But could such a program be developed elsewhere, where community resources aren't as plentiful? Bell thinks it could. It might have different kinds of health providers working within such a program, she says, "but a program like this is totally able to transfer to any community with the assistance of health providers in each community." A general PT might fill in for a therapist with arthritis-specific training, for example, "but that general therapist could consult with a TAS therapist for any specific needs within her program."

Certainly there are already arthritis programs in place across the country, while still others are in the planning and development stages. In Vancouver, for example, The Arthritis Centre (a regional program for all of B.C.) is working on amending the current program, Bell says, "to be a little bit more responsive to immediate community needs." Bell has also been to Winnipeg and Ottawa to spread the good word, and has fielded calls from cities in southern Ontario that have expressed interest in learning more about ambulatory arthritis programs: "I think people across the country are interested in changing the method of care delivery to people with arthritis," she says. "And, as programs move further out into the community, in the end, the patient is the person who wins."

What's the most important consideration in arthritis care? Its effectiveness, Dr. Carter Thorne says—how a given program compares to what's available elsewhere. Because arthritis is a major problem and the rheumatology care community relatively small, what caregivers have to do is adopt some standard measure for patient outcomes, and agree on its appropriateness, reliability, and validity: "We should all approach it the best way we know how, and compare outcomes, then look at how successful we've been and change it," he says, "then do that again a couple of times, and *then* we might have some sense that what we're doing is right. We have to look at health-care services for people with arthritis and decide what should be available, not what's 'Cadillac' or 'Emerald City.' What should be standard? In most instances, that'll be more than anyone has access to right now."

Getting the Message Out

In recent years, Bell says, "we've been lobbying the government fairly strongly about arthritis being Number One as far as long-term needs are concerned. We need to do more of that. We need to empower the public by giving them more knowledge around arthritis and its impact on the community—through public-awareness campaigns, articles in the paper, and trying to get closer to the people who will eventually have arthritis of one kind or another. If people don't understand the impact of arthritis on their own community, it's going to be very hard to get the lobby behind the arthritis movement. So, the more we get out there, the more visible we are, the better we'll do."

ACREU, the Arthritis Community Research and Evaluation Unit in Toronto, has clearly identified the burden of illness due to arthritis in Canada. It's huge, and it's growing. "It's going to be unmanageable by 2020," Bell says, "so we need to start impacting on the public now to increase its level of awareness so we can be prepared for what the future's going to bring. ASMP [Arthritis Self-Management Program] is reaching more people with basic information, and TAS staff and their ability to consult with other health providers and community groups is a wonderful way to educate the public, and, as rheumatologists, we have to get out there and let people know that this is a major problem."

Denis Morrice, president and CEO of The Arthritis Society, sometimes asks people with arthritis which is more important: patient care or research. "Every single person I've talked to," he says, "—and I'm talking about people with serious pain and inflammation—they all say research. They don't talk about themselves. They're concerned about their children and grandchildren. They don't want them to suffer like they've suffered."

There are at least two kinds of research, of course: basic science research, which tries to discern the cause of the various kinds of arthritis and look for cures, and clinical research, where a wide range of health professionals look at current practice and methods of treatment, and assess their value to the person who has arthritis. "While we're trying to prove that certain kinds of programs have benefits for people with arthritis," Bell says, "we're also providing care and trying to shape the kind of care they receive by providing the evidence to back up current practice. We need to support programs, we need to evaluate those programs for their effectiveness and their impact on the person with arthritis—*while* we're doing the basic science research, looking for a cause and cure."

Two million people rely on arthritis medications every day to relieve pain and inflammation, Morrice says, "and 600,000 of them have long-term disability as a result of arthritis. Fifty per cent of those people have incomes less than $20,000, and a quarter of them can't even get out of the house without the help of a relative or a friend who's willing to help."

Yes, he says, "arthritis *is* the sleeping giant of health care. We have to build a lobby group and get people to understand that arthritis is serious. In Canada—and North America as a whole—more people die from the side effects from arthritis medications than all illicit drug use. Those are mammoth numbers. What we're saying is, we have to do something about arthritis, and you can't do anything about it until people start seeing it as serious. More people see their doctors because of arthritis than for anything else except the cold and the flu."

As far as Morrice is concerned, "people with arthritis are being cheated." Everybody, he says—doctors, drug companies, pharmacies—"is making money out of people with arthritis," and that won't end until people begin to accept the magnitude of the problem. Information, he says, is a prerequisite to power, but until people get the full story on arthritis they won't *have* any power over it. How to give people that knowledge and understanding is the problem—certainly government isn't much help.

The Arthritis Society received a grant several years ago to set up the Arthritis Self-Management Program, which has educated thousands of people in managing their arthritis—while reducing the impact of health-care costs to us all. Since then, the program has been running on grants from industry, specifically Searle, the pharmaceutical giant, because government bailed out of the project—and not because they didn't think it was a terrific program: quite the opposite. Morrice was at a health-care conference in Ottawa where health ministry representatives held up ASMP "as a model for other health-care agencies to follow." So, how much does government put into the program now? "Not a dime," Morrice says flatly, "and it wouldn't be operating if we hadn't gotten the money from Searle."

Seeking new ways to get the message out, TAS has since forged a partnership with Meditrust, a mail-order drug company, which agreed to put TAS information into every order it delivers in exchange for an endorsement from the Society. "Getting into bed" with big business is something TAS assiduously avoided in the past, for fear of commercial conflicts of interest, but, with government funding a dry hole, there's little choice. Indeed, the Meditrust deal *did* spark criticism, though mostly from the pharmacy association—a brush fire that was quickly extinguished. The more disturbing question is whether TAS hasn't been forced—by digging up its own, non-governmental funding—to play into government's increasingly tight-fisted hand.

Be that as it might, TAS sees the deal as payback time—an entirely appropriate way for business and industry to give something back to the people it's been getting rich on for so long. And it provides a new platform to talk about ASMP, the Society Aquabics program, new research, new medications, and more. It's also an opportunity, Morrice says, to tell people "all the things they should be upset about, and to encourage them to write letters to the Prime Minister or the Minister of National Health and Welfare—or their MPs and provincial representatives. That's the only way I can see that we're going to get any kind of groundswell coming from people with arthritis, and that they'll ever see any kind of change. That's the only way we're going to get a national strategy or provincial health strategies for arthritis—if people get mobilized and start demanding it. If people can start looking at the *real* numbers."

Those real numbers are both positive and negative, and they're headed in opposite directions. The positive numbers are people— people with arthritis: four million and counting. The negative numbers are dollars for their care, which are shrinking. Any way you look at it, it's an equation that just doesn't add up. Arthritis is a huge problem, and ignoring it won't make it go away. What's needed is more research and the kinds of improved treatment and care that have been advanced in recent years—until the problem is under control once and for all.

RECOMMENDED
RESOURCES

For more information about arthritis, contact The Arthritis Society, at 250 Bloor Street East, Suite 901, Toronto, Ontario M4W 3P2. Call 416-967-1414 (FAX: 416-967-7171), or call the toll-free hotline at 1-800-321-1433. The Arthritis Society is online with its own Internet site, which has a great wealth of arthritis information. The address is http://www.arthritis.ca.

Arthritis News, the quarterly publication of The Arthritis Society, is available by subscription. Send a card or letter with your name, address, and telephone number, with a cheque or money order for $10 (for four issues), to: The Arthritis Society, Subscription Department, 250 Bloor Street East, Suite 901, Toronto, Ontario M4W 3P2. The Arthritis Society also has a range of free brochures on a variety of subjects, including the Arthritis Self-Management Program, osteoarthritis, rheumatoid arthritis, lupus, gout and pseudogout, scleroderma, juvenile arthritis, fibromyalgia, arthritis medications, and surgery, among others.

Ability OnLine (AO) is the support and advice network that began at The Hospital For Sick Children in Toronto. Call 416-650-5411; if you're outside the Toronto area and you have an Internet account, you can avoid long-distance charges by using telnet. The address is bbs.ablelink.org. To reach AO's office, phone 416-650-6207, or write to 919 Alness Street, North York, Ontario, M3J 2J1.

For a copy of RAIV (Rheumatoid Arthritis InVentors), send a stamped, self-addressed envelope to Derry Gardens, 4130 Derry Road West, RR 2, Milton, Ontario, L9T 2X6. Jan Watkins can be reached on the Internet at jwatkins@wchat.on.ca.

For immediate information about arthritis, ask your doctor during a regular visit, or your rheumatologist. Other health-care professionals, such as nurses, pharmacists, orthopedic surgeons, psychologists and social workers, are also a good source of information.

In many communities—especially in provinces where The Arthritis Society can only maintain an information service—local hospitals are the main source of arthritis-related services, including physiotherapy, occupational therapy, and social work and psychological counselling. Some communities also offer services, such as pool and exercise programs, through community centres.

For government-sponsored services, contact Health Canada, your provincial Ministry of Health, or your municipal Social Services office. Most provinces—and many municipalities—offer a range of home care and homemaking services, which may be augmented by non-profit community agencies, such as Meals On Wheels and some therapy services. Some provinces also have government-funded assistive devices programs (as do some private-insurance plans), as well as outreach physio- and occupational therapy programs.

There are any number of commercial outlets and medical supply stores, including some pharmacies, that sell or rent assistive devices, from reachers and grab rails to walkers and scooters. Look under "Hospital Equipment and Supplies" in your Yellow Pages, or ask for a recommendation from The Arthritis Society, your doctor, or another health professional.

Books of Interest:

Camp, Dalton. *Whose Country Is This Anyway?* Vancouver: Douglas & McIntyre, 1995. An eloquent collection of Camp's columns in defense of a more tolerant Canadian society, with a deft skewering of the follies committed in our name by politicians and self-interested parties of every stripe.

Ellert, Gwen. *The Arthritis Exercise Book: Gentle Joint-by-Joint Exercises to Keep You Flexible and Independent*. Chicago: Contemporary Books, 1990. A practical and safe guide to exercise by a former nurse who has arthritis herself.

Fries, James F. *Arthritis: A Comprehensive Guide to Understanding Your Arthritis*. Reading: Addison-Wesley Publishing Co., 1993. A good overview of arthritis, including major conditions, self-management and problem-solving.

Lorig, Kate, and James F. Fries. *The Arthritis Helpbook*. Reading: Addison-Wesley Publishing Co., 1995. Used by the Arthritis Self-Management Program (ASMP) in its classes, this book contains a wealth of practical advice and useful tips.

Maurer, Janet. *How to Talk to Your Doctor: The Questions to Ask*. New York: Simon & Schuster, 1986. A good way to prepare yourself for those all-important doctor visits.

McQuaig, Linda. *Shooting the Hippo*. Toronto: Penguin Books Canada Ltd., 1995. A readable and cogent analysis of Canada's deficit battles and why gutting social programs is the wrong road to national solvency.

Rachlis, Michael M., and Carol Kushner. *Strong Medicine: How to Save Canada's Health Care System*. Toronto: HarperCollins Publishers Ltd., 1994. A superbly researched and critical examination of our health-care system and reform efforts, with an agenda for change that could preserve Medicare for future generations.

Warning: There are numerous books about arthritis on the market. Many contain useful information and practical tips, but be wary of such titles as "Arthritis Can Be Cured" and "There Is a Cure for Arthritis." So far, there *is no cure* for any form of arthritis, and any book, brochure, radio, newspaper, or TV ad that suggests there is is trying to sell you useless information—and it could be dangerous counsel that may interfere with prescribed treatment, or offer strategies that are potentially harmful to arthritic joints.

Provincial divisions of The Arthritis Society:

British Columbia and Yukon Division
895 West 10th Avenue
Vancouver, BC V5Z 1L7
(604) 879-7511
(800) 667-2847
FAX (604) 871-4500

Alberta and Northwest Territories Division
1301-8th Street S.W.
Calgary, AB T2R 1B7
(403) 228-2571
(800) 332-1316
FAX (403) 229-4232

Saskatchewan Division
2550 Twelfth Avenue
Regina, SK S4P 3X1
(306) 352-3312
(800) 667-0097
FAX (306) 565-8731

Manitoba Division
386 Broadway Ave., Suite 105
Winnipeg, MN R3C 3R6
(204) 942-4892
(800) 697-2929
FAX (204) 942-4894

Ontario Division
250 Bloor St. East, Suite 901
Toronto, ON M4W 3P2
(416) 967-1414
(800) 321-1433
FAX (416) 967-7171

Quebec Division
2155 rue Guy, Bureau #1120
Montréal, QC H3H 2R9
(514) 846-8840
(800) 335-6175
FAX (514) 846-8999

New Brunswick Division
65 Brunswick St.
Fredericton, NB E3B 1G5
(506) 452-7191
FAX (508) 459-3925

Nova Scotia Division
2745 Dutch Village Rd., Suite 100
Halifax, NS B3L 4G7
(902) 429-7025
(800) 565-2873
FAX (902) 423-6479

Prince Edward Island Division
P.O. Box 1537
Charlottetown, PEI C1A 7N3
(902) 628-2288

Newfoundland Division
P.O. Box 522, Stn. "C"
St. John's, NF A1C 5K4
(709) 579-8190
FAX (709) 579-8191

I N D E X

ABOUT THE
AUTHOR

Louise Mullie

Roderick Jamer is the editor of *Arthritis News,* The Arthritis Society quarterly, to which he has contributed as a writer and editor for more than a dozen years.

As a long-time freelance writer, he has written science, health, and medical articles for a wide range of publications, including *Arthritis Today, Canadian Living, The Journal of Arthritis and Rheumatism, Disability Today, Future Health, Influence, Chatelaine, Healthwatch,* and *TV Guide.* He has reported stories from across Canada and the United States, Scotland and France.

He is also the associate editor of *CARPNews,* the bimonthly magazine of the Canadian Association of Retired Persons, for which he writes and edits a section on a different health condition every issue.

Mr. Jamer lives in Toronto, Ontario.